D1504063

OVERCOMING

OVERCOMING

The AUTOBIOGRAPHY of W. Harry Davis

Edited by Lori Sturdevant

Afton Historical Society Press
Afton, Minnesota

First edition

Copyediting by Michele Hodgson
Cover and book design by Barbara J. Arney
Graphic layout by Mary Susan Oleson

Library of Congress Cataloging-in-Publication Data

Davis, W. Harry, 1923–
Overcoming: The autobiography of W. Harry Davis / edited by Lori Sturdevant.—1st ed.
p. cm.
ISBN 1-890434-52-3 (linen bound hardcover : alk. paper)
1. Davis, W. Harry, 1923– 2. African American civil rights workers—Minnesota—Minneapolis—Biography.
3. Civil rights workers—Minnesota—Minneapolis—Biography. 4. African Americans—Minnesota—Minneapolis—Biography. 5. African Americans—Civil rights—Minnesota—Minneapolis—History—20th century.
6. Minneapolis (Minn.)—Race relations. 7. Minneapolis (Minn.)—Biography.
8. Boxing trainers—Minnesota—Minneapolis—Biography. I. Sturdevant, Lori, 1953– II. Title.
F614.M553 D38 2002
977.6'57905'092—dc21

2002005023

Printed and bound in Canada

Publication of
OVERCOMING: The Autobiography of W. Harry Davis
was made possible with generous financial support from:

Elmer L. and Eleanor J. Andersen
John Jr. and Sage Cowles
John III and Page Cowles
TCF Foundation

The Afton Historical Society Press publishes exceptional books on regional subjects.

W. Duncan MacMillan
President

Patricia Condon Johnston
Publisher

Afton Historical Society Press
P.O. Box 100, Afton, MN 55001
(651) 436-8443 or (800) 436-8443

email: aftonpress@aftonpress.com
www.aftonpress.com

To my beloved family

my wife, Charlotte,
our children,
Rita, Harry, Richard, and Evan,
and our grandchildren

—

and to the memory of

Cecil Newman,
Gertrude Brown,
and
Raymond Hatcher

Contents

Editor's Foreword

IN THESE FIRST YEARS of the twenty-first century, it's easy for the good citizens of Minneapolis to feel somewhat smug about race relations. This is the progressive, enlightened Upper Midwest, after all, with no history of slavery to live down and little experience of violence between the races. Schools and other civic institutions have long been integrated. The city entered the new century with black women holding three positions of civic importance—mayor, school superintendent, and parks superintendent. Racism, a Minneapolitan might think, is somebody else's problem, someplace else.

That is wishful thinking. Racism still stalks this city, though less visibly than it once did. Evidence of its persistence can be found in the incomes, educational achievement, housing patterns, and health and employment status of nonwhites compared with white residents.

Nevertheless, while racism was not eradicated from Minneapolis in the twentieth century, it was dealt a punishing blow—by a boxing coach. This is his story.

The remarkable life of W. Harry Davis is witness to the fact that a more virulent form of racism lurks not far removed from modern-day Minneapolis. Blatant discrimination in lending practices, public accommodations, employment, and basic services were routine in this liberal city within his lifetime. People still among us, Harry included, were scarred by the overt bigotry that was once interwoven with "Minnesota Nice."

But this book tells of much more than one African American's journey through the changing minefield of Minneapolis racism. It is also the story of one man's tireless struggle to defuse those mines and make the city he loves a place of harmony and justice for all.

In the early 1960s, Harry was a factory worker who had come to local prominence as a successful youth boxing coach. He could have left it at that. Or he could have chosen to capitalize on his coaching ability in the lucrative but risky professional arena. Instead, Harry saw his credibility with people both black and white as a tool he could employ in the cause of civil rights. He chose to become what Jackie Robinson, the Brooklyn

Dodger who integrated Major League Baseball, called a "race man." Harry devoted much of the rest of his career to providing equality of opportunity to every citizen of the city he loved.

The path he chose was not easy. The 1960s brought confrontation and militancy to the fore. Harry is by nature a conciliator who strives to treat every person as a child of God. At a time when mutual mistrust among the races ran high, he preached the power of trust and kindness. When other seekers of justice became bitter, he clung to an inherent optimism and faith in the basic goodness of humanity.

As a result, more strident voices in the black community accused Harry of excessive accommodation to the white majority. At the same time, white voters suspected he would move integration too fast and rejected his bid for mayor. For a time, he was caught in between. It had to be an uncomfortable spot. But he stood his ground, and in doing so, he performed a great service to his city. As his friend and former Minneapolis mayor Art Naftalin said, "Harry was willing to be a human bridge between black and white when this city really needed one. I shudder to think what might have happened if that bridge had not been there."

Listening to Harry pour out his memories, I often wondered, "What if?" What if he had been able to go to college? With his gifts for teaching and organization, it might have been Harry who became the first black superintendent of schools in the city. What if he had run for mayor in a year when white fear about school desegregation had been less strong? It might have been Harry who became the first black mayor. What if he had been able to climb a corporate ladder as far as his ability would let him? He might have become the city's first prominent black CEO.

But the "what ifs" should not minimize what Harry did accomplish. The ten-year-old football hotshot he took under his wing was Richard Green, who became the first black superintendent of schools in Minneapolis. The college student his unsuccessful mayoral campaign inspired was Sharon Sayles Belton, who twenty-two years later became the first black mayor of Minneapolis. The CEOs who came to appreciate Harry's ability at the Minneapolis Urban Coalition made room for people of color in their own corporations.

To this day, scores of grown men still draw inspiration from the lessons Coach Davis taught them as boys. Scores of black city employees owe their jobs to his assault on the color barrier as a member of Minneapolis's Civil

Service Commission. Thousands of Minneapolis adults learned lessons of tolerance at the city schools that school-board member Davis helped integrate. Tens of thousands have been touched by the War on Poverty programs he helped launch in Minneapolis: preschool education, job training, health care, housing support.

This book should lead no one to conclude that racism has been conquered in Minneapolis. But my hope is that it heightens the reader's appreciation of how much has already been overcome—and of one who had a hand in the overcoming.

THIS BOOK WAS INSPIRED by many relatives, friends, and admirers of W. Harry Davis, who asked him repeatedly through the years, "When are you going to write a book?" I asked Harry that question a few times when we chatted at Hennepin Avenue United Methodist Church, where we are both members. It eventually became more than idle conversation. I made it clear to Harry that when he was ready to tell his story, I would be honored to help him write it.

When Harry had heart-valve surgery in 2000, his family began asking the question in earnest. His illness made him realize that such a project could not be forever postponed. He told his granddaughters Chloe and Jaylyn when they visited him in the hospital that, yes, he would write an autobiography. I am grateful that the next thing he did was telephone me.

Harry and I are also grateful to many others who had a hand in our project. It was funded in part by generous gifts from people who have been important in Harry's life and mine: former governor Elmer L. Andersen and Eleanor Andersen, Virginia McKnight Binger, John Jr. and Sage Cowles, and John III and Page Cowles. We were helped greatly by Beverly Hermes, who transcribed our taped interviews. Beverly's personal interest in our project, her research assistance, and her friendship meant a great deal to us.

To supplement Harry's memory, we mined the clips in Minneapolis's *Star Tribune* library with the help of librarian Roberta Hovde. We also called on people who lived Harry's story with him. They include Matthew Little, Josie Johnson, Arthur Naftalin, John Cowles Jr., Steve Keefe, Gregor W. Pinney, Chuck Hales, Asa Grigsby, Jimmy Jackson, Wes Hayden, Ken Rodriguez, John Jacobs, Lawrence Brown, and Danny Davis. Harry's sister

Geraldine and his four children, Rita, Butch, Ricky, and Evan, added their memories and made helpful suggestions. Keyboarding help came from Marlene James of the *Star Tribune* editorial staff. My partner, Martin Vos, proved, as he has before, that electrical engineers can also be excellent proofreaders. Through it all, we had enormous support from the pillar of strength in Harry's life, Charlotte NaPue Davis. We thank them all.

We are also very appreciative of the encouragement and guidance we received from Patricia Condon Johnston and her staff at Afton Historical Society Press. It is an honor for *Overcoming* to be listed among the fine titles produced by this distinguished Minnesota publishing house.

Lori Sturdevant

Introduction

WHEN I WAS A YOUNG CHILD, I used to watch my father, my uncles, and my older brother playing baseball. How good they were! I could hear the crowd cheering as they won their games. But I could also hear the opposing crowd boo and call them hateful names because of their color. I wondered why. Little did I realize how deeply that experience would mold my future.

I remember my mother, Libby, making root beer for us and home brew for my dad in our cellar at 1014 Bryant Avenue North in Minneapolis. I remember Sixth and Lyndale Avenues North—the stores, the people, the churches, the school, and, at the center of my world, Phyllis Wheatley Settlement House.

All of those places are gone now. But lessons my generation and I learned there live on. The neighborhood clergy of our youth—Father Chaney, Reverend Young, Reverend Botts, Reverend Franklin, and Reverend Graham—told us that God loved us and that we were somebody. God gave us a family and friends to teach and direct us, and our neighborhood schools and teachers to educate us. Gertrude Brown and her staff at Phyllis Wheatley were there to be our mentors and leaders. Those of us who were Wheatley kids from the time it opened in 1924 until the old house was torn down in 1971 were richly blessed. We lived, learned, and loved the Wheatley all our lives, and we are the better for it.

I have enjoyed telling my grandchildren stories about the old North Side, Phyllis Wheatley, and the people I knew. My granddaughters Chloe and Jaylyn persuaded me to write an autobiography to preserve some of those stories. My hope is that this book will inspire other Wheatley kids to record their memories about that special place and its extraordinary power to shape young lives. It is important that the Wheatley's wisdom not be lost.

I owe many people thanks for their help in the preparation of this book. The book's editor, Lori Sturdevant, mentions a number of them in her foreword, but it falls to me to express my gratitude to her. Lori is the angel who took my words and turned them into a book. She is a brilliant, lovable writer and a wonderful woman who has filled this book with laughter and lessons that I hope will make people think not only about the past, but also about the future.

I must echo Lori's thanks to Charlotte, my wife, best friend, lover, comforter, partner, and adviser. She has been beside me through good and bad, and her support has shown me the love of Christ. Her contribution to this book is on every page.

My heart is also full of love and thanksgiving for all the people who have helped, encouraged, and inspired me through nearly eighty years of living. I cannot begin to name them all here, but in the pages that follow, readers will meet many of them. The support and friendship I have known from so many have truly been blessings from God. If I have had the knowledge, courage, and strength to do my part, let it be a reflection on them.

May God continue to bless all of his people.

W. Harry Davis

We shall overcome,
We shall overcome,
We shall overcome, someday.
Oh, deep in my heart,
I do believe,
We shall overcome
Someday.

African American spiritual and
civil-rights rallying song

I
GROWING

1
Founding

DRIVERS SEE ONLY DULL PAVEMENT when they cruise past the Olson Memorial Highway and Interstate Highway 94 junction in north Minneapolis today. In my mind's eye, I see much more. I knew that spot as the notorious corner of Sixth and Lyndale Avenues North, where otherwise sedate Minneapolis foamed with speakeasies, tippling houses, gambling joints, and brothels during the Roaring Twenties. Some people called it the Hellhole. I called it home.

I was born on April 12, 1923, at 711 Lyndale Avenue North, in an apartment above a Jewish bakery, just a block from the Upper Midwest's epicenter of vice. Not coincidentally, it was also the home of Minnesota's largest African American and Jewish populations. They were not there because they were attracted to criminal activity. They were there because the majority white population in Minneapolis would not tolerate them elsewhere.

I joined a neighborhood where people down the street were bootleggers and alcoholics, pimps and prostitutes, gamblers and hustlers, pushers and addicts. But side by side with them, coexisting in uneasy but unavoidable familiarity, were dedicated doctors, honest merchants, hardworking laborers, crusading social workers, kind senior citizens, and loving families.

Mine was among the latter. I am the youngest of six children born to Leland C. and Elizabeth Frances Jackson Davis. Like many people of color who made their way to Minnesota in the decades after slavery ended in America, my parents were the products of hardship, endurance, and courage. Their forebears included people of several races who had in common the capacity for persevering love. My parents had to struggle as minorities at a time when majority rule was often harsh. But they had the love and the lessons of their parents and grandparents to show them the way.

My father was known as Leland or Lee Davis as an adult, but that is not the name he was given at birth. The fact is, I do not know that name. He was born on a Winnebago Sioux Indian reservation in Nebraska in July 1887 and was a full-blooded member of that tribe. His mother always said that her Indian name was too hard to pronounce and that we should call her Grandma Molly. She was headstrong, tempestuous, and, I imagine, quite a flirt as a young girl. She was slight of build, with straight black hair and flashing eyes. She was a daughter of the tribe's chief, Golden Eagle. Family lore has it that Golden Eagle opposed a union between Molly and my father's father, who was another member of the tribe. I do not know my grandfather's name, nor anything more about him.

When my father was about five years old, he and his mother left the reservation without my grandfather and moved to Omaha. Molly gave him the name Leland when she enrolled him in public school. Why she left the reservation I do not know. Conflict with her father may have been part of the reason. But the 1890s were bitter years for the Sioux, a time of defeat, loss, hunger, and persecution. Molly may have understood before others in her tribe that the old way of life was gone forever and that she needed to make her way in a different world. The family always described her as rebellious, but that reputation may have been earned by a show of the boldness and grit that a desperate situation demanded. My mother used to say of Grandma Molly, "If she butted heads with a bull, she'd win."

While Grandma Molly was in Omaha, or perhaps even before she arrived, she met a black man with skin nearly the color of hers. His name was Abner Davis. He was a barber and owned his own barbershop in Omaha's black neighborhood. That would have been a point of some distinction for a former slave, which he was. We don't know when he was born, nor where, other than the southern United States. We don't know whether he escaped from a plantation or was freed at the end of the Civil War. He was part of a westward movement of former slaves in the 1870s and 1880s, set on making a new life. Many of them settled in Kansas. He veered north and landed in Omaha.

Maybe the fact that they were both refugees of a sort is what brought Molly and Abner together. They married, and my father took the name Davis. Molly and Abner had a son of their own too, Clarence Davis—my Uncle Dixie.

Molly and Abner eventually moved to Minneapolis. Molly was joined by a kinsman—likely an uncle—who was called Grandpa Mac by me and nearly everybody else as he aged. He lived to be 109. Because he had been a Union Army scout during the Civil War, he achieved some acclaim as the city's oldest living veteran. He even rode in Aquatennial parades, wearing his Civil War uniform.

When I was seven or eight years old, we lived at 1014 Bryant Avenue North. Grandpa Mac used to come to visit on summer evenings and sit on the porch. My grandmother would come with him. My mother would build a smudge-fire so the smoke would keep the mosquitoes away. Grandpa Mac would sit on the floor, Indian-style, with a blanket wrapped around him, and tell the assembled children stories about the Civil War and the buffalo hunts of his youth. We had to listen closely because he talked just above a whisper. He seemed to have a sixth sense, an ability to predict the future. Often, things he forecast would come true. We children were in awe of him.

Grandpa Mac could always remember the name of every child. We noticed that, since a number of our other, older relatives often confused the names of the many Davis children and our Jackson cousins. For some reason, Grandpa Mac called me "Little Pops." Soon Dad was calling me Little Pops too. The nickname stuck.

Grandpa Mac told of the arrival of large numbers of white and black people on the Great Plains, and how the Indians soon noticed that white people treated black people badly. Whites insisted on staying separate from blacks and would tell the Indian leaders to do the same. "They'll steal your daughters," the white people warned. Those warnings only served to make Indians feel a bond with the blacks. The white people were treating the Sioux in the same demeaning way they treated blacks, Grandpa Mac said. In Nebraska and elsewhere on the frontier, blacks and Indians developed a kinship that included more than a few instances of marriage.

Both Molly and Abner lived long enough to know some of their grandchildren. Abner used to cut and style the hair of my older brother and sisters. Molly lived at Eleventh and Dupont Avenues North and often walked all the way downtown. She refused to ride the Minneapolis streetcar; she considered it unnatural and unhealthy. Even if she were offered a ride in a car, she would not accept it. Ironically, her insistence on walking downtown ended her life. She was hit and killed by a car at age seventy-five.

Like my father's family, my mother's people were touched deeply by events in American history. Their patriarch was John Wesley Harper, my great-grandfather. Born in 1839 in Wheeling, Virginia, he was the son of a slave-owning family. From time to time, his father would travel to Norfolk, Virginia, to buy slaves. Young John Wesley may have joined his father on one fateful trip in the 1850s, when the purchases included a young girl who had been forced off her plantation home in Opelousas, Louisiana, Frances Ann Frazier.

Frances Ann was unwanted property on the plantation where she was raised because she was plainly not the daughter of a black father. Her fair skin and Caucasian features told the story of her conception. While her mother was a slave, her father was likely a member of the plantation owner's family, perhaps the owner himself. By all accounts, Frances was a beautiful and spirited girl, hotheaded and tough when she needed to be. She took the name of her owners, Frazier, and a fair amount of Creole culture with her on her journey to the Norfolk slave market.

Frances and John may have met as slave and owner, but their relationship quickly developed into something much more positive—though it likely was viewed differently in the eyes of John's family and society. We can only assume that the disapproval of the Harper family propelled the young couple's move to Zanesville, Ohio, about the time of the outbreak of the Civil War. Ohio was a free state and a haven for refugees from southern slavery. Daring and passion must have been required for these two young people to run away from the lives they had known and start life over together. My grandmother used to say that her father was a little bit crazy. Maybe that helped.

When the war broke out, John enlisted in the army. When the war ended, he stayed in uniform—a decision suggesting that even after the war, during which West Virginia had sided with the Union and the wretched practice of owning human beings ended, the Harpers felt they could not return to John's home. John Wesley Harper became a career sergeant and took his wife with him to a series of army posts on the nation's frontier.

Soon the Harpers were parents of a large family. My grandmother, Armintha Alice, was the second of their children to survive infancy; she was born at Fort Bliss, Texas, on March 8, 1872. Her youngest sister, Evelyn Belle, came twelve babies and eighteen years later, on September 18, 1890, at Fort Snelling, Minnesota. It was the last assignment of John's army career. The nomadic Harper family had come home.

It was at Fort Snelling that fair-skinned, fiery-tempered Armintha met and married William Henry Jackson in the early 1890s. I regret not knowing more about my Grandpa Jackson. He was a black soldier, born five years after the end of the Civil War in a place unknown to my generation. As a black man, he was not eligible to become an officer. He made his career in the army as a barber. His life came to a premature end at age fifty-two, the year before I was born. He liked to gamble and had taken to frequenting gambling parlors on Washington Avenue in Minneapolis, a white man's street where high-stakes poker was played. He hung out at a place called the Persian Palms. One night he apparently won more than some of his fellow gamblers thought a black man should. A group followed him out of the parlor and, a few blocks away, jumped him. They beat him to death.

The Jacksons had fourteen children, twelve of whom survived past infancy. My mother, Elizabeth Frances, was the third surviving child and the second daughter. She was born January 11, 1898. Even as a young girl, she was a favorite of my grandmother, and she was raised almost as part of the Harper family. Her younger aunts and uncles were close enough to my mother in age to be her girlhood playmates.

Most of the Harpers lived in St. Paul, though some lived in Minneapolis. They were a close-knit family, almost to the point of being clannish, and my grandmother was their master sergeant. Both the Harpers and Jacksons jumped to attention every time Grandma Armintha came into a room. She was smart; she was strong; she was strict. When she told you to do something, she meant it and you did it. If she saw a grandchild acting badly, she would say, "See that tree out there? See that bush? You go out there and get me a switch." You knew what was coming, but you had to obey. She used that switch on your legs. My mother would stand and watch as Grandma's punishment was administered, never daring to intervene.

But Grandma was loving too. After my grandfather died, it didn't take her long to remarry. Her second husband and the man I knew as Grandpa was Sam Bell, a black horse doctor at Fort Snelling. He had been a friend of Grandpa Jackson and was well acquainted with our large family before he joined it.

What a cook Grandma was! She had learned a southern-cooking style from her Louisiana-born mother. In our Minnesota household, we were used to eating many kinds of greens, plenty of fried potatoes, and the traditional meat dish from the slave cabins: chitlins. My grandmother could fix chitlins (from the small intestines of pigs) and other pig meat, including the ears and feet, with black-eyed peas and greens and make it taste out of this world. She taught my mother to cook the same way.

First Grandma, and later my mother, became somewhat famous locally for their home-brewed beer. Grandma learned how to do it from her mother and would brew beer for her dad to serve when he entertained his fellow soldiers from Fort Snelling. She passed on the skill to only one of her children, my mother. Their brewing talent was especially appreciated during Prohibition. The Jackson and Davis families were full of athletes. They would come home from games and look in our cellar for those big quart bottles. That's where the brewing was done, where there was a dirt floor to absorb the consequences of the inevitable "pop!"—the signal that a batch of beer was ready to drink. Grandma was both brew master and brew drinker. My mother, a devout churchwoman, abstained from alcohol, but did not mind brewing beer for others to consume.

Besides brewing, Grandma passed on another talent to my mother, one she learned from her own mother. They were the "doctors" in the family, the practitioners of the folk medicine and old African remedies employed in the slave cabins of the American South. They knew how to make things like cough syrups and ointments to rub on sore joints and muscles. Those remedies were often quite effective, or at least thought to be so. They were in demand in our neighborhood.

Grandma Armintha was a force to be reckoned with in the community. Big as her family was, everybody knew her and she knew everybody. She was considered a trusted friend by our Jewish neighbors; she even learned to speak Yiddish. She would arrange odd jobs for my cousins and siblings and me, like turning on the gas for the Banks family when they were away.

Kid Cann, the gangster kingpin of Minneapolis in the 1920s, knew Armintha and the Jackson family through athletics. Grandma encouraged four of my younger uncles—Kenneth, Harold, Edgar, and Theodore—to get involved in baseball. She figured that if they were playing baseball, they wouldn't be hanging around on Sixth Avenue. They became excellent ballplayers. Kid Cann used to support their teams, and they competed with white teams in the region. I suspect he reaped a profit from the bets placed on those games.

Grandma was a familiar figure to the other racketeers on Sixth Avenue too. When she would take her sons or grandsons to get a haircut or something, the pimps on the street would say, "Here comes Mrs. Jackson. Watch your lip. Watch your mouth." They knew she was the mother of six strong sons who were not afraid to stand up to anyone who bothered their mother. They also knew she would cuss them out on the street if they said anything unfit for us to hear—and if that did not end the discussion, she would raise her own fists. My mother was accorded the same respect because she was one of the Jacksons.

My mother, whom the family called Libby, spent most of her girlhood in north Minneapolis. But the connection the Harper and Jackson families had with Fort Snelling in the years before World War I gave her a somewhat larger world than many of her neighborhood-bound peers. For example, she occasionally went with her father or other male family members to semiprofessional baseball games at old Nicollet Field on the city's predominantly white South Side. It was there, at an exhibition game between the Minneapolis Millers and the Kansas City Monarchs of the Negro League, that she was spotted in the stands behind the Monarchs' dugout by the team's catcher, Leland Davis. Leland was twenty-three; Libby was just twelve. The year was 1910.

By that time, my father had been playing Negro League baseball for at least four years. He started playing ball for money with a famous touring baseball team called the House of Davids. One of the team's trademarks was that all the players wore beards, real or otherwise. The House of Davids included good ballplayers, so good that Babe Ruth, disguised in a phony beard, once toured with them briefly between seasons with the New York Yankees. My dad got a tryout with the House of Davids when they came to Omaha to play an exhibition game at a time when they were short a catcher. My dad's school coach recommended him to the team's owner.

Not long after he joined the House of Davids, the team played an exhibition game with the Kansas City Monarchs. Along with the Chicago American Giants, the Birmingham Black Barons, the New York Black Yanks, and several other teams, the Kansas City Monarchs were early mainstays in the Negro League. The Monarchs went on to be the league's most successful and most prominent team—but that was years ahead of our story.

The Monarchs were impressed by my dad's play and also by the fact that his bronze skin left people guessing about his race. He did not look out of place on an all-black team.

It was as a Monarch that he met my mother at Nicollet Field. She must have made quite an impression, for what happened that day could have been little more than flirtatious chatter between ballplayer and fan. Names and some additional information must have been exchanged. Both Leland and Libby resumed their very different lives after that first meeting. But something significant had happened for both of them that day at the ballpark.

Later that same season, my dad was traded—sold, actually, for they treated the players like livestock—to the Chicago American Giants. As he did at the end of every season, he looked for a job. But this time, he came to Minneapolis to find off-season work—and to look up pretty Libby. The job he landed was as a driver, first of a team of horses, later of a truck, for Rose Brothers Lumber and Cleveland Wrecking Company. It was on Girard Avenue North, between Sixth Avenue and Glenwood, close to my mother's neighborhood. He became the first Native American truck driver in Minnesota.

Few men of color in Minneapolis had better jobs in those years. The best jobs open to blacks at that time were on the railroad as Pullman porters, waiters, or chefs. Next best was to hold a similar position at one of the big downtown hotels. At some of the downtown corporate buildings—Pillsbury, First Bank of Minneapolis, Northwestern National Bank—blacks were hired as doormen. My uncle, Harry Jackson, worked as a checker at the door of the Minneapolis Athletic Club for forty years. Some men had shoeshine stands inside the doors of downtown office buildings, such as the Baker Building. Those deemed most trustworthy would stay in the buildings after hours and clean them. The African American people with those jobs were the fortunate ones. They made good wages for their time, enough to modestly support a family. But there were many more black people in Minneapolis than there were such jobs.

Maybe it was because my father had two impressive positions—truck driver and professional baseball player—that Armintha and William Jackson agreed to let their second-eldest daughter marry him when she was only fourteen. Maybe, after a protracted courtship, they had come to know my quiet father as the dependable man he was. Maybe they simply became resigned to a romance they could not stop. At any rate, my parents were married on August 6, 1912.

2
The Davis Family

MARRIAGE DID NOT IMMEDIATELY end my father's baseball career. It was too lucrative. When he was playing, he was able to send home twenty-five dollars every other week, a comfortable amount of money for those years, even for a family that was growing rapidly. Four children, three girls and a boy, were born to the Davis family in quick succession between 1913 and 1917.

Charlotte Elizabeth came first, in 1913. We called her Dooney, for reasons I do not know. She was an attractive young lady, with high cheekbones that revealed her Native American heritage and wavy black hair that Grandma Molly loved to braid. She was petite, pert, and kind—and had a lot of suitors, to my dad's dismay. As the oldest daughter, Dooney was assigned the greatest share of household responsibility and got the fullest lessons in cooking, sewing, and medicine-making from my mother. She was the one we younger children had to obey when our mother was not home. She was a stern but compassionate baby-sitter who took seriously her family duty.

Two years later came my only brother, Leland Clarence, whom we called Menzy. He was a great athlete and a wonderful brother to me. When I was small, he was like a second father when my dad was not at home. It was Menzy's job to cut wood and bring in coal to keep our stoves going in the winter. He hated that job, but he did it well. He was responsible, strong-tempered (a family trait), and big and strong enough to scare you when he was riled up. But he was kind to me. We shared a bedroom.

Geraldine Frances was born next, in 1916, just a year after Menzy. She was fair-skinned, pretty, soft-spoken, and sensitive. She cared a lot about her looks and about boys. That made her kind of wild as a teenager. She would sneak down to Sixth Avenue and visit one of my mother's younger sisters who frequented the hot spots, much to my grandmother's chagrin. My aunt made sure that nobody bothered Geraldine, but my dad would be furious when he found out where she had been.

My third sister, Marie Melrose, was born the next year, in 1917. The family called her Retie. She was naturally pretty and a happy, sweet girl. Sadly, she lived just ten years. She was playing on a swing at Sumner Field playground when some tough older boys, including two brothers, came to the park to drink a bottle of moonshine. They started teasing and pushing her swing. One of the brothers pushed her too hard, and she fell out of the swing and landed on her head. She went into convulsions and died.

That was a horrible time for our family. We all loved Retie so much. I was only four when it happened, but I remember still how awful she looked when they brought her body home from the hospital. Menzy was just twelve, but he bolted from the house, found the boy who did it, and nearly beat him to death. The funeral home took her body, then brought her back home for reviewal. In those years, it was customary to place a casket in the front window of a house and have people walk by on the front porch to pay their respects. That went on for three long days, and then we took her body to Wayman Methodist Church, at James and Sixth Avenues, for a funeral service led by the Reverend Claybook. That was my mother's church. My dad went with us to church sometimes, but he was not a member. Retie's death put a sad pall on family life for a long time.

It was after Retie's birth that my dad retired from professional baseball. My mother's insistence clinched his decision. She announced that a man with four children in his household had no business traveling the country as a ballplayer five months a year. It turned out that one of the last big-league games he played was against his old team, the Kansas City Monarchs. The rookie pitcher that day was Satchel Paige, who went on to be, arguably, the best pitcher of all time.

From then on, Lee Davis was a full-time truck driver. Years later, at about the time of the Minneapolis truckers strike, he became a member of the Teamsters Union—the first person of color to do so in Minneapolis. When he left the Chicago American Giants he also left his winter job with Rose Brothers Lumber and the Cleveland Wrecking Company and started driving full-time for Como Nut Company and, occasionally, for that business's next-door neighbor, Parson's Meats. In those years in Minneapolis, a lot of grocery stores, restaurants, and specialty stores sold cashews, stuffed dates, and other nuts and snack foods. My dad was a trucker for a chain of such stores and restaurants owned by two Greek families, Zaker and Boosalis. It was unusual then for a nonwhite man to have a job like that, but the Greek families in Minneapolis had some connections with Sixth Avenue. His new employers probably knew my dad, at least by reputation, before they hired him. When I was small, Dad would sometimes take me along on his route. It was a big thrill to ride with him in his truck.

Dad still played a little baseball for recreation and pocket money. He was joined by John Donaldson, a pitcher who had been his teammate on the Chicago American Giants before settling in Minnesota. Donaldson was a powerful pitcher. Dad used to say of him that he would walk the bases full and then strike out the next three batters just to show off his skill.

My dad was a great baseball organizer and coach. He got to know black ballplayers in Minneapolis and St. Paul, players with real talent who were barred from the white teams in town because of their race. Minneapolis and St. Paul both had black teams, and they would play against each other. My dad recruited the best players from St. Paul and Minneapolis and created a new, more competitive team called the Twin Cities Colored Giants. That team became an attraction. Dad found a fellow from St. Paul, George White, to book games for the team. He also had help from Harry Crump, who was married to one of my younger aunts, Ruth. Harry Crump was manager of the Midwest squad of the Harlem Globetrotters and had a good head for sports management. My dad preferred to be the talent scout, coach, and captain on the playing field. He was a tremendous coach of young players—quiet, serious, and very much respected. A look from him was all it took to keep his players in line. When the Kansas City Monarchs came to play an exhibition game, my dad's team would play them. The Monarchs were sufficiently impressed with my dad's teams that they would hire some of his players on the spot.

My brother, Menzy, joined them when he was thirteen or fourteen. Dad encouraged it, partly to help Menzy deal with his anger and grief after Retie's death. Menzy was about six feet tall and, even as a kid, weighed nearly two hundred pounds. My dad had taught him to be a pitcher, and he was a good one. And, man, could he hit a baseball! When I watched him play in Shakopee one day, he hit a ball out of that city's roadside ballpark and onto Highway 169! Another time, Menzy played an exhibition game in the old Nicollet Ballpark, at the corner of Nicollet Avenue and Lake Street. He hit a ball that crossed Nicollet and crashed through the awning on a store window and broke the window. The awnings were there to protect the windows, so that balls would bounce off of them, but they weren't strong enough to withstand Menzy's slam. Only a handful of other players—Joe

Hauser of the Minneapolis Millers was one—ever broke one of those store windows.

I was always so proud to watch Dad and Menzy play. Even when he was past his prime, my dad could do what great catchers like Yogi Berra bragged about: he could throw a ball quickly and accurately to second base without leaving the catcher's crouched position. Dad was not a tall man—he was about my height, five-foot-seven—but he was powerfully muscular. And strong! He used to roll fifty-five-gallon barrels of peanut oil in and out of his truck and throw around bulging sacks of peanuts. He had such physical and mental ability that he surely would have been a star in Major League Baseball, if only he had been allowed to play.

Teams in the white Southern Minnesota League—Shakopee, New Ulm, Sleepy Eye, Mankato, places like that—used to hire my dad and Donaldson; my mother's brothers Ted, Ed, Kenny, and Harold; and, later, Menzy and some of the other Colored Giants to play for them. The money was good. When my dad was hired by the Shakopee team, he could pick up $150 for one game. He used to put benches in the back of his Como Nut truck and drive his players to Shakopee. He installed shades on the open sides of the truck so the players could change into their baseball uniforms when they arrived. They were not allowed to change with the white players.

I was along one fall day in Shakopee when Dad and John Donaldson were playing for that team in a championship with the team from Prior Lake. They won the game for Shakopee. I watched as all the other players joined the fans afterward for a big party with plenty of food and drink. Dad and John didn't go along; they stayed on the diamond. Eventually, someone brought them a plate of food, and they stayed on the diamond to eat.

I asked Dad, "Why don't we just go with everybody else? You just played for them and everybody cheered you." He said, "You don't understand." Dad and John were not welcome to eat with the rest of the team, even though they had just won the game for them. It was the same in other towns, I later learned. When they traveled farther from home and had to stay overnight, no hotel in those Minnesota towns would accept them. They had to sleep in their cars or in Dad's truck.

By that stage in his life, my dad had come to accept some forms of discrimination as a fact of life. I knew him as a quiet and reserved man, and not much involved in the community other than through baseball. My mother used to say of him, "Still water runs deep." He had inherited a hot temper from his mother, but by midlife he had learned to control it, with a little coaxing from my mother. My mother was a loving person who brought out the best in the people around her. She had a beautiful smile and could make friends just walking down the street. When she'd smile, you couldn't help but smile back.

But my mother was a strong person too. She worked hard, raising a large family and taking care of her younger brothers and sisters as well. Her relationship with her brother Johnny reveals something about the kind of person she was. Johnny was very intelligent, nearly a genius I think, but he had a terrible addiction to alcohol. By the time I was a boy, he was out of control. Someone would say to my mother, "Lib, Johnny's lying down in the alley down on Bassett Place. He's drunk and stinks, and people are going to get the police to come and get him." Then my mother would get my father or my brother or one of her brothers to fetch him and bring him to our house. She would put him in the bathtub and clean him up. She would wash his clothes and press them. She would be there to give him food and coffee after he had slept off his drunkenness.

I once heard them talking at a time like that. He asked her, "Lib, are you having a tough time?" She said, "Johnny, we're making it." She was not one to complain. He was observant and noticed that we were without power that day. "Did they turn off your electricity because you couldn't pay?" he asked. He then went outside, climbed up the utility pole, and hooked up the electricity to our house. Any other person would go up there and get electrocuted, but Johnny knew what he was doing. It was his way of showing appreciation for my mother's care.

When we paid our light bill and Northern States Power came to turn the power on, the man from NSP said, "Somebody's been fooling around with your lights up there." My mother replied, "Well, there's none of us dumb enough to get up there and fool with that electricity." The NSP man said, "Yes, I'm sure of that, Miz Davis. You're too smart to get up there on that pole."

Dad's restraint and my mother's sunny disposition were both put to a terrible test in 1920. Our neighborhood included some horrible characters. One was a large black man with a reputation as a sex maniac and a murderer. Word was that he had slit more than one throat. One late-winter day, when my dad was working and my mom was home with small children in the house, this man came into the house and raped her. As a result, she became pregnant with the sister closest in age to me, Eva Juanita. My mother was only twenty-three when Eva, her fifth child, was born.

Understandably, my dad went into a rage and set out to kill the man who attacked my mother. But as word of what happened got around the neighborhood, the system of rough justice that ruled the Hellhole took over. Ben Wilson, a racketeer who was sometimes called "the mayor of north Minneapolis," intervened. He found the offender and told him to get out of town, right now, and stay out, or he was a dead man. He said he would blow his brains out—and Ben Wilson would have. My dad or my mother's brothers would have too if they had found him first. The rapist complied with Wilson's order. My family never saw him again.

My parents gave no serious thought to calling the Minneapolis police. In 1920, our neighborhood was essentially without police protection. What little attention the police paid to the Hellhole was aimed at lining their own pockets. Racketeers paid the cops to look the other way.

Not many years later, the neighborhood got a more dedicated police officer, a plainclothesman named Leonard Colston. He was about six-foot-four or -five, weighed at least 250 pounds, and was black but fair-skinned. He was married to a white woman and lived in northeast Minneapolis, so he was either passing for white or intimidating anyone who might give him difficulty. He was so forceful that the racketeers on the Avenue were afraid of him. He saw his role differently than did the cops who had come before; he believed he was there to protect the families in the neighborhood. To us kids, he was a friend. Oftentimes, he would go into the drugstore and buy candy like Mary Janes, Chocolate Soldiers, and Green Leaves and give them to the neighborhood kids.

My mother's rape says a lot about the North Side of eighty years ago. It was a dangerous place, but at its core it was a close-knit community. Justice was crude and homegrown, but it could be quite effective. Ben Wilson was a racketeer, involved in a variety of illicit activities, but he would not tolerate molesters of his employees or of any of the respectable women in the neighborhood. After all, he lived there too. If a man was discovered to be a molester, he did not stay around the neighborhood long. If he went after children, he risked a quick death sentence. If it had been a young girl that my mother's attacker had raped, he soon would have been lying in the street. The other men would have seen to that. Flamboyant gay men who lived in the neighborhood were tolerated but told, "Don't fool with any kids." A lot of the hoods who hung out on Sixth Avenue had a similar sense of respect, almost of protection, for their neighbors. They would be loitering in front of a smoke shop, admiring their fancy cars and talking over their "business," when my mother and some of us children would walk by. I would hear them say, "Here comes Lee Davis's wife. Watch your language."

Just a few blocks away from the vice of Sixth Avenue was the best of our neighborhood, the Phyllis Wheatley Settlement House. A partnership of sorts developed between Ben Wilson and Gertrude Brown, the first director of the Wheatley. If any of the unsavory elements from the Avenue drifted into the Wheatley, she would tell them to either get out or she would call Ben Wilson—and sometimes she did just that. Wilson would respond just as efficiently as any beat-walking police officer.

The circumstances of Eva's conception and birth bothered my dad a great deal, and I think they changed him. He blamed himself for not being there to protect his family. He always felt that he should have exacted revenge himself, that Ben Wilson should not have interfered. But to his great credit, Dad raised Eva as if she were his own daughter. My mother too loved Eva as much as any of her children. In fact, I think my mother favored Eva a little, out of compassion for her. As a result, the whole family protected her, and people in the neighborhood did not regard her as anything other than one of the Davis kids. She was a pretty girl who lacked the high cheekbones that Dooney and Geraldine had, but she had their sweet temperament. She was our sister.

Some years later, my parents also took into their home the youngest child of my mother's older sister, Frances Pettiford. Frances had nine children and died giving birth to the last, a girl named Joyce. By then, my mother had six children of her own. She had four other sisters who might have stepped forward to raise Frances's orphaned daughter. But my mother always played the role of the responsible big sister in the Jackson family, the same role Armintha had played before her and Dooney would take on later. My mother accepted the responsibility and raised Joyce as a sister to us.

I think I am here in part because of the circumstances surrounding Eva's birth. My mom and dad did not want a child conceived the way Eva was to be the last child born into the Davis family.

3
Little Pops

I WAS BORN ON APRIL 12, 1923, and christened William Harry, after my mother's eldest brother. My arrival was much like that of any other North Side child that year. The birth was at home, attended by one of the neighborhood doctors who practiced medicine of both the legitimate and illegitimate kind in second-story offices above drugstores. The physician who delivered me, a Dr. Red, had a fate that says much about the precarious nature of life on the North Side. While I was still a child, he was murdered.

Shortly after my second birthday, an epidemic of infantile paralysis—later called polio—swept through the Twin Cities. The contagious disease had ravaged other parts of the country earlier but had largely spared Minnesota until then. Hundreds, perhaps thousands, of Twin Cities children were stricken. I was one of them.

My mother, Libby, had been reading about the epidemic in the newspaper, so she responded with alarm when I started complaining about numbness and pain in my legs. She took me downtown to Minneapolis General Hospital (now Hennepin County Medical Center). Doctors in the emergency room recognized that my symptoms were the same as a number of cases they had seen recently. They diagnosed my disorder as infantile paralysis, but they had no idea how to treat it. They turned me over to more experienced doctors, but they were similarly in the dark about what to do.

Meanwhile, my pain had turned to paralysis. My legs could not move from the hips down. Even though I was only two, my memory of this is vivid. I had been an active toddler who loved to run, and all of a sudden I could not. I was frightened and I was in pain. The ache in my legs was severe enough to make me cry.

Libby was the family medicine woman, and her medicine was as good as anything the doctors could prescribe. From years of treating my dad's sports injuries, and from generations of her foremothers treating the sore muscles of field slaves, she knew that heat and massage could work wonders on disabled limbs. So that is what she tried on me. She would fill a tub with water and heat it on the stove until it was piping hot, but not hot enough to burn me, and she would put me in the tub and massage my legs. Then she would make a salve of wintergreen, goose grease, and alcohol, and rub that on my legs from my hips to my toes. She repeated this treatment three or four times a day.

At bedtime, after the same regimen, Libby wrapped my legs in hot Turkish towels. Then she went over the Turkish towels with a hot iron for what seemed a long time to me, keeping a steady application of heat to my legs. No doctor told her to treat my legs that way; she was merely applying the medical skill passed down to her from her mother and grandmother. But the treatment the acclaimed Sister Kenny recommended for polio victims many years later wasn't much different. My mother was doing the right thing.

I could feel the life gradually coming back into my legs. My left leg responded first and more fully, and before long I could hop around on it. My right leg remained rather numb. I could feel the hot packs on that leg, but after it cooled I could not feel a pinprick.

After about a year, some feeling returned to my right leg, but primarily the feeling was pain. My right foot was stiff and curling up toward my shin. The tendons in my foot were shrinking and drawing it up. When I cried in complaint, Libby would make some kind of syrup. Using the name Grandpa Mac gave me, she would ask, "Little Pops, does your leg hurt?" If I said yes, she would give me a teaspoon of the stuff she had brewed. I never knew what it contained, but it worked as a pain reliever and muscle relaxant.

Libby may have been practicing folk medicine, but it was highly regarded in our family. Whenever any of the aunts or uncles or cousins had a cold or a stomachache, they would show up in our living room, asking for advice and medicine. Libby always had time to provide both.

Her treatment of my right foot provided temporary pain relief but could not cure the problem. I could hop on my left leg and hobble around a little on the heel of my right foot, but I could not walk normally. I was deemed a crippled child, and as such I was assigned to start school at age five at the one public school in Minneapolis devoted to the education of handicapped children: Michael Dowling, at 3900 West River Parkway, far from my neighborhood. Every child at that school had a physical disability, often involving their limbs. When I enrolled there in 1928, I was the only child of color in the school.

Michael Dowling in those years was part rehabilitation center, part school. Some teachers were nurses, but several other nurses worked at the school every day. A special bus—navy blue with a white stripe—picked up Dowling children at their homes. My brother, Menzy, used to carry me and place me safely on the bus in the mornings. After school, either Menzy or one of my uncles would be there to carry me off again. The bus driver and a female bus attendant were trained to deal with medical emergencies that might arise with their passengers and give them any assistance they might need. They were nice to the kids.

I was examined when I first got to Michael Dowling and was told I should use a brace on my right leg. It was a metal brace with a special shoe built into it. When I put the brace on, I stepped my foot right in the shoe and tied it up. In the heel there was a metal part with rubber on the bottom, which allowed me to walk on my heel more easily. The brace was uncomfortable at first, but it helped me use my right leg, which was already noticeably smaller than my left.

With the brace, I became one of the more mobile students in my kindergarten class at Michael Dowling School. At first, I thought that was why I was always left behind on Tuesdays and Thursdays, when groups of children would go to the nearby Shriners Hospital for heat and massage therapy on their ailing limbs. Later I learned the real reason I did not go to Shriners: in those years, black children were not treated at that hospital.

I felt less left out after school, when I was back in my neighborhood and able to play at Sumner Field, near our home at 1014 Bryant. A wonderful mixture of kids of all races and religions would show up to play at Sumner Field—Irish, Scandinavian, Jewish, Mexican, African American. I was a little bit of a curiosity to the other kids because of my brace and limp, but I joined in the play all the same.

I was in second or third grade when my teacher announced the arrival of someone at Michael Dowling School who would change my life. "We're going to have a visitor here for quite a while," she said. "His name is Dr. Paul Giessler."

Paul William Giessler was an orthopedic surgeon. Though he was born in

Minneapolis in 1885, he spoke with a thick German accent, so much so that for years I believed he was an immigrant. He trained at the University of Minnesota, served as a captain in the army medical corps during World War I, and then came home to practice and teach. He was both a professor at the University of Minnesota and the head of orthopedics at Minneapolis General Hospital. He was also a founder of Michael Dowling School. He had acquired renown for developing a surgical technique involving the tendons of paralyzed feet and hands that restored movement to the affected limbs. It was said to work especially well with children, whose bodies were still developing.

I met Dr. Giessler a few days later when the principal brought him into each classroom and introduced him to us. He was something of a fascination to us. His German accent made him hard to understand, but I was drawn to this gentle man with his nice smile. He flashed that big smile when he examined me and said German words I couldn't understand. His touch was so tender, you could tell that he had love in his heart.

Some days later, the principal came and said a few words to my teacher, who then read the names of six children at our school whom Dr. Giessler believed he could help. All of them had paralysis in their legs and arms. My name was on the list. I went home that day, wondering and worrying, "Gee, what is he going to do with me?"

It was not long before I found out. Dr. Giessler reappeared on a Tuesday, when the rest of my class was at therapy at Shriners Hospital and I was left behind. He was walking by my room when he noticed me sitting alone. He came in and asked me, in his accent, "Heddy, vat are you doing? You're supposed to be at the Shriners Hospital?" I said, "I don't know, Dr. Giessler. They don't take me." He smiled and put a big hand on my head. "You and I are going to have a good time," he said. "Starting next week, we're going to ride downtown in a car, and you and I are going to be together."

That sounded fine to me. The next Tuesday, as he promised, Dr. Giessler came for me. Outside the school, a big old Packard drove up. It had been furnished for our use by a local charity. I felt very special to be able to ride in a car like that with Dr. Giessler. The other Dowling kids were impressed.

It was the first of several weekly trips I made with Dr. Giessler from school to Minneapolis General. He made them fun. During our rides, he said, "Heddy, I vant you to be my teacher." I'd say, "OK, if I can, Dr. Giessler." He said, "Vhen I mispronounce a vord that you know, I vant you to tell me vhat the vord is." So I tried to help him conquer his accent. I would say, "Instead of 'vell,' say, 'You're getting well,' like well water." Then he would laugh and laugh. Our driver would join in the merriment. Any nervousness I had about the treatment I was to receive was quickly dispelled.

Dr. Giessler told me that he would do for me what the doctors at Shriners Hospital were doing for my classmates. He had a device that looked like a metal shield, covered on the inside with light bulbs. He put me on a table, covered my leg with a Turkish towel, then placed this shield on my leg. He said, "I'm going to pull this switch and all the lights are going to go on, and you'll feel the heat on your legs. That's what they do at Shriners Hospital." I recognized that it was much like what my mother had done for me since the start of my affliction.

One day he took me into an examining room, put me on a table, and held my foot. He felt where the tendon on the top of my foot was tight. He studied it for a while, then took an indelible pencil and drew a line on the top of my foot. It was where he would make an incision. I was to have surgery. He did that examination for about three successive weeks, not always drawing the line in the same place, as if he was uncertain how to proceed. On one of our drives from school, he advised me, "Today, I'm going to have some other doctors come in, and they are going to draw some pictures on your foot too. It won't hurt you; it will just tickle."

Then he started to explain to me: "What I'm going to do, Heddy—inside your foot, there is a tendon, like a muscle, that moves your foot back and forth, like you do your other one. What has happened is that tendon in your right foot is shrinking. It's attached to the front part of your foot, so your foot is curling back. I'm going to open that up and cut the tendon and add some catgut to the two sides and stitch them back together so that your foot will drop down. After that heals, we're going to give you some exercises to make you move your foot back and forth. You tell your mother that when we do this, you won't go to school for a while. When we schedule the surgery, I'm going to pick you up at your house in one of these cars, and we're going to go directly to General Hospital. Tell your mother we want her to go with us."

So that was the plan. I was asked to fill my mother in because we did not have a telephone, but it seemed that my mother always knew what Dr. Giessler was doing. Perhaps there had been an exchange of letters or a visit at our house that I did not know about.

I felt proud one day at the hospital when I overheard Dr. Giessler say to another doctor, "Look what his mother did to the left leg and look what she's done to the right leg. You can move it. Just think of the knowledge she had—to understand that there was soreness in the legs and it had to be treated." I am convinced that my mother saved my left leg. Her medicine had but one limitation: Nothing she did could lengthen that shrinking tendon. Only surgery could do that.

On the big day, I was scared. So many strangers were looking at me, fussing over me. But Dr. Giessler was wonderful in explaining every detail of the surgery to me and to my mother. He said, "Heddy, we're going to take you into this little room on the side. We're going to put a gown on you and a thing on your head. Then we're going to take you into a room, and I'll wheel you underneath a bunch of lights. There are going to be nurses and doctors all around. What I'm going to do is cut open your foot. When I reach these tendons, I'm going to cut them and attach this catgut"—or whatever—"to each end, so that your foot will drop down. We're going to hold that so you can't move it until it heals. When it heals, we're going to see if you can move your foot back and forth. . . . We're going to put something over your face." Of course, that was the ether. "Then you will go to sleep. When you wake up, we'll be all through with all of this."

There was never anything said about paying for the operation. All I know is that my family did not pay and could not have paid. Dr. Giessler took a special interest in me. I suspect that he provided his services for free.

The procedure lasted five or six hours. It was a long and fretful day for my mother. I was her baby, after all. She stayed in the waiting room the whole time; my dad joined her right after he got off work. He drove his Como Nut truck downtown because we did not have a car. He parked the truck in front of the hospital. By the time he got there, I was out of surgery.

All I could see, when I came to, was a cast from my hip down to my toes. It kept my leg straight and perfectly still. I was awake when Dr. Giessler came to inform my parents about the surgery. He used a pen to draw a little diagram on the cast to illustrate what he had done, then he signed his name to it. That signature was something to brag about when I got back to school. I'd tell all the kids, "Look! Dr. Giessler signed my cast."

The cast stayed on for six weeks and nearly drove me nuts. My leg itched terribly, but I could not scratch it. The cast was awfully heavy. I used crutches with it and got pretty good with them; I could spin around on one crutch.

I was a happy boy when Dr. Giessler announced, "Tomorrow, Heddy, we're going to take the cast off." He did that procedure right at Michael Dowling School and arranged for my mother to be present. He took us into a small room where he used some big, scary-looking scissorslike things to cut the cast all the way down the side of my leg. When he pulled it open and looked, he saw that my leg had shrunk. It was smaller than my left leg.

He asked me to move, and I started to move my foot up and down. Dr. Giessler watched for a moment, then declared, "Your right leg is going to be shorter and smaller than the other, but you're going to be able to walk!" I looked at my mother and she was crying. Dr. Giessler was so happy, he was shouting. I was too. What a moment that was!

I walked on crutches for another month. Almost every day, Dr. Giessler would come to Dowling School and check on me. After a few days, he would take the crutches away and ask me to walk short distances. I still was not allowed to go to Shriners Hospital for therapy, so Dr. Giessler became my therapist as well as my doctor. He would not let me go without the care I needed just because of prejudice. He gave me wonderful encouragement as I learned all over again how to walk, then how to run.

I was walking steadily and running a little within six or seven weeks, and running pretty well within three months. At first I had no clear memory of what it was like to run; I had not run since I was two years old. You forget even the most basic skills if you don't practice them. My mother took me to Phyllis Wheatley Settlement House after school so that I could practice running in a supervised setting. I was sometimes discouraged, but then those kind instructors at Phyllis Wheatley would say, "Let's have a hopping contest." They knew that I could outhop any kid who was used to having two good legs.

Before the end of fourth grade, Dr. Giessler had a talk with my teacher and principal at Michael Dowling School. "Harry is doing well enough now that he won't have to stay here," he told them. "He can go to his neighborhood school now." They didn't wait until the end of the year to move me; I was told I would start at Sumner School the following Monday. My teacher cried as she said good-bye to me that Friday afternoon, saying over and over, "I'm going to miss you here. I'm going to miss you." The principal came in to say good-bye too. Then in came Dr. Giessler. He hugged me and said, "I don't want you to forget me. I won't forget you."

With that, I was off to Sumner School and a more typical life as a north-

Minneapolis kid in the 1930s. I was the first child in the history of Minneapolis Public Schools to be mainstreamed. And with that, Dr. Paul Giessler, the man who saved me from a life as a cripple, went out of my life, only to reappear many years later. It was 1946 and I was a young man, married and a father, trying to piece together a living after having been laid off from a defense-plant job. With another man in a similar fix, I went into the household-maintenance business. Our specialty was removing storm windows in the spring and replacing them in the fall.

One day when we were working at a big, imposing house on East Lake Harriet Boulevard, I noticed I was being watched by a man in a wheelchair inside the house. As I moved from window to window, he moved too, watching me closely. I smiled and waved at him and he returned the gesture. Finally, he motioned for me to raise the window, which I did. He said, "Young man, I cannot help thinking that I know you. What is your name?" When I told him, his jaw dropped, then he burst into a big grin. "Harry, I'm Dr. Giessler!" he said. I did not recognize him. He had aged beyond his years and was himself now unable to walk. Heart disease had shortened his career; he had been retired since 1936.

We renewed our friendship that day, and I stayed in touch with him, making occasional visits and phone calls, for the rest of his life. He lived only a few more years, dying in 1951. I felt blessed to be able to return some of the kindness he had shown me.

Polio left me with a right leg that would always be shorter and weaker than the left. But the physical damage was no great handicap. I could not be a runner, but I could high-jump well. I could play quarterback in football, pitch a mean softball, and hold my own for short bursts on the basketball court. The more significant impact of childhood polio may have been on my developing personality. I had learned early how to endure pain, how to get along with others from a position of weakness, and how to find happiness even in adversity. I saw the worst thing that had ever happened to me overcome through the knowledge and kindness of another human being. Polio made me believe in the power of kindness.

4
Hellhole

MY MOVE TO SUMNER SCHOOL in fourth grade narrowed my world to the neighborhood that some people called the Hellhole. It was a place unlike any other in Minneapolis—more diverse, more dangerous, more disadvantaged, but also, somehow, more alive.

My neighborhood's center was the junction of Sixth and Lyndale Avenues North. Sixth Avenue was the street dominated by retail shops. Lyndale, which was also Highway 65, was more of an entertainment street with restaurants. Lyndale, in that part of Minneapolis, grew up to be Interstate Highway 94; Sixth Avenue is now Olson Memorial Highway.

Then, like now, they were thoroughfares into downtown, the South Side, and St. Paul. But in the 1920s and 1930s, they were something more: they were an after-dark destination for people throughout the region who were looking for a less than legal good time. Prohibition did not get in the way of business in the Hellhole. Beer parlors stayed open, allegedly selling only nonalcoholic near beer. But each owner would have a relationship with a bootlegger who would be on hand to sell his patrons a mickey. Buy a bottle of near beer, pour some in a glass with a mickey, and you have a drink more potent than pre-Prohibition beer ever was. Kids regularly saw people staggering when they left near-beer parlors.

Sixth and Lyndale probably had more vice per square foot than any place west of Chicago. But during daytime hours, more of the business activity on those streets was legitimate than illegitimate. The speakeasies and brothels would go into operation at night. Some storefronts had a split personality. For instance, a tailor shop would also sell policy, an illegal numbers game. Or a drugstore would offer both kinds of drugs, depending on the proprietor's level of trust in the customer.

Jewish people owned most of the neighborhood's businesses, but blacks owned a few businesses too. Woodard's funeral parlor was a successful one. White funeral parlors did not cater to blacks, so in Minneapolis and black neighborhoods in cities around the country, black-owned funeral parlors prospered. The Woodards also owned a grocery store on Sixth and Bryant Avenues, and they were prominent in the Elks Club, Phyllis Wheatley, and other community organizations.

The neighborhood was loaded with drugstores, one every block or two. Some were on the up-and-up; some were fronts for the underworld. The one right on the corner of Sixth and Lyndale had a doctor's office upstairs that was known for treating a lot of prostitutes. Next door, going west, was Sam Schuere's clothing store. Then there was a little alley, and a little place called the Bright Spot, which sold cigarettes, candy, and pop and served as kind of a cabstand for a jitney, an unlicensed cab. A crap game was generally going on in the back room. Kids could come in the front part of the Bright Spot, but one of the men would stop them if they tried to go in the back. Next to the Bright Spot was Feldman's grocery store. That was one of the most popular grocery stores because the Feldman family lived right there, sent their kids to Sumner School, and extended credit to a lot of families during the 1930s.

The next building was large and ran all the way to Aldrich. It had upstairs apartments where people of the night lived—prostitutes, racketeers, musicians. On the street level was Howard's Steak House, a restaurant that featured live music and things going on in the back room that kids weren't supposed to know about. It was owned by Howard Walker, a black fellow from the neighborhood who was a tap dancer and a drummer. His restaurant served mostly people from other parts of town who came to the Avenue for a night of fun. Those of us who lived there couldn't often afford a steak dinner at a restaurant; but Howard used to let some of his neighbors know that, for a birthday or special occasion, they could come into his restaurant early in the evening—before the musicians and the bootleggers came in—and he would serve them dinner at a reasonable price. Howard was one of several black restaurant owners in the neighborhood. Others owned the chicken shacks and barbecues, like the Monarch Barbecue, that dotted the area.

Next to Howard's was Sam Bass, a clothing store a little larger than Sam Schuere's. I knew Sam Bass well. He knew all the families in the neighborhood and was well liked. He gave my mother credit when things were hard for my family and I needed new shoes. Next on the street was a Chinese laundry, whose owners lived in the back room of the store and sold a little policy on the side. A lot of the Chinese-owned laundries in the city in those years had the same sideline, all organized by my neighborhood's native son, Isadore Blumenfeld, better known as the mob boss Kid Cann.

Another drugstore, on the corner of Aldrich and Sixth Avenues, was owned and operated by a man I remember as Benny. His was one of the legitimate drugstores, interested in serving the neighborhood. It had a soda fountain where teenagers could hang out. Benny took an interest in the neighborhood kids and encouraged a number of young men to consider a career in pharmacy. My friend Archie Givens, who grew up to own several nursing homes, got his start working for Benny.

There were good relationships between many of the Jewish merchants and their black customers. Another popular store was Adlin's Grocery Store on Bryant Avenue. The Adlins were a wonderful family. One of their sons, Hymie, grew up to be one of the founders of several casinos in Las Vegas. He married several times, once to a black girl with whom I went to school. Interracial couples were not uncommon in our neighborhood. They got nasty stares only if they went downtown, which none of us often did. We had everything we needed or could afford right there.

Above Adlin's was the office of a Jewish doctor named Dr. Labosky. He treated a lot of the families in the neighborhood, white and black, as did the doctor who treated our family for decades, W. D. Brown. Dr. Labosky lived in the neighborhood too. In some respects, our neighborhood was decades ahead of the rest of the city in terms of integration.

The neighborhood included a Jewish-owned department store, Swatez, on Girard Avenue. The high-quality store sold dressy clothes as well as shoes and underwear, and it drew customers from beyond the immediate neighborhood. It was big enough to employ some people from the neighborhood. So did a window-shade company next door to Adlin's Grocery. On the corner of Sixth and Colfax, a used-furniture store also sold the stoves most homes used for heating. We lived for a time in the apartments above that store.

On up the street, at Sixth and Dupont, was a smoke shop where the big-shot racketeers hung out and played high-stakes games. Sometimes groups of black pimps would be in there too. It was a dangerous zone. Right next door was the Liberty, our neighborhood movie theater, where we used to go on Saturday afternoons to see cowboy movies and adventure serials—Buck Jones, Tom Mix, and all of those. One afternoon, when I was about ten, my friends and I came out of the Liberty Theater and saw a group of racketeers and gangsters standing in front of the smoke shop. A car came careening down the street at high speed, and a guy in the car poked a submachine gun out a window. We heard the sound of repeating shots. Several guys on the street were hit; one was killed. We saw the blood jump right out of him, and he fell over in the gutter. If we had come out a little sooner, we would have been in the line of fire. The gunman started shooting before he had careful aim. He didn't care who else he mowed down.

That wasn't the only murder I witnessed. We would sometimes see men in fistfights on the street, and then, suddenly, one of them would drop. Someone had pulled a knife or a gun to settle the dispute. One kid I knew watched as his father tried to break up a fight and was shot as a result. That kind of thing was unusual during daylight hours, but at night the activity on the streets was different. When the sun went down, you would hear the mothers along Aldrich, Lyndale, Lyndale Place, Colfax, and Bassett Place calling kids into their homes. The lights would be lit on Sixth Avenue, the music would start, and the mothers would want their children home. It wasn't all that rare to see a corpse on the street in the morning.

But criminal episodes did not dominate life on the Avenue, which is what we called Sixth Avenue North. They were just that—episodes, against a backdrop of families trying to make a living, educate their kids, and get ahead. A lot of big families lived in the neighborhood, people with six or seven kids. The Hammond family was like that, and the Robinson family. There were the Demrys, the Lacys, the Strawders, the Barbies, the Pattersons, the Bells, the Givenses. You would not be acquainted with just one member of the family; you would know them all, and their mothers would know you. The moms of those families had permission from your mother to spank you if you got out of line while you were in their yard or by their house. There were clear community standards of discipline, and they were enforced.

Similarly, a store was not just a store to us but had an owner we knew, from a family we knew, who most often lived close by. Absentee ownership of a business was almost unheard of. Typical was Eisenstadt's grocery, near Sixth and Emerson. The grocer was one Eisenstadt brother; upstairs was the office of his twin brother, a doctor. We knew them both and their other relatives too. Similarly, we were acquainted with the owners of the neighborhood's gas station, a Pure Oil station, on the corner of Sixth and Emerson. Those were families that went on to some prominence in the city—the Ratners and the Wolfensons. Harvey Ratner and Marv Wolfenson are business partners to this day, having founded and sold the Minnesota Timberwolves and founded the Northwest health-club chain.

As a boy, I knew some of the racketeers rather well. Ben Wilson, the so-called mayor of north Minneapolis, was someone I could greet by name. So, of course, was my uncle, Scotty Williams. He played the drums in a jazz band, controlled a harem of prostitutes, and owned three or four fancy cars. That was one way we kids came to recognize the racketeers—by their cars. The legitimate people in our neighborhood drove Fords and Chevys and Plymouths, if they owned cars at all. The pimps and bootleggers drove Cords and Auburns and Packards. Whether they were illegitimate or legitimate, the people I knew were friendly and nice. They seemed genuinely concerned about the safety of neighborhood kids.

Most merchants lived either in their stores or in houses on the streets that ran north and south from Sixth Avenue. Those streets were as integrated as any place in the Upper Midwest in the 1930s. Blacks and Jews predominated—blacks as renters, Jews as landlords—but there was a smattering of Irish, Latinos, and Scandinavians too. The houses they lived in were two-story, wood-frame structures that had been built between 1870 and 1900. They were long, narrow houses, always with a porch in front. They all had living and dining rooms, kitchens with cookstoves that burned wood or gas, small yards, bedrooms upstairs, dirt floors in the cellars. They were well-made houses, but by the 1930s they were showing their age. Few houses had central heating. The old stoves that provided heat in the winter also guaranteed a cold start to every morning six months of the year. Most houses had indoor plumbing, but when the weather turned cold the pipes would freeze. Someone would then go to the basement with a newspaper, roll it up, light it, and run it like a torch along the pipes to break the ice jam. All of the houses had electrical power, though it was sometimes cut off when a family failed to pay its utility bill.

In the middle of it all, just a block from Sixth and Lyndale, stood Sumner School. It was a large building, taking up half of a full city block and serving kindergarten through ninth grade. Sumner's principal and teachers saw themselves in a day-to-day battle of sorts for the futures of the neighborhood's kids. The Avenue offered one way of life to them; Sumner School offered another, and was prepared to use some force to keep children from straying. Children weren't permitted to leave the school grounds during recess and lunch hour in those years. If any student did, he or she could and would be spanked. Parents gave their permission for spankings, and most did not hesitate to do so. After a child turned ten years old, a parent could give permission for him or her to be spanked by the principal with a belt. Not many kids got that treatment, but we all knew the consequences for misbehavior.

Sumner's student population reflected the neighborhood fairly well. It was about a third to half black. Finnish and Scandinavian kids from Glenwood Avenue and Mexican children from over by Seventh Street mixed with Jewish and black kids from our neighborhood. Students of various races and backgrounds got along well. There were few fights along racial lines. Sumner School created a natural feeling of togetherness among the children and convinced us not to worry about each other's color.

The teaching staff, by comparison, was all white. But I have no complaint about the quality of my teachers or their sense of social and racial justice. I had wonderful teachers at Sumner School. I held them in the same esteem as I did my parents. Teachers like Miss Blakely and Miss Hood were just like our mothers. They provided an extension of the discipline we had at home. They would correct students, usually in the nicest way. They would talk to you like this: "Really, Harry, what good was the fight? I see you've got some bruises. They hurt, don't they?" "Yes." "Well, if you don't get into a fight, you don't get bruises." Then, if you were bad enough, they would say the ominous words: "I'm going to talk to your mother."

My parents, and all the parents I knew, were very satisfied with their children's experiences at Sumner. Teachers and parents had close relationships in those years, even though not many families had telephones. When a teacher wanted to speak with a parent, she would call the Phyllis Wheatley Settlement House and ask the staff there to relay the message. If the parent didn't come around to get the message, an older brother or sister almost certainly would and be pressed into service as messenger. A message from a teacher was a grave matter and treated with utmost seriousness.

When I started at Sumner School, I was the new kid, even though I was sitting beside children I had seen and played with at Sumner Field for years. I was different. I was small for my age, and my right leg was markedly shorter and weaker than my left. My hair was wavier than the other black kids' hair. My mother fussed over me and made sure my hair was brushed just so. She would wash my face until she had almost sandpapered it. She dressed me in a nice white shirt and neat little blue pants, fancier than those other kids wore. My brother said, "Lib, don't dress him like that. Those kids are going to beat him up." My mom replied, "That's my baby. He's got to look nice when he goes to school."

Menzy was right, of course. The other kids teased me, and worse. My mom eventually got the message and stopped her grooming routine, but the teasing and taunting and occasional fistfights continued. Walking home from school became a misery for me.

I was in fifth grade, still enduring this treatment, when I came home one springtime afternoon to a surprise. My dad's younger half-brother, Clarence, whom we called Dixie, had arrived for a visit. He was a professional boxer, a nationally ranked middleweight who contended twice for the world championship. He was in his mid-thirties then, maybe a little past his prime but still very much an active boxer. His visits with us always came after important professional bouts; he would stay with us to rest, heal his wounds, and begin to train for his next fight. I had come bruised and limping into the house that day, but I quickly forgot my own wounds when I took a look at Uncle Dixie. He was in much worse shape than I.

Still, I must not have looked too good. "Little Pops, what's the matter?" he immediately asked. So I told him about the trouble I was having with school-yard bullies. "I still can't run too fast. I can't get away from them," I said. "Little Pops, you don't need to learn how to run faster," he said. "You need to learn how to box."

I was an eager pupil and my uncle was a good teacher. That very day, we began daily lessons in the manly art of self-defense. I quickly learned that the thugs who were on my tail after school were merely fighters; all they did was throw punches. I was being trained to be a boxer, and that was a far better thing. Boxing begins with the basic punches and stances, but then teaches leverage and balance. It teaches how to move the body to get the most leverage and what position to be in to throw the fastest and hardest punches. A boxer learns to bob and weave, to dodge punches and counterpunches.

Uncle Dixie would hold up his hands, and I would practice my punches on them, with him giving me steady feedback and instruction. I learned all the basic punches. There's the straight punch, the one that you throw straight ahead. There's the cross-punch, thrown from right to left or left to right. There's the hook, where you get out and around and strike your opponent on the side of the face. There's the uppercut, which lands underneath an opponent's chin. There's the looper, where you kind of throw your right hand and loop it over and down so that it lands on the top part of the opponent's face. I learned what position I had to be in to throw each of the punches. I learned the counterpunch variations on the basic punches so I could deflect punches thrown my way. Fighters simply throw any old punch without thinking. A boxer is always thinking to make sure his legs and arms move and work together, to make sure he always has balance and is in control.

I found Uncle Dixie's lessons fascinating because I was not just learning what to do, but why. Rope-skipping is an example. People think skipping rope builds endurance, and it does. But the main reason a boxer skips rope is to build the muscles in his lower calves, ankles, feet, and toes. A boxer needs strong feet and toes for speed and agility. He needs to be surefooted.

Uncle Dixie's stay in Minneapolis was a long one that year, and my lessons ran well into summer vacation. Those lessons were my first serious attempt to become physically skillful. Polio had deprived me of a lot of the physical-skill development other kids routinely acquire. What I discovered that summer was that as I learned to be a boxer, I was also becoming a better batter in baseball. I was concentrating on my stance and the leverage that comes with a proper swing. I could throw a ball farther and stronger because I thought about how to set my foot for maximum leverage. I applied the same ideas to football and learned how to fake a defender out of position. That summer brought about my transformation from crippled child to athlete.

Part of the fun of that transformation was the closeness I developed with Uncle Dixie. He was single and had no children of his own, but he seemed to have a natural gift for teaching and relating to the young. He spent a great deal of time with me, patiently giving advice, praising me when I did well, hugging me to show how much he cared. He was training for his next fight, and he involved me in that. Sometimes I ran with him when he did his roadwork. We would talk about how to move our legs and feet and how to breathe. When he would compliment me on being a fast learner, that would make me run all the harder and faster. Uncle Dixie was not just teaching; he was giving me the ability and the desire to learn. That made a big difference.

Finally, the day came when the lessons were over. "The time is up," Uncle Dixie said. Both of his wounded eyes had healed and cleared. He had an appointment for another fight in another city. As for me, school was about to start. I was soon going to have to face the bullies at school. Two boys in particular had been my tormenters. I concocted a plan for dealing with them if they had not dropped their interest in me over the summer.

Sure enough, those two were on my tail after school the very first day. I put my plan into action. I still could not run as fast as those bigger boys, but I could do pretty well for a short distance. I decided to run down Bassett Place, a short, alleylike street between Bryant and Aldrich Avenues. I waited until I knew they were following me, then took off down Bassett Place toward Eighth Avenue. Between Bassett Place and Bryant were several buildings, including one that housed the Knitting Works, an underwear manufacturer. That building had a large red-brick chimney in back and a narrow passageway just big enough for one person to come through. I led them to that place because Uncle Dixie had advised me not to try to fight two people at once. Try to get into a situation that permits facing your adversaries one at a time, he had said. That passageway was just such a location. I ran and positioned myself between the building and the chimney. They ran right in after me, one at a time, exactly as I had planned. Then punches flew—and, boy, did the punches and leverage Uncle Dixie taught me work wonders! My punches landed fast and hard. That day, finally, I was not the one to come home bloodied and crying. In fact, they had not been able to land a blow on me.

When I got home that day, my mother was waiting. "How come you're late?" she asked. "I was kind of fooling around," I said evasively, which never fooled Libby. "Tell me the truth now. How come you're late?" So I told her what had happened. Even though she knew what grief those boys had caused me, she was less than pleased about my vindication. She said, "Mr. Everson [the principal] will probably be calling me because their parents will say that you started it and you beat them up."

Libby was right. The next day, my teacher, Miss Hill, said, "Harry, Mr. Everson wants to see you." She asked the boys I had fought to join me in the principal's office. Then, as I passed by her on the way out the door, she whispered to me, "Nice going, Harry." She had heard what had happened and knew what I had been through the year before. Mr. Everson seemed to know too. He lectured the three of us in general about not fighting and warned us that our parents would be called if any further incidents occurred. But he did not suggest that I had been an instigator of trouble.

There were no further incidents. As word got around school that I had bested those two toughies, everybody else left me alone. I felt as if I was finally welcome in my own neighborhood.

5
Phyllis Wheatley

THERE WAS ONE PLACE IN my neighborhood where I always felt welcome. It was Phyllis Wheatley Settlement House, my second home.

The Wheatley was always part of my life, or very nearly so, since it was founded on October 17, 1924, when I was eighteen months old. It was a settlement house, much like ones established a decade or two earlier in other parts of the city to acclimate new European immigrants to Minnesota. This settlement house was not intended to serve new Americans, but the descendants of the Africans who had come to the New World in shackles. It was named after one such immigrant. Phyllis Wheatley was an eighteenth-century slave girl who had the good fortune to be raised as the foster daughter of an enlightened white Boston family and given an education. Wheatley wrote poetry that was highly regarded by the likes of George Washington and Tom Paine.

It's fair to say that Phyllis Wheatley House is what made the African Americans of north Minneapolis a functioning community. There were black people living there for a generation or more before the Wheatley was founded, but they were just living there, not living together. The Wheatley provided those people with purpose, insight, and motivation. It provided relationships. It taught people to get along, to help one another, and to raise their families successfully in a challenging environment.

The Wheatley Settlement House was founded not by black people, but for black people by the all-white Women's Christian Association. This group of affluent, well-educated churchwomen sincerely wanted to better the lives of people in their city. Theirs was perhaps the oldest social-service organization in the city, founded in 1866 with the mission of collecting clothing to distribute to newly freed slaves in the South. The organization founded in 1888 the still-thriving Jones-Harrison home for the elderly on the shores of Cedar Lake and established numerous boardinghouses for single women and downtrodden men throughout the city. The association's members were troubled by the poverty, prostitution, chemical dependency, and other ills they saw in the city's black community, which was growing in Minneapolis as it was in other northern cities after World War I.

From today's vantage, it's easy to fault the churchwomen for prescribing and implementing a solution to my community's problems without consulting and involving my community first. But for their day, the members of the Women's Christian Association were as progressive and socially conscious as any members of the white ruling class in Minneapolis—and probably more than most. They were trying to be helpful to my community, and when they founded the Wheatley, they were helpful indeed. They showed me and other kids in my neighborhood a more positive side of white people than we were exposed to in other settings.

Originally, the mission of Phyllis Wheatley House was to redeem the lives of the prostitutes, prospective prostitutes, and former prostitutes along Sixth Avenue North. It would seek to turn young women away from the oldest profession toward less dangerous, more respectable careers. But the vision of the Wheatley's first director, Gertrude Brown, was much bigger. She saw the need for a one-stop help center for all the black people in the neighborhood who were trying to make a living and raise families on the legitimate side of the law. Her talent and the force of her personality were both as big as her vision. In just thirteen years as the house's director and head resident, she made Phyllis Wheatley the lively heart of the north-Minneapolis black community.

The Wheatley was able to assume a large role in part because so many of the community's basic needs were otherwise unmet. For example, black students could enroll at the University of Minnesota, but they could not live in dormitories on campus. So they were housed at Phyllis Wheatley, often for free but in exchange for their commitment to tutor or coach children in the Wheatley's programs. Likewise, when black entertainers came to Minneapolis in the 1930s, they were welcome to perform downtown, but not to stay in downtown hotels. They too stayed at Phyllis Wheatley. Kids coming to activities at the Wheatley after school might bump into members of Count Basie's or Duke Ellington's orchestras, jamming in a vacant classroom, getting ready for a performance that night.

The Wheatley got its start in an old, two-story wooden structure on Bassett Place that had been previously occupied by the Hebrew Talmud Farah School. My first memories of going to Phyllis Wheatley are of that building and my mother pushing me there in a buggy when I was three or four years old. But that building was too small to house Gertrude Brown's vision. In 1929, with the substantial support of the Women's Christian Association and the businesses of its members' husbands, an imposing three-level brick structure was built to take its place. It consumed nearly half a city block, between Eighth and Ninth Avenues on Aldrich, and cost $32,000 to build—a large sum in those days. The building was designed largely to Miss Brown's specifications. She wanted a large commercial kitchen capable of serving several dozen people on a routine night and several hundred people for banquets with some frequency. She wanted most of the building's top floor devoted to dormitorylike rooms to house the black students, entertainers, and visitors who could not find lodging anywhere else in the city. She wanted a gymnasium where young people could receive training from the university athletes who stayed upstairs, as well as a balcony to accommodate the crowds that might come to watch them compete. She wanted a library filled with the works of black authors and classrooms outfitted for lessons ranging from music to home economics to grooming. One large room would contain a nursery school; another would house a used-clothing distribution center, an important place for large families during the Great Depression. The building also included an apartment, where Miss Brown lived. She was never off duty.

Gertrude Brown was a statuesque, striking woman who never married. Born in Ohio, she was educated at Columbia University in New York, then worked in Charlotte, North Carolina, before coming to Minneapolis at age thirty-five. She was intelligent and opinionated, her principal opinion being that black Americans are first-class citizens, deserving the same rights and bearing the same responsibilities as white Americans. Some people called her a troublemaker, for she did not hold back her views; she left no doubt about who was in charge at Phyllis Wheatley. But she was as kind as she was forceful, and she was especially gentle to the children who were Wheatley regulars, like me.

Miss Brown's greatest strength may have been her organizational skill. She planned. She would plan programs for a whole school year before the previous school year had ended. She would be in contact with the university and other organizations to know what resources they might have that she could appropriate for the Wheatley. Were entertainers scheduled to come to town whom she could get to perform at the settlement house? Were some lawyers available to do pro bono work or medical professionals able to donate a day of their services? Could a law firm give a summer internship to a promising young man or woman? Might a librarian be available to join a Wheatley library committee, or could a teacher serve on the education committee?

Miss Brown was always in the know and never afraid to ask anyone to do almost anything for her house or the people it served.

She quickly positioned the Wheatley on the front line of the neighborhood's defense against the vice of Sixth Avenue and mounted a day-by-day battle for the hearts and minds of the neighborhood's children. After school, boys and girls who did not go straight home had only two choices: they could wander down to the Avenue, where they could see what was happening with the pimps, gamblers, and bootleggers, or they could go to Phyllis Wheatley, where the boys might join a pickup basketball game and the girls might have a cooking or grooming class. No other after-school programs were available for school-age children in those years. The neighborhood had a park, but its only organized activities were sponsored by Phyllis Wheatley: College students who stayed at Phyllis Wheatley taught neighborhood kids to play tennis on Sumner Field's courts. Summer band concerts at Sumner Field were performed by people connected to the Wheatley. The only competition with other youth sports teams was that arranged by Miss Brown and her staff with the directors of the other settlement houses in the city. The neighborhood parents and Sumner School teachers applauded Miss Brown's work and urged the children to participate. But it was up to Miss Brown and her staff to make the Wheatley's offerings fun, interesting, and inviting. If they had not done that, no amount of cajoling by parents and teachers would have kept the young people there.

When I first went to Phyllis Wheatley after school, at age five and six, it was with my older sisters. All of them were involved in the programs there, as was my brother, Menzy. They kept me close to them because of my handicap, and, as a result, I got to know a number of kids older than I. They were all so excited about the new building and the expanded programs that it made possible. Little guy that I was, I absorbed their enthusiasm for the place and concluded that Phyllis Wheatley was *the* place to be.

A lot of adults in the community were coming to the same conclusion in the early 1930s. The Minneapolis chapters of the National Association for the Advancement of Colored People and the Urban League were founded before the Phyllis Wheatley Center opened, but they were small and ineffective before they connected with Miss Brown. She allowed them to make the Wheatley their headquarters and assisted them with membership recruitment and organizational development. She put them in touch with educated people who could give them direction. Similarly, she summoned black ministers in the city to a meeting and encouraged them to form a ministerial alliance to work together on community problems. With her as their adviser, those organizations took off.

The black community in Minneapolis in the 1930s was actually two groups: one in my neighborhood and the other, a more middle-class and better-educated crowd, clustered close to Central High School on the city's South Side. Miss Brown set out to bridge the several-mile gap that divided the two. She became acquainted with people who lived on the South Side and offered them meeting space and Wheatley resources for their professional organizations. She showed those who were interested in service projects the needs that existed in their own city. Before long, Phyllis Wheatley was drawing able, educated people from all over the city into my neighborhood, providing young people like me with a wider range of role models than Sixth Avenue could.

Miss Brown was very persuasive; some would call her bossy. At the beginning of every school year, she would get all the kids and their parents to come together to a meeting in the Wheatley's gymnasium. Even those who lived on the borderline of the law showed up. It was an unusual family in my neighborhood that chose to stay away, and if one did, Miss Brown would make it her business to know why. She was interested in serving the children, no matter what the occupation of the parents, legal or otherwise. She would tell them outright, "Do you have children? I want to see your children here. If your children come, you come." But she would add a warning: "When you come here, you act like you're civilized. I don't want any stuff going on, or I'll put you out, and you can't come here anymore."

At the annual meeting, Miss Brown would go through the program for the year, not asking, but telling, you to participate. "Here's what we're going to have for your children this fall and this winter," she would say. "Here are the organizations and the Ministerial Alliance that are going to be here. If your minister is not a member of the Ministerial Alliance, please, have him get in touch with me. You'll have medical examinations for your children required by the school system here. You can bring them in at such-and-such a time. We're going to have scheduled, organized sports groups that will be taught by Horace Bell, who is a University of Minnesota football player. . . ." The speech would be long, but no one would stir or interrupt. "If you're looking at improving your cooking, or if you don't know how to cook certain things, we have classes for you at Phyllis Wheatley. We want your teenage girls to come and learn and attend the cooking classes. We want your teenage sons to come too. Mrs. Jones is going to have a housekeeping class on how to keep your house clean, how to make your beds." Problems at school? Tell us at the Wheatley—we can help. Medical worries? A doctor will be here on Saturdays, seeing people at no charge. Toothache? The dental clinic is in two weeks. A retarded child? We've got the connections to get the help you need. Pimps bothering your daughter? Tell Miss Brown. She'll see that it stops.

In my young eyes, Miss Brown was the very definition of leadership. It seemed she had a hand in everything good happening in my neighborhood. For example, she was acquainted with all the teachers at Sumner School and met frequently with the principal, T. O. Everson. "How are the kids getting along?" she would ask him. They developed strategies together for steering wayward children onto the straight and narrow path. She was heavily involved in the design and organization of the city's first public housing project, at Eighth Avenue between Aldrich and Dupont Avenues, in 1936–1937. She was the one who met with the aldermen. She helped screen the families who moved into the new housing. She ran classes to teach those people how to use a gas stove rather than a woodstove and how to operate a shower when all they had had before was a washtub for baths. She made sure that people knew how to care for those houses, and they followed her instructions.

Miss Brown was not a civil-rights leader in the sense that the people who came a generation later were. But she was preparing us to take our rightful place in society when that opportunity came. She made sure every child who came to Phyllis Wheatley got the message that he or she was just as good as anyone else. She saw to it that every child was taught black history and exposed to books by black authors. She prepared us to show respect and to be respected. She would say, "Although the Lord says, 'Turn the other cheek,' that's pretty hard. You'd better learn how to take care of yourself." She knew that teenagers from our neighborhood sometimes did not get the attention they deserved in high-school extracurricular activities, so she backstopped them with the Wheatley's own drama, debate, music, and sports programs to develop their skills to the fullest.

It was important to her that we learn the manners of polite society. One of her standard speeches at assemblies of children would go like this: "Phyllis Wheatley is your second home. When you walk into your house at home, do you take your cap off? Do you use any foul language? Do you show your parents respect? When you come into Phyllis Wheatley, I want you to do the same thing. If you're a boy, when you come into Phyllis Wheatley, you take your cap off. People on my staff or a volunteer, you address them as Mister and Missus or ma'am and sir." That's what we did too. If you did not, the instructors took note. You could get demerits and get kicked out of Phyllis Wheatley. That would be the worst thing in the world.

To Phyllis Wheatley we brought our questions about the way people of color were treated in the larger world. Those episodes have a way of staying with a person. I remember going downtown with my mother when I was still quite small. It was a hot day, and we sat on a bench downtown for a long time, waiting for the streetcar to take us home. I wanted to go into one of the lunch counters to eat and to have something cold to drink, but my mother said, no, we could not do that. We were not permitted there, because of the color of our skin. If we wanted to go to a movie theater downtown, the State or the Orpheum or the Pantages or the Lyric, we had to sit in the balcony. Farther south, on the lower part of Hennepin, theaters like the Aster or the Bijou would let us sit anywhere we wanted. But those theaters did not have the best reputation, so we took a little chance going there. Nearby was the Marigold Ballroom, a dance hall that brought big-name bands to town. African Americans were not welcome there until long after I was grown and married. But we didn't care. We had a dance hall almost as big as that one at Phyllis Wheatley in our gym. We had better entertainment than they had downtown. In the summer, we had dances outdoors—Friday Night Socials, we called them—with great bands, food, and soft drinks. The best local black bands played there because Miss Brown gave them free rehearsal space.

Miss Brown helped shape our attitudes about white people in a way that kept us from becoming racists. When we would come to her with a story about some incident of discrimination that someone had experienced, she had a ready response: "That was terrible, and the people who did that are bad people. But not all white people are like that. When you see our board of directors, these are the good people that are coming in. These are the people that care about you. These are the people that built this building so you could come and learn." If we said something disparaging about downtown businessmen, about their hiring practices or some such thing, she had a comment to keep us from overgeneralizing: "That company is headed by a board member's husband. They contribute money to Phyllis Wheatley every year."

I will admit that I had an especially close relationship with Miss Brown. I think she felt that I was a special child because of my handicap. It was the same with another disabled child in the neighborhood, Hardy White, who was maybe four years younger and the brother of future Minneapolis City Council member Van White. Miss Brown paid extra attention to Hardy and me. When she saw me come in to Phyllis Wheatley, she would hug me and ask me how I was doing.

Her extra attention became all the more important to me after a dark day in 1935. We were living then on the corner of Colfax and Sixth Avenues. After school that day, I went to Phyllis Wheatley for an hour or so. When I came back home, I saw my dad carrying boxes out of the house and loading them into his truck. The boxes contained his clothes. I went upstairs and found my mother sitting there, crying. I said, "Mom, what's the matter?" She said, "Your father just left. He moved out." "Why did he move out?" "We haven't been getting along too well lately. I'm sure you've heard us arguing after you went to bed." I had, but I hadn't thought much about it. Strong tempers were a characteristic of our family.

I was stunned by the breakup of my parents' marriage—stunned, angry, confused, and sad. I felt caught in the middle. I admired my dad. He was so strong, and though he didn't play with us a lot, he did teach us things. He didn't talk a lot, but we knew he loved us. He worked hard to support us. But I loved my mother very much. The help she gave me in combating polio drew us very close. She had raised us kids, often with little help, it seemed.

The tension in my parents' marriage had several sources. One of them was unresolved grief over the death of Retie Marie. My dad became more withdrawn after that. I think he felt he had failed to protect his family. Another was my dad's pattern of repeated absences. Long after he quit playing professional baseball, he continued to be gone on spring and summer nights and weekends, playing and coaching. He was also involved in his union, the Teamsters, which he was finally allowed to join during the tense time of the violent Minneapolis truckers strike of 1934. The strike put a financial squeeze on the family. My mother came to resent my father's absences and would go out with some of her single friends to get back at him. Another source of trouble likely was the eleven-year difference in their ages. My mother had given up some of her girlhood to marriage and motherhood. In 1935, not yet forty years old, with her two eldest children married and others almost ready to be on their own, she was wondering about the fun she had missed. My father, on the other hand, was nearly fifty. He was practically from a different generation. He worked very hard, and when he came home he was tired and quiet. He did not give us children much time or attention, and he was not a lively companion for my mother.

I did not understand all of this at the time. These insights came much later, when, as an adult, I learned more about the complexities of relationships. When my parents' breakup was a fresh, raw wound, I was a mixed-up kid. Not long after they separated, my father took up with a girlfriend and my mother entertained a boyfriend. That bothered me very much. Before the breakup, my mother used to talk about marriage as something permanent and holy. "Harry, when you get married, you're speaking before God," she would say. "You're making a pledge before God that nothing will break up this marriage unless it's death." Did she really mean that? What did God think now?

Of course, Miss Brown knew what had happened at the Davis house. She had a way of knowing everything in our neighborhood. She was especially kind to me in the weeks after it happened. I think she knew that, as the youngest child in the family, I was more affected by the change than my siblings. She said to me, more than once, "If you need anything, Harry, or if you need to talk to somebody, please come and see me." Sometimes, I would go and ask her questions. "Why is my dad with this lady? She's not my mother. My mother is with some other man." Miss Brown would gently explain to me that when two people can't make it together, they have to find another partner. Her words eased the pain but did not cure it.

My own living arrangements changed soon afterward. At first, the Davis house was Libby's house. Then she moved out and Dad moved back in with another woman. My mother moved into an apartment on Sixth Avenue and went to work selling policy, the illegal numbers game. I no longer felt comfortable in either place with either parent. My oldest sister, Dooney, by then married with two small children, came to my rescue. She arranged for me to live with her, just a few blocks away, with the continued financial support of my father. At Dooney's house, I had my own bedroom. I had a good relationship with my sister. I had responsibilities, like bringing coal from the coal shed to the stove that provided central heat. But I also had fun, as I took the role of big brother and playmate to Dooney's children.

Dooney's kindness helped me through several rough years. I suffered a fresh blow in 1937, when Gertrude Brown left Phyllis Wheatley. I never knew whether she left voluntarily or was pressured to leave by some of the powerful people in Minneapolis who were not prepared in the 1930s to deal with a strong, smart, outspoken black woman. Her whole life had been Phyllis Wheatley since 1924. She lived right on the premises. She knew what the settlement house's needs were and was unafraid to bluntly ask that they be met. She wanted to build a center that would train young black people for leadership in the community, for college and professional positions. Some of the people she asked for help thought that she was overreaching and that her goals for the young people at Phyllis Wheatley were unrealistic. Her nature was not to avoid an argument and not to accept any sort of demeaning comment without a response, no matter with whom she was dealing.

We sometimes overheard heated discussions between Miss Brown and the board, all of whose members were chosen in those years by the Women's Christian Association. By 1937, pressure was building for her to leave. And by then, I am convinced, she felt she had accomplished much of what she set out to do. She may have concluded on her own that the time was right for her to move on. She moved to Washington, D.C., where twelve years later she would be killed in an auto accident.

I felt her departure keenly. She had been a part of my life since I was a tyke and had been especially important to me in the days and weeks immediately after my parents separated. Her decision renewed the feelings I had then, of loss, uncertainty, and abandonment.

But she left behind a new head of boys' programs at Phyllis Wheatley who proved to have an equally profound influence on my life. His name was Raymond Hatcher. He came to Minneapolis from Ohio as something of an expert on teen organizations; he also came highly recommended by the NAACP and the Urban League in cities he had served. He could relate to people, to teenagers and adults alike. He was a no-nonsense, extremely organized person, but he had such a warm personality that even when he was scolding you, you would not get angry with him. He was about thirty years old when he and his wife, Mae, came to Minneapolis, shortly before Miss Brown left. They had no children. Mae became head of the girls' department at Phyllis Wheatley.

Ray Hatcher's idea was that every boy at Phyllis Wheatley older than nursery-school age should belong to a club, a group of anywhere from ten to forty boys close to his own age. Ray's clubs were not casual affairs; they became the structural backbone of the Wheatley's youth program. Clubs were well organized. Ray taught us how to operate them, then watched each meeting and coached us afterward about how to improve. The clubs elected officers and learned the responsibilities of a president, vice president, secretary, and treasurer. They learned Robert's Rules of Order and followed them in meetings. They paid dues, usually a nickel a meeting. They kept minutes. They decided what activities to pursue each quarter. They took on work projects around Phyllis Wheatley and in doing so earned points they could redeem for special activities or privileges. The clubs taught us a great deal—organization, group dynamics, parliamentary procedure, discipline, service. My club, organized the year I was fourteen, was called the Brown Bombers, after heavyweight champion Joe Louis.

In organizing the Bombers, Ray's timing could hardly have been better for me. Something happened during the summer of 1937, when I was fourteen, that put me much in need of a structure like Ray was creating.

I was one of several younger teens that summer who liked to get together on hot days and walk west on Sixth Avenue all the way to Theodore Wirth Park, which we called Glenwood then. The lake beckoned to us in those days when air-conditioning was scarce. When we went that far west, we were venturing out of our neighborhood and into the territory of another youth gang—not like today's gangs, engaged in dope dealing, but a bunch of tough kids who believed in protecting their territory. Walking out to Glenwood was risky for us. We knew that we could encounter a hostile gang and that we had to be prepared to either run or fight. I noticed that some of the guys made a point of having me with them. If a fight developed, they wanted me along. I was sort of feeling my oats that year. If someone wanted to see how I threw a punch, I would be glad to oblige him.

One day toward the end of summer, it happened. About six of us got into a fight with about the same number of kids, all about the same age as we were. I was in the thick of it. One of the kids I punched was knocked unconscious. He was out cold, lying on the ground. His friends got scared and ran home to tell their parents what had happened. Naturally, the parents called the police. Meanwhile, we retreated to Phyllis Wheatley. That's where we were when the cops came with some of the boys we fought. They identified me as the one who had thrown the knockout punch. The cops did not believe them at first. "It can't be—he's the smallest one of the bunch!" they said. The boy I knocked out was much larger. We all were ordered to appear in juvenile court a short time later.

I was scared to death. It was the first time I had any kind of trouble with the law. I told my mother, and she was willing to go with me downtown to the courthouse. So, bless him, was Ray Hatcher.

The judge asked us what had happened. We explained, "Judge, each little area has a gang, and as you go out to Glenwood, you'd better be prepared to fight or you'd better be prepared to run. That day, we decided we weren't going to run. They were going to stop us from going out to the lake, so we got into a fight." He said, "Which one of you fought this kid right here?" I raised my hand. The judge looked first at the kid I fought, then at me, and said, "It can't be." He was assured that it was. Then he uttered a threat that I later learned was a standard scare tactic. He said, "What we're going to have to do is to send some of you to Glen Lake"—a juvenile corrections facility. The line worked with me. I was terrified that I would be sent away. I knew of kids who had been sent to Glen Lake and who wound up just a few years later in juvenile reform schools in Red Wing or St. Cloud, or in the penitentiary in Stillwater.

But then the judge mentioned the alternative he really favored: probation, under the supervision of a probation officer. Ray Hatcher spoke up. He said, "Judge, I'm the boys' director at Phyllis Wheatley." He explained his new club system and that I would be part of a club called the Brown Bombers. "What I'm going to do is, I'm going to teach them not to fight in the street. The *Minneapolis Star* has started a program called the Golden Gloves. We've signed up with the *Star* for the Golden Gloves. What I would like you to do is, if you're going to put them on probation, let me be their probation officer." The judge agreed. I was to be on probation for six months. Ray Hatcher was to report to the judge periodically on my behavior. Ray invited the judge to come to Phyllis Wheatley and watch the Brown Bombers box. The judge allowed that he just might do that. "I especially want to see what that little guy is doing," the judge said, meaning me. "If he can already handle the big guys like that, he must be pretty good."

I left that courtroom very curious about the boxing program Ray had mentioned. I couldn't wait to find out more about the Golden Gloves.

6
Boxer

THE GOLDEN GLOVES AMATEUR BOXING program started in Chicago and New York, under the sponsorship of the *Chicago Tribune* and the *New York Daily News,* in the late 1920s. Its roots in Minneapolis were not particularly auspicious. In 1929, a promoter named Nick Kahler started a youth boxing program called the Diamond Belt as an expansion of a tough-man competition he had operated for some years in the bars and speakeasies in the Seven Corners neighborhood of Minneapolis. Kahler had the support of the firefighters based in the firehouse that is now home to the Mixed Blood Theatre. Some of them knew how to box and were willing to teach what they knew to neighborhood kids. Kahler encouraged that fire station to challenge other stations to enlist boys in a boxing program. Their organization was small and crude, but it was a start.

The program's organization improved dramatically when the largest of the city's three newspapers, the *Minneapolis Star,* took over the program in 1935 and called it the Northwest Golden Gloves. The paper was following the lead of the *Chicago Tribune,* which was showing in that city that newspaper-sponsored youth boxing was good for the participants and good for the community, not to mention good for newspaper circulation and advertising. The *Star*—which in 1939 would take the name the *Star Journal* and, in the early 1940s, become the sister paper of the *Minneapolis Tribune*—brought professional organization, adequate funding, and an assurance of adequate promotion and publicity to the boxing program. The paper set up competing Golden Gloves units in community centers not only in Minneapolis but also throughout the Upper Midwest.

It's hard to appreciate today how popular boxing was in America in the 1930s. There were fewer sports for sportswriters to cover and fans to follow. Basketball was in its infancy. Hockey was a purely local fascination, bigger in northern Minnesota than in the Twin Cities. Football was dominated by the college rather than the professional game. Baseball was called the nation's pastime, but the big leagues were centered on the East Coast. Boxing got a lot of attention on the sports pages. It had its detractors even then, and for good reason. Organized crime was heavily involved in professional boxing; the mob controlled fighters and dictated the outcome of bouts. But many fans of the sport didn't know that, or if they did know, they didn't care. They chose to believe that boxing was a sport that rewarded ability and hard work, and nothing more. At the amateur level, it did just that.

The Golden Gloves program was the first organized amateur-boxing program with more than a local reach. It was still in its infancy when Ray Hatcher brought it to Phyllis Wheatley, and to me, in 1937. That was when the *Star Journal* was inviting the city's eleven settlement houses to join the Golden Gloves network. Ray happily obliged, recognizing the sport's value for boys like me. Whenever he would catch a couple of boys fighting in or around Phyllis Wheatley, he would make them come to the gym, put on boxing gloves, and box, not fight. He insisted on observance of the Marquis of Queensbury rules: no dirty punches. He had help from a heavyweight professional boxer named Webster Epperson, who somehow or another had convinced Miss Brown to let him stay at Phyllis Wheatley while he was in town training for his next fight. Miss Brown had made her standard arrangement: "If you're going to stay here, you're going to have to provide something." He was a boxer and nothing else. Ray, on the other hand, was not a boxing coach. He supervised Web Epperson and the other boxing coaches who came after him. Even before the Golden Gloves started, Web was teaching some of us kids how to box. In my case, he picked up where my Uncle Dixie left off in my training. When he first asked me to throw some punches, Web said, "You're going to be a good boxer some of these days." But after he got a good look at my right leg, he said, "I don't know. Maybe you won't be able to go those long rounds."

I heard that again when the Golden Gloves program got under way at the Wheatley. People would doubt that I could box competitively because of my bad leg. But Ray Hatcher believed in me. "He's good enough to fight in a tournament," he would say. "Just watch him."

I made believers of the skeptics, at least at Phyllis Wheatley. The first year, I won the right to represent the Wheatley in the city Golden Gloves tournament in the featherweight class. I weighed 126 pounds and had been seriously training as a boxer for only a few months. I was starting to think that my leg was no handicap to boxing success. But the city tournament showed me otherwise. At that time, the tournament sometimes required a boxer to fight twice in one evening. By the second of two matches, my right leg would begin failing me. I would be too tired to box well. I won a few matches in the city tournament but did not impress many observers.

The next spring, I entered North High School as a beginning tenth-grader. In those years, there were eleven high schools in Minneapolis, each serving grades ten through twelve. Classes were staggered, with some beginning their academic year in the fall semester and some in the spring. I was in the spring-semester class in 1939.

North was the largest high school in the state of Minnesota in those years. Today, it is racially well integrated. It was less so in 1939. Perhaps 10 percent of North High students were African American. North also drew from the Finnish population living along Glenwood Avenue, the Italians from Penn and Sixth Avenues, the Jews from Plymouth Avenue, and the Swedes and Norwegians from north of Broadway. Each of those groups tended to be clannish, so tensions arose between groups of students at North High. Some Jewish students came from well-to-do families—the Winters, the Schlottlers, the Ratners, and the Bergers, owners of the Lincoln Del. There was some resentment of the rich kids by the rest of us.

Each city high school had a boxing team. That's partly because the *Star Journal* encouraged the high schools to take up boxing. In only a few years, the *Star Journal* had its Golden Gloves division better organized than any other in the country. Charlie Johnson, the newspaper's legendary sports editor, took on the program as a pet project and became its great advocate. He hired Ed Haislett from the athletic department at the University of Minnesota to be the coordinator of the Golden Gloves, along with two other winter-sports programs the newspaper backed: the Silver Skis and the Silver Skates. Ed Haislett was a terrific organizer. He designed a structure for the Golden Gloves that lasted for decades. He worked with Chet Rowan of the Minneapolis Park Board to involve the settlement houses and park programs in Golden Gloves. He then appealed to the high-school athletic directors to offer boxing and to involve the boys who did not play basketball in the winter. Ed knew full well that a lot of those boys were already Golden Gloves boxers. He thought the additional training and discipline that came from a high-school program would improve their skill and bring our Golden Gloves division more championships. We boys always heard it said, "If you win the high-school tournament, you can win the Golden Gloves." Golden Gloves encouraged its boxers to be part of their school teams. I wanted to be a North High School boxer, and Ray Hatcher wanted that for me too.

I made the North team, and between Golden Gloves and school I fell into a much more disciplined and rigorous training regimen. The North athletic director, Tom Kennedy, and I got along well. Many of the kids he coached had not been trained for boxing; all they wanted to do was get in the ring and knock the other guy out. Kennedy's job, of course, was to teach boxing skills, and I was a receptive student. "I like the way that you box, even though you've got a bad leg," he said. "You box the way I'd like to have all my kids box." As a result of my experience at the first Golden Gloves tournament, I had a better sense of the demands of such competition. I also knew what losing felt like, and I did not like it. I resolved that, as a tenth-grader, I would be a winner.

That year, I won the right to represent North High in the city high-school boxing tournament as a 126-pound featherweight. I then won the 1939 city tournament in my weight class—the first time I had scored a personal triumph in an athletic competition. If I was not already hooked on boxing, winning that tournament set the hook for good. The following year, I won the school tournament again, this time in the 135-pound weight division. I was what was known as an aggressive counterpuncher. It's the style of a boxer and a fighter combined. A counterpuncher studies the boxing style of the other fellow and knows when and where he's going to punch. Then he beats the other fellow to the punch. He has to be both quick and strategic in his moves. That's the way Sugar Shane Mosley recently beat Oscar de la Hoya for the world welterweight championship. It's also what Uncle Dixie had taught me in fifth grade: Don't go out and just bang away on the other fellow. Get the other fellow to start, then beat him to the punch with faster hands.

At North, I was also enjoying academic success. My grades were good, especially from my junior year forward. I qualified for a new club called the Pinnacle Society, a sort of honor society for African Americans led by a teacher I admired named Miss Quelo. She was one of the few teachers at North who participated in activities at Phyllis Wheatley. I was the first president of the Pinnacle Society. Miss Quelo's goal was to raise our sights higher to see larger possibilities for our future than we might otherwise perceive. She talked often about being prepared to go to college, saying, "Don't think because others recommend that you not go to college that you should give up on that dream. You're as bright as anyone. You should go to college." She was the nicest person, and she seemed to take a special interest in me. She had a brand-new 1940 blue Plymouth. She would say to me sometimes, "Harry, why don't you drive my Plymouth up to the garage and get gas and get it washed?" That was a favor I gladly performed.

I was a good student but not a perfect one. I was known to skip school now and then, especially when the weather turned warm and sunny in the spring. That's when Wirth Lake, then called Glenwood, would beckon to us. Some of us would meet before school on Plymouth Avenue and Fremont. One person would say, "Boy, I'd like to sit down at Glenwood today." Then another one would say it, and the next thing you knew, you had six or seven kids going down Plymouth Avenue toward Glenwood. The trick then would be to forge a note of excuse from our mothers to give to the attendance clerk at school the next day so we could claim an excused absence for playing hooky. Having a girlfriend with handwriting like a mother's was a great help.

Of course, I also continued with the Golden Gloves program during those years. Several members of my Brown Bombers Club boxed with me. I competed in Golden Gloves at the city level but never advanced into the regional tournament. My leg held me back—that, and the concern of my Golden Gloves coaches about not overtaxing me. At Golden Gloves tournaments in those days, boxers would sometimes compete two or three times a night. But I was able to play other sports recreationally, with the Bombers—basketball, football, and baseball. Ray saw each activity as an opportunity to teach us organizational skills. We made a budget for every activity and helped arrange the competition schedule. We competed with other clubs close to us in age and with groups from other settlement houses around the city. As we got older, we played American Legion baseball. Ray gave us a hand in selecting our coach from among the volunteers and college students working with his programs. For example, as our football coach, we were able to get Horace Bell, a University of Minnesota football player who was staying at Phyllis Wheatley. He was a placekicker and as strong as a bull. We would hold a ball for him at Sumner Field right near Bryant Avenue, and he would kick it all the way to Dupont Avenue.

Anything we chose to play, we were obliged to help finance. Ray gave us suggestions about raising money through fund-raising projects and odd jobs. We did our share of work projects around Phyllis Wheatley. Our club became close-knit and very important to me. One of the Bombers, Hank Majors, eventually was best man at my wedding. Newton Campbell, Bobby Miller, Russell Everett, Doug Moses, Narvel Brooks, Jack Bell, Jack Strawder—all were clubmates, schoolmates, and very good friends. Even the two boys who caused me such grief my first year at Sumner School became Bombers and friends when we all were at North High.

The relationship that meant the most to me in those years, though, was with

Ray Hatcher. We became very close. He knew all about my circumstances at home. He saw how well I got along with kids my own age and with younger children, like my nieces and nephews. He was more of a teacher than a coach, and what he was teaching me, more than anything, was how to teach. I came to understand and admire his interest in structure in any program, boxing included. He taught me that winning was not a matter of luck, but of preparation and consistent work. You have to study for it. You have to train for it. You have to condition yourself for winning in three crucial areas—body, mind, and spirit. And whatever you gain, Ray always said, you're obliged to pass along to someone else, someone younger.

Ray was not just teaching boxing; he was always weaving in lessons for life. He had a consistent message, one that came to mean a great deal to me: "Pay attention to three things, your body, your mind, and your spirit. If you treat them right, they'll treat you right. Don't misuse or abuse them. If you do, they won't be there when you need them." He was very firm on that. He would hammer away: "Your mind, your brain, should be full of knowledge. The only way you can get it is by reading and listening and seeing. Listen to the people who have knowledge. Ask them questions. Watch what they do and try to imitate them. . . . Your body needs to be physically developed to keep up with your mind. If you're feeling sick, it creates a problem with your brain. Keep your body in good shape." He would stress regular exercise and direct us to participate in sports, no matter what our physical condition was. He wanted every boy at Phyllis Wheatley to learn sportsmanship and keep his body in shape. He always added: "None of these things is any good if you don't have a relationship with God. You can't love someone else if you don't love yourself."

One of Ray's annual lessons involved a bus trip for the fourteen- to sixteen-year-old boys to Stillwater State Prison or the Boys' Reformatory in St. Cloud. Ray would arrange for our Golden Gloves team to put on a boxing exhibition for the inmates. He also arranged with the warden for us to tour the place. He wanted us to stay just long enough to sense the stifling feeling of confinement there and to see some of the faces we knew from our neighborhood. Ray knew them too, and he would point them out on our tour. "Remember that smart guy? There he is. If you want to be like him, you can be right here. Remember how he used to fight?" He wanted us to see the penalties that could result from the life some people on the Avenue led.

The Avenue was not beckoning me the way it did some of the other kids I knew in the neighborhood. I was busy at school and at Phyllis Wheatley. Besides, I did not care for what I saw and heard on the Avenue. One of my mother's younger sisters was married to a jazz drummer who was also a pimp, Scotty Williams. Scotty, for all his vices, was kind to us. He would occasionally let my cousin Cecil Taylor or me drive one of his cars. In the middle of the depression, he always had two or three brand-new cars. At one point, he owned a 1937 Lincoln Zephyr, a 1936 Buick Special, and a 1938 Packard—that's how good business was for him. I got to know other pimps through him, but I didn't think too much of them. They used foul language of the sort I did not hear at Phyllis Wheatley. They called women names I considered demeaning. After being around Ray Hatcher and Gertrude Brown, I knew better. I could always hear Ray's voice in my head, saying, "Mind, body, spirit." I did take a little moonshine once, and, boy, did I get sick! I said to myself, "What fool would want to drink this stuff and get sick every day? Something has to be wrong with that person." That kept me off of moonshine. Cigarettes? I'd see guys smoking who would cough and cough. "What fool would smoke these cigarettes?" I thought. Then, of course, around the after-hours joints you would see beautiful women, "working" women. They weren't for me, either. I thought, "She belongs to that pimp over there. He's not going to let you get near her without paying. He'd kill you."

About the only thing that appealed to me on the Avenue was the chance to see a big-name musician who might eat at Howard's Steak House or show up at the Clef Club, a late-night hangout, or at the Elks Club restaurant. They wouldn't let teenagers into those places after 10:00 p.m. But if the people at the door knew you and knew that somebody special was there—say, the drummer Chick Webb—they might let you in to listen to the music or just long enough to try to get an autograph.

Like Gertrude Brown before him, Ray Hatcher was a whirl of energy and ideas. He used to say to us, "I don't worry about you from September to June, because you're in school and you come directly here from school. But I worry about you from June until September, when you have no school to go to, to keep you disciplined." He came up with a solution and one day announced, "We're going to have a camp." Somehow he learned about state property that wasn't being used southwest of the city, between Shakopee and Savage, along the Minnesota River. It was a former military camp and was then controlled by the state's Old Soldiers' Home. Instead of cabins, it had barracks, about six of them, each able to house about twenty kids and furnished with double bunk beds. The barracks were well insulated, so they could be used in both winter and summer. The camp also included a great big dining hall, a kitchen, a well with a pump for plumbing, a big recreation room, and baseball diamonds and playing fields. It had everything one would want for a summer camp, except campers. Ray was intent on filling that void. Sometime during the winter of 1939–1940, he persuaded the Phyllis Wheatley board to enter into a ninety-nine-year lease with the state for use of that property as a youth camp.

When spring came, a bunch of us teenagers and young adults went to work to turn that deserted campground into Phyllis Wheatley Camp. We cleared the roadway and the unkempt grounds, cleaned and painted the buildings, and repaired whatever needed fixing. Meanwhile, Ray and Mae Hatcher were planning an ambitious summer camping schedule: a week of younger girls, a week of younger boys, a week of older girls, a week of older boys, and so on. The Bombers (by then sixteen- to eighteen-year-olds) and another youth club, the Olympians, were to be the crew that ran the place. We would be camp counselors and maintenance workers.

I was given a particular responsibility. Since I had taken bookkeeping at North High School, I was to be the bookkeeper for the camp's canteen. It sold candy, cookies, and pop to the campers. I was to keep track of the inventory and the canteen revenues, and to work out a system of credit for some of the canteen's customers. "Some of our campers can pay for their snacks, but we've got some kids who can't pay," Ray explained. "So we've given them jobs. I want you to keep a record of the jobs they do. When they come to the canteen, they get paid with a bottle of pop, a candy bar, or whatever. That way, they will get the same treats as the other kids." My duties extended to the supervision of some of the work assigned to the campers in exchange for canteen privileges. We raised chickens at the camp, for example, with the idea that, at the end of the summer, we would serve the campers and their parents a chicken dinner. One of the canteen jobs involved feeding and tending those chickens. I made sure that job was done right.

It was a good system that Ray had established, and I was pleased to be able to administer it. It gave me a chance to get better acquainted with a lot of the campers. There was one female camper I was particularly interested in knowing better: Charlotte NaPue. Ray caught wind of my feelings. One day he said, "See that little Charlotte NaPue sitting over there?" She was sitting by one of the cabins. "Why don't you go over there and sit down and talk with her?" I tried to feign disinterest. "We're not supposed to be fraternizing with the campers," I said. But Ray was persistent. He said, "I'll give you permission to do that. I'm going to have Mae"—his wife—"sit there and watch you." With such encouragement, I could hardly refuse. I got to know Charlotte that summer. Of course, Mae spent little time sitting and watching us. But it felt good to know that these two special adults were taking note of my personal life.

By the end of my junior year, Ray let me know that he wanted me to consider taking a new role in the Golden Gloves in my senior year: He wanted me to be his assistant coach and join in meetings with the senior staff at Phyllis Wheatley. It was an offer I could not refuse. I recognized that, because of my handicap, I would always face rather serious limitations as a boxer. But I thought I could do well as a teacher. I wanted to be like Ray. So when I was a senior at North High School, I didn't box in the high-school tournament. I spent most of my time at Phyllis Wheatley working with the ten- to fifteen-year-olds in the program we started to call the Junior Golden Gloves. It was a formal responsibility. I not only worked with the boys, I wrote reports of my work that went to Ray and then on up to the Wheatley head resident.

A big part of what attracted me to coaching at Phyllis Wheatley was the chance to coach alongside Ray. He had taught me a great deal about how to teach, but I still had a lot to learn, and I wanted to learn it from him. That was not to be. During my senior year, Ray and Mae Hatcher resigned to take a better-paying job in Detroit. That was a real blow to me. I felt some of the same disappointment and disillusionment that I had known when my parents separated. But I stayed with the path Ray had set me on. I discovered that I enjoyed coaching. (Years later, Ray and Mae moved back to Minneapolis. They said they wanted to retire near "their kids," meaning me and my contemporaries at Phyllis Wheatley.)

I also was enjoying the chance to develop another talent that I had been honing at North High and the Wheatley: singing. I came to North High in 1939 with strong vocal-music training at Sumner School. Sumner had a wonderful choir, led by a music teacher named Juanita Erickson. I was among the boys she included in a quartet and a double quartet that she drew from the larger school choir and then trained to sing at special events. Miss Erickson arranged some of those events through Phyllis Wheatley, so we performed at Women's Christian Association social events, churches, and other public gatherings. Before I went to North, Miss Erickson told the North choir director, Mr. Tenney, that she was sending him a promising tenor, soon to be a baritone, who ought to be in his choir. I became one of two African American kids in the North choir and held my chair all three years.

Choir provided me with a great opportunity to make friends with kids from outside my immediate neighborhood. Our choir competed in statewide contests that strengthened the bonds between choir members. When you compete together, you depend on one another. You work together to make sure the harmony is there. Mr. Tenney had us try out for seats in the choir, with ten seats for each section. He moved us around a lot, so we had a chance to sit and sing next to a lot of kids. He would have the tenors and the basses in the back row and the altos and sopranos in the front, close together, so they could hear you sing and you could hear them sing. The girls I sang with became my friends. We practiced a lot as Mr. Tenney pushed us to aim for perfection. We tried to help each other satisfy him.

We sang mostly classical music at North, whereas I was exposed to jazz, blues, and gospel music at Phyllis Wheatley. I came to enjoy classical music, but I was pleased one day when Mr. Tenney asked for my help in finding gospel music that would be suitable for the North High choir. I went to the music teacher at Phyllis Wheatley, Jeanette Dorsey, and asked her to send some suitable music to Mr. Tenney.

One of the reasons I showed promise as a singer was the music training I was getting at Phyllis Wheatley at the same time. Miss Dorsey taught drama as well as music and was a tremendous pianist. She organized those of us who liked to sing into a choir called the Southern-aires at first, then later the Wheatley-aires. We learned to sing not only gospel music but also light operas and operettas. This was more than recreation; it was a serious vocal-music program. It included a big public performance each spring, featuring dance and music of high quality. I was a soloist in some of those programs. Those of us who sang for Miss Dorsey became close to her and to each other. Some of the young people she trained went on to be professional musicians.

Of course, we had inspiration from the real thing at Phyllis Wheatley, courtesy of the color bar that existed at downtown hotels. The Mills Brothers and the Ink Spots had to stay at the Wheatley when they came to town to perform in the 1930s and early 1940s. So did Marian Anderson, Roland Hayes, and Paul Robeson. They would practice there too, in the big assembly room. Their practices were concerts for us—if we sat quietly and behaved ourselves. If we did not, we were out, fast. We would tiptoe in, sit on the floor, and soak in that great music. Just imagine!

Music had such appeal for me in those years that I was willing to engage in a little illegal behavior to hear a good concert. Along with a bunch of friends my age—Hank Majors, Bobby Miller, Newton Campbell—I'd sneak into the Orpheum Theatre when big bands performed there. Admission might be as little as twenty-five cents, but money was dear to all of us. One of us would come up with twenty-five cents and buy a ticket and go in. Then he would go to the sand-filled ashtrays provided for cigarette butts in the theater lobby. A lot of people put their ticket stubs in there. He would help himself to a bunch of those stubs and sneak over to the exit doors on the Orpheum's west side, the darker side, where the rest of us would be waiting to come in. If an usher questioned us, we could say, "Here are our ticket stubs!" and look legitimate. We'd run down and take orchestra seats. That was how we heard Duke Ellington, Cab Calloway, and Ella Fitzgerald. If girls we knew were there, we would sometimes get up and start dancing in the aisles. Nobody seemed to mind. We began to think of ourselves as quite an attraction.

At Phyllis Wheatley, Miss Dorsey liked to organize vocal quartets. I was part of one of them, along with David Faison, Charlie Waterford, Hank Majors, and later Rufus Webster. We called ourselves the Four Notes. We used to sit on the stairs that led up to the students' quarters and sing a cappella, imitating the Ink Spots and the Mills Brothers until we convinced ourselves and quite a few others that we sounded as good as the real thing. Miss Dorsey took an interest in what we were doing and coached us a bit. Before long, she had us performing at Wheatley programs. One night, she told us she wanted the Four Notes to sing for the Wheatley board. By then, the board was racially integrated. It included not only Women's Christian Association members, but also able local people recruited by a capable board chair named Charlie Fisk. With some trepidation, we went into the meeting room and did our imitation of the Ink Spots. Then we switched tunes and imitated the Mills Brothers. Oh, my, did we get applause!

One of the board members was Mim Himmelman, whose husband was the manager of Brown's Clothing Store, a substantial dry-goods retailer in the city. She sought us out after the board meeting. "How would you like to do a radio commercial for Brown's Clothing?" she asked us. "You could use one of the songs you just sang." We eagerly accepted and were soon at the recording studios of WDGY Radio. Mrs. Himmelman was there too, just as proud and protective as any agent or talent scout might be.

Then she told us about another opportunity: "You know, the Ink Spots are coming to the Orpheum Theatre in a couple of weeks. They're going to have a contest to see who can best imitate them. The award for the winner is a two weeks' engagement at Curly's," a night spot on Sixth Street in downtown Minneapolis.

We entered that contest, and sure enough, we won. But that presented a problem. We were all in high school. We weren't supposed to be in a place that sold liquor. Miss Dorsey played the piano for us when we won the contest, but she refused to accompany us at Curly's. She wanted no part of any place that had liquor. But we were intent on keeping that engagement at Curly's. We thought it might lead us toward more lucrative engagements—and all of us needed the money. So we all grew mustaches and convinced ourselves that they made us look much older than seventeen and eighteen years old. We convinced our friend Rufus Webster to replace Miss Dorsey at the piano. Beyond that, we kept quiet about our ages—and we sang at Curly's for two full weeks.

We got to meet the real Ink Spots when they came to town. Charlie Waterford had been told by many people that he sounded just like the Ink Spots' tenor, Billy Kenny, but when he heard that from Billy Kenny himself, he began to believe it! We were encouraged when the Ink Spots said, "You sound so good." But they added some good advice: "Don't imitate us. Get your own style."

We were trying to do just that in the summer of 1941, as we got one gig after another. After Curly's it was the Flame, an operation with a bar in Minneapolis and a bar in St. Paul. We spent one week in each place. At Hennepin and about Seventeenth Street, a place called the Happy Hour gave us a two-week engagement. But just when some of us were beginning to think singing might make a career for us, world events intervened. Draft notices arrived for David Faison first, then Hank Majors, then Rufus Webster. Meanwhile, Charlie Waterford was lured into another group and began to sink into the temptations of the Avenue. Already when we were at Curly's, we'd have to get him out of bed in the late afternoon so that he could perform that evening. The Four Notes had a short career.

During my sophomore year, I also had a brief but promising career as a civil-rights activist. The famous contralto Marian Anderson came to Minneapolis that February to perform at the Minneapolis Auditorium. It was just a few weeks before she became the central figure in a notorious bit of discrimination in Washington, D.C., where she was denied use of the DAR's performance hall because she was black. First Lady Eleanor Roosevelt resigned from the Daughters of the American Revolution in protest and arranged for Anderson to sing at the Lincoln Memorial instead. Her Easter Sunday open-air concert in 1939 became a triumphant celebration of liberty and justice for all, and sealed her place in the nation's civil-rights history.

The events in Minneapolis in February foreshadowed that episode. Marian Anderson had been in Minneapolis before and had stayed at Phyllis

Wheatley. But this time, she tried to reserve a room at the Dyckman Hotel, one of the city's finest, on Sixth Street between Nicollet and Hennepin. Her request was denied. The Women's Christian Association, to its credit, was the first to register a public protest. I heard about it at Phyllis Wheatley the afternoon the story broke. With us were Wheatley staff members Leo Bohanan and John Thomas, who said, "You guys are teenagers now. You've come through the NAACP leadership program. We've taught you about civil rights. We want the youth chapter of the NAACP to go with us to picket the Dyckman Hotel."

We could not say no to them, nor to Marian Anderson. Some of us had come to know her a little when she had stayed at Phyllis Wheatley during earlier visits to the city, and we sat in on her rehearsals. She always spoke to us kindly. She was a gentle, wonderful lady whom we all admired.

The next day, we were downtown carrying picket signs in front of the Dyckman Hotel, and either that same day or the next at the Minneapolis Auditorium. It was the first time I had done such a thing, and it felt good. We walked alongside members of the senior NAACP organization, as well as a number of white people who supported our cause. I met the legendary Rabbi Roland Minda of Temple Israel on that picket line and recognized some of the Women's Christian Association members whom I had seen at Phyllis Wheatley. The adults took care to position us young people in such a way that they could shield us if trouble should erupt. A little did. We attracted a crowd that taunted us, spit at us, and threw a few things at us. It was my first encounter with racism that ugly. It was frightening. But it gave me an understanding of the intensity of people's feelings about race.

A few days later, we got word that the Women's Christian Association had negotiated with the Dyckman Hotel and that Marian Anderson would be able to stay there. At first, the Dyckman asked that she enter the hotel in back and ride the freight elevator to her room. But John Thomas and the members of the Women's Christian Association who were negotiating on Anderson's behalf would have none of that. Then the great Dyckman Hotel backed down and made Marian Anderson a guest, the same as any other. Of course, that meant that the other hotels in town would be obliged soon to follow suit and admit black guests. We were pleased and proud that we had played a role in making that change. We had been given our first inkling that, if we applied the right sort of pressure, we could change the way our city treated its black citizens. A seed had been planted.

U.S. Army sergeant John Wesley Harper, my great-grandfather.

Frances Frazier Harper, my great-grandmother.

Armintha Harper Jackson, my grandmother (left), and her sister Frances Murray.

Elizabeth Jackson Davis, "Libby," my mother, circa 1941.

This is the only photo I have of my father, Leland Davis, and it was taken late in his life.

Me, at age fifteen months. Photographers went door to door in Minneapolis in the 1920s, offering parents photos of their children in goat carts. I was stricken with polio less than a year later.

Sumner School, on Olson Memorial Highway between Aldrich and Bryant Avenues North. It was built in 1876 and last used as a school in the 1940s.

Gertrude Brown, founding director of Phyllis Wheatley, with some of the neighborhood children. My three sisters, Charlotte, Geraldine, and Marie, are in the group.

Ray Hatcher, boys' program director at Phyllis Wheatley and my mentor.

Phyllis Wheatley Settlement House, 809 Aldrich Avenue North.

My ninth-grade graduating class from Sumner School, January 1939. Our teacher was Lilah Sullivan; I am in the second row beside her.

II
MATURING

7
Charlotte

CHARLOTTE JEAN NAPUE came into the world on August 20, 1926, and into my life fourteen years later. She has been there ever since.

Charlotte was born in Topeka, Kansas, the second oldest child of John and Omagina NaPue. John NaPue was originally from Tennessee, the son of Liza and Henry NaPue. Omagina's mother's name was Mary Officer; Charlotte did not know her maternal grandfather or his name. John and Omagina had six children, and John struggled to support that large family, first as a cook for the Soo Line Railroad, then as a car salesman, and later as a laborer for the New Deal's Works Progress Administration. Eventually, like Lee Davis, he earned his living as a trucker. In his later years, he worked in a shoe shop in the old Pillsbury Building downtown.

In 1930, when Charlotte was four, the family moved to Minneapolis's South Side, on Garfield Avenue near Lake Street. That's the site of her earliest memories—of her big sister going to Horace Greeley School and of her little brothers being born. She lived in one of the city's few mixed-race neighborhoods at first, but that did not last. By 1934, John NaPue had suffered a reversal of fortunes, and the family moved to Eleventh Avenue and Seventh Street on the North Side. They relocated again not long afterward, to Eighth Avenue and Emerson, close to Phyllis Wheatley.

I had little chance to know Charlotte when we were children. I attended Sumner School; she went to Grant. By the time she arrived at Sumner for junior high, I had moved on to North High. Her family went to Border Methodist Church; my mother and I went to Wayman Methodist, though later my sister and I attended Zion Baptist, near Charlotte's house. I spent most of my free time at Phyllis Wheatley in the boys' department; Charlotte did not come to Phyllis Wheatley as often as I did. She was needed at home to help with her younger brothers and sister. When she did go to the

Wheatley, it was for activities like tap dancing and ice skating, not to watch the Golden Gloves practice.

But it was Phyllis Wheatley that eventually got us together—at camp, during the summer of 1940. I was seventeen. Charlotte was just fourteen, but she was a sober, steady, mature fourteen. Her mother had died suddenly two years earlier, and Charlotte had assumed the role of the responsible big sister, holding family life together for her younger siblings. Her youngest brother was only three or four when their mother died, so plenty of work fell to her at home. Her dad relied on her and was strict with her. It would be a stretch to say that we had a summer romance. I was a camp counselor; she was one of the campers at girls' camp week, enjoying some rare relief from her domestic responsibilities. She was very attractive, with dark curly hair and an assured, self-contained manner that I liked. We met that summer and took an interest in each other.

The romance started the next year, when Charlotte began to come to the Friday Night Socials at Phyllis Wheatley. It was a dance that cost a nickel for admission, with music provided either by a live band or a disc jockey playing records. Several young musicians who later became prominent jazz saxophonists—Percy Hughes, Irv Williams, Chet Christopher—would perform at Phyllis Wheatley on Friday nights. The socials were intended to give kids someplace other than Sixth Avenue to go for entertainment and socializing and to keep young girls away from the older men who would prey on them on the street. Families felt good about sending their daughters to Phyllis Wheatley on Friday nights because they knew the staff would keep an eye on them. I had a lot of female friends, and I always enjoyed their company at the dances. One might say I had dated a few of them. But during the fall and winter of 1940–1941, I started looking for just one girl at the Friday Night Socials, and I got the sense that she came looking for me too.

Charlotte was not like the other girls I knew, who were silly and giggly and aggressive with boys. She was known to Ray and Mae Hatcher as "one of the good girls." That was important to me. She stood apart and behaved like a lady. She was always well groomed, choosing clothes that were becoming but not elaborate. She waited to be asked to dance. When some fellows asked her to dance, she would say no. When I asked her, she said yes. She was a very good dancer. We would jitterbug in our own style. There was also a dance called the jelly-roll blues, a slow dance to the blues when couples would do what they called the belly rub. During that dance, Ray used to come around and put his hand between couples, saying, "No closer than this." He never needed to interrupt Charlotte and me. She wouldn't let me get that close. She had firm ideas about how to conduct herself. If conversation turned to racy behavior of various sorts, she would announce, "I don't do those things." Usually, as the dance ended, word would spread about a party somewhere that we could attend. Sometimes those were loud, wild parties where drinks flowed. I'll admit that I sometimes went to those after-dance parties. But I never saw Charlotte at one.

I asked others about her and learned quite a bit about her family circumstances from the pastor at Border Methodist, the Reverend Damon Young. He was a friend of Ray Hatcher and, in many respects, was a ministerial version of Ray—intelligent, dynamic, and attuned to the young people in the community. He was often at Phyllis Wheatley, where I met him. He invited me to come to Border Methodist's Sunday-night youth program. He was a tremendous speaker and had kind of a glowing way with children. He knew how to explain things to them. He had a deep baritone voice that made his message stronger. He had Bible-study sessions for young people, at which he would show us how the Bible related to our lives. He encouraged us to be involved in the community, to work, and to study, but he said, "Remember, life is made because of God's involvement. The church is his house. You have to come back here to get regenerated and refueled, and to learn how to meet worldly conditions." I took a liking to Reverend Young. His messages helped me understand what was going on around me. He told me about Omagina NaPue's untimely death and about Charlotte's sense of duty to her family. I heard from him how strict John NaPue was and how he depended on his daughter for help at home. That explained why I sometimes went days without seeing her at Phyllis Wheatley.

That information also provided the basis for a bond between us. Like Charlotte, I had been forced to grow up quickly at age twelve after my home life was shattered. I was still seeing both of my parents in those years, but ours was no longer a regular parent-child relationship. My dad was working a great deal. He had hooked up with a young lady and lived with her. I never felt comfortable around her. My mother was living by then on the Avenue with a boyfriend, selling policy (the racketeers' numbers game) and providing a home for my sister Eva. When I visited my mother, her boyfriend was usually around and he treated me in a friendly manner. Sometimes he offered me the use of his car for dates with Charlotte. It was a big old Packard that shifted like a truck.

My parents were never legally divorced, but their separation lasted for the rest of their lives. Their situation always left me feeling a little bad, even after I became old enough to better understand it. Though my parents were still part of my life, I felt that in some ways they had left not just each other, but me.

I liked Reverend Young, and between my attraction to him and to Charlotte, I found myself going to Border Methodist most Sunday nights. Before long, Reverend Young followed Ray Hatcher's lead and moved on, to another parish. But my connection with Border, as with Charlotte, would last.

In the spring of 1941, I had the lead role in the annual operetta at Phyllis Wheatley. My big solo number was "Tangerine." I sang to a full house, but in my mind there was only one person there: Charlotte. She was wearing her first long formal gown that night and looked stunning. I can see her still.

We became schoolmates at North High for just one semester, during the fall of 1941. She was a sophomore and I was a last-term senior, due to graduate in January 1942. By then, we were getting serious in our feelings for each other. I had lost all interest in other girls, and she refused offers of dates from other boys. Most of our dates were at Phyllis Wheatley or some other destination in the neighborhood. For those occasions, we could just meet casually. After Phyllis Wheatley closed for the night at 10:00, we might go to a little spot called the Highway, where kids could have Cokes and hamburgers or hotdogs in a room apart from where beer was sold. When I wanted to take Charlotte on a real date, say, to a movie downtown, I had to speak to her father.

Charlotte was a movie buff and had a standing date with a girlfriend from Border Methodist, Bonnestelle Jones, to take in the early matinee at the Aster Theater on Sundays after church. That pattern was interrupted on Sunday, December 7, 1941, when Bonnestelle was hospitalized for an appendectomy. I happily filled in for her and was sitting beside Charlotte at the Aster when the theater's manager stepped onto the stage before the film began. He announced that the Japanese had attacked the U.S. fleet at Pearl Harbor, Hawaii. The damage was extensive. I looked at Charlotte with a chill. She did not fully understand the implications of what we had heard, but I did and I explained: it meant war.

Our world suddenly changed. I graduated from North High School in January as planned. I had a new suit for the occasion, a gift from my mother that I knew she had to stretch to afford. I had been thinking about finding some way to go to college the following fall. I was thinking in terms of the University of Minnesota, even though the staff at Phyllis Wheatley pushed all of us to consider the black colleges of the South—Fisk, Lincoln, Alabama

State, Grambling, Howard. They felt that those places would prepare us best for the world we would face as adults. Some fellows who were only slightly older than I—Lawrence Brown, Earl Miller, the twins Cozelle and Barnelle Breedlove—had taken that advice. I had not ruled it out, though I was concerned about the discrimination that people of color faced in the South. The local university seemed a better bet, I thought, but now those plans had to be set aside. I fully expected to be drafted and to be in the army by fall. A number of my friends got draft notices very soon after Pearl Harbor.

Relationships suddenly grew serious. Couples we knew who had seemed to be only casually dating were quickly getting married. Guys who were going into the service wanted to make their girlfriends their wives before they left. They wanted to make sure their girls would still be there for them when they got home. They did not want to miss out on any part of life. People's attitude about marriage was different in the 1940s than it is today. It was not thought right back then to live together without being married. A long period of bachelorhood was not considered normal or desirable. It was an uncertain time, when people wanted to create as much certainty for themselves as possible. Charlotte and I began to talk about what we would do after I was drafted.

My draft notice did not come until July. I had spent the months since high-school graduation working on the staff at Phyllis Wheatley, picking up what singing gigs I could downtown, doing a little cleaning work at a ladies' shoe shop called the Nicollet Slipper, and wondering what lie ahead. My brother, Menzy, had been drafted but deferred because he was working for the Onan defense plant. He made me aware of a possibility I had not initially considered: I might not qualify for military service because of my polio-weakened right leg.

My draft notice required me to report for examination and induction at Fort Snelling. I went through that procedure and very shortly afterward got the verdict: 4F. The condition of my leg disqualified me from regular duty in the armed forces. In a way, it was disappointing news. All my friends were going into the military, and I wanted to do my part and go too. But I was also relieved because I was increasingly reluctant to leave Charlotte. I figured, if I can't be any good there, maybe I can be of some good to the war effort here at home. I was informed that I had a choice: find a job in a defense plant or be inducted for what the military called "limited service"—in essence, a corps for the disabled. Defense-plant work sounded more interesting and more promising for the future. Further, defense-plant work would keep me in Minneapolis. Several options were close at hand: Honeywell, Minneapolis Moline, International Harvester, FMC (Federal Munitions Corporation), and Onan. Within a day I put in an application at all of those places, but my efforts and hopes quickly focused on Onan.

I thought of the Onan Company as a neighbor and a friend. Its plant was then adjacent to our neighborhood, on Royalston and Highland Avenues and right off Lyndale, where the Farmers' Market is today. It was then a higher-income area than our neighborhood, and it had a lot of trees. We called it Tangletown because the streets had no alphabetical or numerical order. When I was small, a number of us boys would go to that area to play Tarzan or cowboys and Indians, mimicking our Saturday-afternoon matinee idols.

The Onan family owned one of the large houses in Tangletown. When we were playing, D. W. Onan Sr., the founder of the company, would be out in his fenced backyard wearing overalls and working on small engines. They made a "pop, pop, pop" sound and spewed strange-smelling smoke. He used one to operate a portable power saw. As he tested these engines, he would call to us, "Could you kids please play someplace else while I'm testing this? It can be dangerous." Our mothers taught us to respect requests like that, so we complied. Then, later on, when he was through, he would walk up the street to find us and whistle to get our attention. He would give us each a little Baby Ruth candy bar. We thought that was a great treat.

The small engines Mr. Onan was testing became the basis of his company's declaration as a defense plant. The army wanted his portable power saw and another Onan motor as an electricity generator for its camps. Onan designed a diesel-powered generator that could be installed on the back of a pickup truck and was powerful enough to provide electricity for an entire camp. In addition, during the war, the company developed an electric igniter for launching rockets from any location. In the 1930s, the Onan plant was little more than a small-engine shop in Mr. Onan's garage. By the 1940s, it was a company with several plants—one on Royalston, where the original garage had been, and a much bigger one on Stinson and Broadway Avenues, where Menzy worked as a spray painter.

I talked with my brother. He had a positive experience working for Onan. He was the star pitcher on the company's softball team and was popular with his coworkers. He was well acquainted with the head man at the Stinson Avenue plant, Palmer Stark, and the assistant plant manager, Gene Bursch. Menzy said, "Why don't you come with me when I go to work? I'll take you to see Gene Bursch and Palmer Stark, let them know that you're my brother and that you were told to get into a defense plant." That's what I did. Gene Bursch interviewed me on the spot and asked me not only about my education and work experience, but also about my ability on the softball field. He invited me to start work on the following Monday, July 6. I would be working in what they called the wash-and-paint department, at fifty cents an hour. He told me, "You'll work twelve hours a day, five days a week." I tried not to let my face show my disappointment at those long hours. Then he seemed to change his mind. "We'll shift that around," he said. "For the day jobs, we need people to work on Saturday, so we're going to shift from the twelve hours a day during the week to ten hours a day and nine hours on Saturday." The night crew was twelve hours a day Monday through Friday, five days a week. Either way, those were rough hours, but there was a war on. The Onan plants were running around the clock, six days a week. My job initially was to clean the grease off newly manufactured engines and generators before they were painted with olive-drab, army-green paint. I was to clean them, put them on a dolly, and wheel them to the booths where painters would spray them. But Mr. Bursch took note of my high-school diploma, which few of his employees had, and soon decided I could do more. I was taught to do the painting too. He also hinted that my education might make me a candidate for promotion in the future.

Menzy would soon help me in another way. His deferral was ending and he was about to enter the army. He had a 1935 Ford two-door that had been embellished with a Continental kit—extra chrome, wire wheels, and so forth. He sold it to me for $300. I didn't have that kind of money and was too young to sign for a loan. My mother came to the rescue. She signed a loan agreement for me. Because I worked for a defense plant, I had an advantage in gas rationing. I could get as much as I needed. That solved my transportation problem.

My living arrangement changed at about that same time. I moved back in with my mother, in part because she lived in an upstairs apartment at 1223 Sixth Avenue, right across the street from where Charlotte lived. The second floor of that building included one full apartment, a half-apartment with a kitchen and a bedroom, and one separate bedroom. All of that was shared by my mother, my sister, and my mother's second-youngest sister, Evelyn Turley. Evelyn's husband, Sam, was in the army's tank corps, based in California. Evelyn had the full apartment, with a bedroom, a living room and dining room combined, and a kitchen; my mother had the half-apartment; and my sister Eva was in the single bedroom. In the fall of 1942, Evelyn was eager to go to California to be with Sam. She proposed that I take over the rental of her apartment and buy the furniture she did not care to take west.

She offered to let me pay twenty-five dollars a month for the furniture, with no interest, until it was paid for.

By September, I was a nineteen-year-old high-school graduate with no worries about the draft, a good job, a car, and a furnished apartment. I thought I would make Charlotte NaPue a good husband. That was the case I took to her father. Because Charlotte was only sixteen, we needed his written permission to marry.

John NaPue was not crazy about the idea at first. Charlotte was his oldest daughter at home. He depended on her for help raising her three younger brothers. I pointed out that I coached those boys at Phyllis Wheatley and had a good relationship with them. I would be able to help with them if I joined the family. That may have been the argument that won him over. He reluctantly agreed to the wedding. We also needed my mother's permission, which she gave happily. I had been quite independent for some time, and she trusted my maturity and judgment.

We were married on October 3, 1942, in a small evening ceremony in our apartment. The officiating pastor was the Reverend Henry Botts of Zion Baptist, the church I attended while I lived with my sister. Reverend Young had left Border Methodist, and we were not yet well acquainted with his successor, Reverend Howard. My mother was there, and Charlotte's dad. My best man was Hank Majors; her maid of honor was Marcella Hogan, whom Hank was dating at the time. A few other friends, the few who were still around, were there. Afterward, we went to a neighborhood restaurant, Carver's, on Olson Memorial Highway (Sixth Avenue had just been given that more distinguished name, in honor of the late Minnesota governor Floyd B. Olson). We had a chicken dinner. There was no honeymoon trip. Afterward, we went home. It's hard to imagine a simpler wedding, yet it meant everything to me.

Charlotte and I were ready to create a stable and loving home. After difficult years as teenagers, that is what we both wanted, more than anything. We understood, perhaps better than most of our contemporaries, the gravity of the commitment we were making. Some of our friends had advised us not to marry at such young ages; they said to our faces that they doubted the marriage would last. They were wrong. In 2002, we have been married for sixty years. All the people who predicted that our marriage would not last are dead and gone. It's a pity. I'd like to be able to say to them, "See, I told you!"

8
Laboring

AT THE ONAN COMPANY in 1942, I found myself in a situation that was new for people of color in Minneapolis. The work I was doing was dirty and somewhat menial, to be sure. But there I was, working on the line of a factory, side by side with white people who a few years earlier would never have believed they would have a black coworker. That was the opportunity that the end of the depression and the intense production demands of World War II created for me and people like me throughout the city. It was not that employers were becoming more enlightened about race so much as that they badly needed every worker they could find.

Young African American men were encouraged to jump at the chance at good-paying jobs in white-owned defense plants. The *Minneapolis Spokesman* newspaper regularly listed the opportunities at places like FMC in New Brighton, as well as Minneapolis Moline, International Harvester, Honeywell, and Onan in Minneapolis. The Urban League of Minneapolis also began to function as an employment agency, teaching people how to look and apply for jobs and how to conduct themselves once they were hired. It's a function the Urban League still performs today.

Some of the new black hires in defense plants felt as much discomfort as did the white people working alongside them. They too had led racially insular lives. But that had not been the case with me. From the time I started Michael Dowling School as a kindergartener, I frequently had been in situations in which my skin color was different than those around me. Every school I attended was integrated. Meanwhile, at Phyllis Wheatley, I had experienced the comfort and confidence-building that comes from associating with people of my own race. Through Wheatley athletics, I met white kids from other settlement houses around the city. I learned what it meant to show respect to all people. I began my working career with determination and considerable optimism that my stay at Onan would be positive.

Onan was a straightforward, no-nonsense business during the war. Hours were rigidly observed. Security was tight. Employees had to wear a badge and check in and out with security every day. The niceties of making sure a new, young black worker would fit in were not on the minds of managers. Getting along was up to me. There was a war on, and it was management's job to produce the engines and generators that the war effort required, as quickly and flawlessly as possible. Managers were there to give orders and my job was to take orders. It was made clear to me that if I did not comply, they would find someone else for the job. But I was also assured that if I performed well, I would be rewarded with raises and a quick promotion.

Our long shifts meant that I got to know my coworkers quickly. I found them to be likable, friendly people. Bud Harr, a man about the same age as my brother, was my foreman; Pete Peterson and Clifford Howard were spray painters, as was Menzy. There were a few other black workers in my area, Vic Wright and Julius Andrews Sr., both a good deal older than I. Mel Godman was a colored worker in the machine shop and a friend of Menzy's. He was a smart guy and very good mechanically. Onan had been among the first manufacturers in town to employ blacks, I suspect because the Onan family lived close to my neighborhood and established the company's first plant there. They knew that good people lived there too.

I was in the wash department, spraying newly assembled engines with carbon tetrachloride degreaser and wiping them clean by hand. I would then deliver the cleaned product to the spray painters. I became acquainted with people in other departments during lunch hour, when workers brought their bag lunches and ate together, and sometimes threw a ball around together. I became aware that I had met some Onan people earlier through settlement-house competitions in sports and music. Some of the fellows I worked with were well past draft age. Others were like me, people who were deferred from military service as long as we were working in a defense plant. For us, the work had a serious edge. We knew if we messed up, we would be out of a job and into the service, somewhere far from Minneapolis and our families. Most of us were married; some had children. We did not want to leave town.

It was not long before I renewed my acquaintance with the Onan coworker whom I had known the longest: D. W. Onan himself. Onan managers often walked through the plant and conversed with their employees. Gene Bursch and Palmer Stark did not believe in holing up in the front office. Mr. Onan's visits to the Stinson plant's factory floor were less frequent, since his office was at the plant on Royalston Avenue. But an appearance by him was not uncommon either. One day I was in the rear of the plant in the warehouse, where trucks would back in with the biggest generators Onan produced. The generators would be placed on pallets, then moved with forklifts to an area with a large drain where I would degrease them. I had learned to operate the forklift too. I was at the controls of the forklift, about to move a big generator, when I heard somebody down the hall say, "Watch it! Watch it! We're coming through." So I stopped, lowered the pallet, and got off the forklift. There was Mr. Onan. "Hi, Mr. Onan," I said. He said, "Hi, young man. How are you?" I said, "Fine." He said,"Are they working you hard?" I said, "Oh, yes, they do it all the time," and he kind of laughed. Then he and the manager he was with, either Palmer Stark or Gene Bursch, walked away. But after twenty-five or thirty steps, he stopped, said something, and strode back to me. "Young man, I know you from somewhere," he said. I said, "I know you too, Mr. Onan." I told him about playing in Tangletown when I was a youngster and meeting him on several occasions when he was working in his backyard. "We sure liked those Baby Ruths that you gave us," I said. He laughed and said, "I thought I knew you. Your body has changed but your face hasn't."

After that exchange, Mr. Onan made a point of speaking to me every time he came through the plant. He must have asked Gene or Palmer about me too, because the next time we talked, he knew I had graduated from high school and had taken accounting and bookkeeping. He hinted that my background might be useful to the Onan Company someday.

It must have been a month later when Bud Harr, the foreman, said to me, "Harry, we're getting awfully busy, and I'm in charge of the night crew. I've got to get the night crew started and OK the hiring of these painters and show them what to do. So I'm going to teach you how to make out the daily reports." I was being promoted to lead man among the spray painters. Bud showed me how to keep track of each worker, how many hours he worked, how many units he processed, and so forth. Each day, I was to take those reports to Palmer Stark's office in the production area. Bud described my new responsibility with great seriousness and detail, as if it were a complicated matter. In fact, I had been watching him all the time. It was easy for me to take on that extra duty.

Being lead man in my department included one very pleasant chore. Friday was payday, and on that day the ladies in the front office would come around with checks and give them to the foreman or the lead man for distribution. It would then be my job to pass them out and answer any questions I could about hours or wages. I referred those I couldn't answer to Bud,

Palmer, or Gene. It gave me a chance to become even better acquainted with my coworkers, as well as with the women who prepared the payroll checks.

With my new responsibilities came an extra twenty-five cents an hour. I was up to seventy-five cents an hour. Remember, this was 1943. A top factory wage then was $2 an hour. Plus, that was the wage for the first forty hours. Everything over forty was time-and-a-half, and we were regularly working fifty-four and sixty-hour weeks. So seventy-five cents an hour was a respectable wage for a twenty-year-old. After the raise, my take-home pay was about $55 a week. Rent was $20 a month; we were paying off the loan for my brother's car and $25 a month to my aunt for furniture. We were getting by.

I went home all excited and announced, "Charlotte, I got a raise!" The extra financial breathing room it brought was very welcome: Charlotte was pregnant. Our first child, Ritajean Marie, was born October 26, 1943. She was born at Fairview Hospital, the first private hospital in Minneapolis to allow black doctors to practice on its premises. Dr. W. D. Brown, a leader in both medicine and civil rights in Minneapolis, delivered Rita. When I saw her for the first time in the window that fathers had to peer through in those days, it was such a thrill. What an angel she was! I was so proud, passing out cigars at work the next day.

I had become especially close to my teammates on the Onan softball team. Gene Bursch, our plant manager, was also our company's softball-team manager. He recruited me personally for the team right after I was hired. My brother, who would leave for the service in the fall of 1942, was the team's star pitcher. Mr. Bursch wanted another Davis in his lineup. I wasn't sure my right leg would let me get past tryouts, but I made the team. I found myself in the company of a lot of fellows who knew Menzy well and who I already knew, at least casually. A couple of them were department heads at Onan—Johnny Swanholm of the parts department, Knobs Jolst of the generator department, and Cliff Johnson, a production manager. Hoppy Vernon was a pitcher and assistant coach. All of them were a little older than I was. Most were married; some had children; all were white. I was pleased that I blended in well with the team.

We had a great time playing softball. Our games were family affairs, with wives packing picnic baskets and bringing young children to watch the practices and the games. We generally played either at Logan Park, near Edison High School, or at the ball fields near Parade Stadium, just west of Loring Park and downtown Minneapolis. With Menzy pitching, the Onan

Stinson-plant team won the Commercial Blue League, the softball division for teams from midsize companies, two years running.

In 1943 we were elevated to the Commercial Red League, for teams from larger companies. By then, Menzy was in northern Africa, serving with the army quartermaster corps. A year later, he was part of the Anzio Beachhead invasion of Italy. He was sent north through France and got caught in the Battle of the Bulge in the winter of 1944. Fortunately, he came home in one piece. I always believed that his physical strength and athletic ability to run and jump kept him alive in those dangerous situations.

Even without Menzy, we stayed competitive in our league. But it was when we played softball teams from the other three Onan plants that we had the most fun. Our Onan intramurals concluded each year with an Onan tournament. Mr. Onan and his son Bud would come to watch and cheer, usually for their headquarters plant on Royalston Avenue. But I could always hear Mr. Onan yelling, "Come on, Harry!" when I was up to bat. The University Avenue plant was Onan's biggest and our favorite rival. We beat them all the time. Gene Bursch and Palmer Stark would come and cheer for their Stinson team and get a bet going against the other plant managers. Those bets would often involve the purchase of beer for the team after the game. After the game, the managers and even Mr. Onan would join in as the picnic baskets and cases of beer were opened. A wonderful closeness developed among those players and managers. I would go home after a night like that thinking I had landed at a great place to work.

I soon had more encouraging evidence of how far Onan would go in standing up for its black workers. One night after a softball game, Gene Bursch invited the whole Stinson plant team to join him for a beer at the Streamline Café and Bar on Broadway, right off Washington Avenue. It was a good-sized place, popular with the Onan crowd. I had been there before with groups of fellows from Onan but only to cash our paychecks on Friday night, not to have a drink. I never liked to drink. I rode to work with older fellows from my neighborhood who were just as disinclined to drink alcohol as I was. But this time, to be sociable, I decided to have a beer with my teammates. The team was all white except for me. Gene ordered a round of beers for the whole team. The waiter came back with beer for everybody except me.

Gene noticed what had happened to me. "Harry, you didn't get your beer yet?" he said loudly, so the waiter would hear. I said no. He said, "Everybody else has got their beer." Then he hollered at the bartender,

"Hey! We've got another ballplayer over here. Where's the beer for him?" "We don't serve him" was the answer. Gene said, "What do you mean, you don't serve him?" He said, "No, we don't serve Negroes." Gene was put out. "Do you mean to tell me that this young man, whose brother is over fighting for your freedom, who works in our defense plant, which is supplying the material for the army, you won't serve him?" The bartender said, "No, my boss told me not to." He said, "You tell your boss that Gene Bursch of the Onan Company is going to file a complaint with the city of Minneapolis."

He did just that, with the full backing of Mr. Onan. After a few days, I got a call from someone in the front office, telling me to come to a meeting. The owner of the Streamline was present with his lawyer. Mr. Onan and Palmer and Gene were there too, as was our corporate lawyer. The Streamline people said they had come to apologize in person, to deliver a letter of apology, and to pay us a modest sum of money. I cannot remember how much it was, so it must have been small. But I will never forget that apology and how good it made me feel. Charlotte's reaction, though, was also telling about the times and the fear we lived with. She worried that somehow, someday, the Streamline people would retaliate against me.

They had little chance. I was not spending my after-work hours at cafés and bars. I was where I had always been, at Phyllis Wheatley. I was elevated to head boxing coach at the Wheatley in 1943 and was initially paid $35 a month for the three-hours-a-day, five-nights-a-week job. My attachment to that job and the satisfaction I got from it were way out of proportion to that low salary. It was a big part of my life.

People at Onan were well aware that I was moonlighting at Phyllis Wheatley with the Golden Gloves program. Their reaction seemed quite positive. They would inquire about my boxers' progress. When I would come to work the morning after a tournament, everybody would ask, "Harry, how did your team do last night?" Eventually, the success of my Golden Gloves team brought a little publicity to Onan. When we won, the newspaper account the next day would identify me as coach Harry Davis, an employee of Onan's Stinson Avenue plant. A mention like that would make me a celebrity for a day at work.

By 1945, I was happily settled at Onan and content to stay there for a long time. Of course, I knew that the United States was winning the war, but even after V-E Day, all of us expected the fighting in the Pacific against the Japanese—and the military's need for Onan engines—to continue for some time. We were astonished at news of the atomic-bomb attacks on Hiroshima

August 6 and on Nagasaki August 9, and of the swift end of the war less than two weeks later.

I thought that with three years of seniority, my job was secure. Bud Harr told me as much. I don't know who was more surprised, Bud or me, when my name appeared on the layoff list a few months after the fighting ended. Bud insisted that a mistake had been made and that he would set it right. But there was no mistake. The problem was that jobs were owed to fellows who had been Onan employees before the war and who had been away in the service, fellows like my brother. A lot of men in my department had been with Onan through much of the war, but that didn't matter. The law required that returning servicemen could claim their old jobs. Bud himself was affected. Instead of continuing as a foreman at the Stinson plant, he wound up at the University Avenue plant, demoted from foreman to lead man. He vowed to keep his eye out for an opening for me to return to Onan. But in his new role, he lacked the authority to do much on my behalf.

Suddenly, my sideline job at Phyllis Wheatley was my only job—and not a very lucrative one at that. After my layoff, Phyllis Wheatley matched the thirty-five dollars a month that the *Star* and *Tribune* paid me and gave me a part-time staff position. But even with our frugal lifestyle, $70 a month would not cut it. Not with a two-year-old in the family and another baby on the way. Our son Harry William, whom we call Butch, was born April 15, 1946.

One opportunity I had to make more money was to train my more promising young boxers for professional careers. I would sometimes go down to Potts Gym at Sixth and Hennepin, over the old Aster Theater, to work out. That was where the local boxers who had turned professional trained and where promoters would come to recruit new talent. I was aware that promoters would pay for me to coach and manage some of my boxers into the professional ranks. But through my Uncle Dixie, I was also aware of the seamy side of the professional sport. I was wary of getting involved with it.

Boxing connections landed me another job. One of the regulars at any local boxing match was Reuben Bloom, a car dealer in the neighborhood who was a huge fan of boxing. He used to sit ringside during matches and holler at me. He took an interest in one of my boys, a bantamweight named Mel Hammond. Mel was a terrific boxer, capable of keeping up with the pros at Potts Gym. Reub Bloom asked me one day, "Harry, what are you going to do with Mel Hammond?" "I don't know," I said. "Mel's kind of small. He hasn't won the Golden Gloves yet." Reub said, "When he does, I'd like to be his manager." I said, "I don't really like professional boxing. I just take my kids to Potts to work out with some of the pros because they need tough competition." He seemed surprised at that. He asked me a few more questions, then said, "Harry, where do you work?" I explained that I had recently been laid off at Onan. He said, "I own Broadway Motors." It was a DeSoto-Plymouth dealer on Broadway and James Avenues. "Why don't you come up and see me? I'll give you a job. What can you do?" I told him I could do anything—wash cars, grease cars, undercoat cars, put on seat covers. He said, "Come up and see me."

I went the next day and was hired to do all the things I had mentioned to Reub and more. My spray-painting skill transferred nicely to the undercoating of cars. Reub and his brother Emer gave me a cut of the profit on every undercoating job because I spared them the need to hire an outsider to do that work. The job had another benefit: a discount on the purchase of a car. I traded in my little 1935 Ford for a 1940 Dodge. They worked out a payment plan for me that would not strain the family budget.

Broadway Motors was a small, friendly place to work with a strong family feeling. Reub and Emer Bloom, parts manager Howie Boyer, salesmen Clair Strett, Fred Streen, and Jack York, and Gert, the office manager, all became good friends. Jack York had a son named Bob who always wanted to box. On Saturdays, when I would come in to the garage to clean up and get the grease rack ready for another week, Bob would be there, asking me for a boxing lesson. He was a southpaw and a quick study. We became very close. I was so proud six or seven years later when I heard that he made the boxing team at the University of Minnesota.

When Bob grew up, he was successful in real estate and securities, and we stayed in touch. Once, in the early 1960s, he asked me why I had never joined the Minneapolis Athletic Club. For years, blacks were not welcome there; when they were, I couldn't afford to join, though I really wanted to. I had worked there as a waiter at one point, and I enjoyed the contact I had with Golden Gopher football players and other athletes. Bob said, "Harry, how would you like to become a member of the new Decathlon Athletic Club? That's going to be right out by Metropolitan Stadium," home field for the then new Minnesota Twins and Minnesota Vikings. I said, "If they voted on me, they would probably turn me down." He said, "There is no vote. You just pay a fee and become a member." Then he offered me a very kind gift: he would pay my initial membership fee. "If I buy it and give it to you, they can't turn you down," he said. That's how we became members of the Decathlon Athletic Club and how it became one of the first racially integrated social clubs in the Twin Cities. Eventually, I served on its board of directors. And I helped stage a boxing show at the Decathlon Club of the type put on at fancy clubs in New York, where members of the audience wore tuxedos and formal gowns. It was the first formal boxing match conducted in Minnesota.

During my lean postwar years, I had another moneymaking activity on the side: a home cleanup service. A friend named Harry Miller and I painted our names on the side of a little red pickup truck and went into business cleaning and doing odd household-maintenance jobs for people who could afford such a service. We were busy in the spring and fall of 1946 and 1947, either taking down or putting up storm windows on large houses.

Between my work at Broadway Motors, Phyllis Wheatley, and my cleaning service, I was keeping groceries on the table at home. I had one more venture for a while. Mel Hammond did indeed turn pro, with Reub Bloom as his manager. Reub was paying me to work with Mel as a coach, to prepare him to contend for the world featherweight championship. I was pretty busy, maybe busier than a father with young children should be. It was a hectic life.

That's why I was very pleased with the news Charlotte had for me one fall day in 1948 when I came home for lunch: she had received a phone call from Onan. I learned later that Menzy and Bud Harr had been talking about me, and they had decided to say something on my behalf to Palmer Stark. When I returned the call, I was invited to meet with Jack Shea, an Onan vice president.

Onan had a job for me at its University Avenue plant, one of the two plants it still operated after postwar downsizing. I was to be a spray painter again. But I was offered $1.50 an hour—fifty cents an hour more than I had been making at Broadway Motors—plus health insurance for me and my family, plus an enticing promise: after six months, I would be a junior foreman. And I would get training that would count as college credits, should I ever decide to pursue a college degree. It was awfully appealing. Much as I enjoyed Broadway Motors, there was no chance for advancement there. At Onan, I thought, I might someday rise out of the dirty-coverall, menial tasks I had been doing and become a manager in a shirt and tie. I talked it over with the Bloom brothers, and they said, "Well, Harry, you go ahead and take that opportunity." I did.

Menzy was back in his old role as the star pitcher of the plant's softball team. As soon as I was hired, coworkers started saying, "You played with the famous Stinson Onan team. Try out for this one." I did, and I made the team as a second-string pitcher and a fielder. It was a strong team that included a number of holdovers from our old Stinson-plant club. We played at Parade Stadium, under the lights, against Honeywell and other big corporate teams. We did well, and once again I discovered how valuable athletics could be in building human relationships. Through that team, I became well acquainted with people throughout the plant.

My new foreman in the wash-and-paint department and the finish-paint department was Ralph Markwood. Within only about four weeks of rejoining Onan, I became Ralph's junior foreman. I had a desk and a phone, right in the middle of the production areas. I would receive calls informing our department how many of which items were coming through on what schedule. I would in turn assign the pieces to the lead man in each department for processing. It was a juggling act that I got pretty good at performing.

Some time after that, my brother encountered trouble in the finishing department. He and a coworker had a disagreement that turned nasty and came to the attention of Ralph Markwood. Menzy assumed that Ralph would be his friend and defender, but he assumed wrong. Markwood took the matter to the personnel office with a recommendation that Menzy be fired. The result was a permanent strain in relations between Markwood and me.

Nevertheless, we had to work together. The company was just then installing a big conveyor system, much like auto-manufacturing plants use. It went in first in our department. Everything that came into Onan had to be cleaned before it went to be painted or dipped in a rust-retardant material. New engine parts would arrive in our department and be put on a line to go through a degreasing machine, then a bonderizing process, then rustproofing, then painting, then on to assembly. Ralph had to learn the operation of the entire system so he in turn could train his workers to use it. He was sent to Chicago several times for training to the factory that made the conveyor system we were installing. The new system was complicated but interesting, and I wanted to learn everything I could about it so I could help teach our coworkers. Ralph did not appreciate my assistance. He would snap at me and say, "You've got to do this" and "You've got to do that." After a number of days of that treatment, I finally spoke up in reply: "Ralph, I'm a grown man, just like you are. I was trained in this just like you were. If you will talk to me like I'm a man, then I don't think we'll have any problems."

That exchange may have cleared the air for the moment, but the tension between Ralph and me did not lessen through the years. If anything, it got worse. My Golden Gloves teams were making a name for themselves, and that meant I was getting publicity along with them. The Onans appreciated that and told me so. When Mr. Onan came through our department, he always made a point of stopping at my desk to chat. The Onans made sure I had time off work to go to national Golden Gloves tournaments. They sponsored an "Onan Nite" at the Upper Midwest tournament. Members of the family would sometimes come to tournaments and award banquets to show their support. The company even hired some of my boxers, including Danny Davis, Roger Frazier, Wes Hayden, and Johnny Bible. Ralph was not pleased.

I had also joined the Onan Chorus, a companywide men's glee club. Billy Fisher of the personnel office recruited me. He remembered me from the North High choir and knew me when I worked at Broadway Motors. Cliff Howard and I became the only black singers in the Onan Chorus, yet we fit in easily with what was a large, friendly, sociable group. The Onan Chorus sang at all the company events and performed in competition at the Minneapolis Aquatennial. We won that competition several years running and then were flown in the company plane to the Chicago Musicland Festival. We won that contest too! The Onans were very much involved in the Aquatennial and so proud of us choristers.

Then, starting after the election of Minneapolis mayor Art Naftalin in 1961, I became active in the civil-rights movement in our city. Naftalin appointed me to the Minneapolis Civil Service Commission. Again, I had the strong backing of the Onan family.

Ralph did not appreciate any of that. He was also unhappy that I was acting foreman while he was laid up for a time after back surgery. I don't want to suggest that the problem between us was entirely his fault; it was a two-way street. I had trouble forgiving him for what happened to Menzy. I often said to myself that I shouldn't think ill of him. He may have had reason to dislike me, because people in the plant so often bypassed him and came to me with questions or issues about work, and I may have encouraged them to do that. I tried to apply the lessons I learned from the Golden Gloves to my trouble with Ralph, lessons about treating people with respect and doing unto others as you would have others do unto you. I reminded myself often that God is the creator of us all and that we are called to be as close to his image as possible. That concept is at the core of positive human relationships.

In about 1965, Ralph finally made a move to get rid of me. He went to Jerry Olson in the personnel office and said he could no longer tolerate me as his junior foreman. He offered some trumped-up reason why I should be fired.

I was told later that Jerry said, "Ralph, I can't do that. He's respected by the Onan family, and, incidentally, Ralph, he's done an outstanding job. He runs most of the production in your department. We don't have any complaints from any of our foremen or department heads about production in your department." From what I understand, that exchange started a series of high-level conversations at Onan about my future. Not long after Ralph's complaint, I was called into the personnel department to meet with the director, Ralph Hanson. He said, "Harry, Ralph has asked that you be removed as a foreman." I said to him, "Does that mean that I'm going to get fired?" He said, "We have nothing to fire you for." I said, "Could I ask you why he asked me to be removed?" He said, "To be honest with you, we can't figure that out either. Your production rate is higher than it's ever been, and all the foremen and the other department heads like you." He then told me that Jack Shea and Bud Onan were inclined to offer me a different position, if I was interested in leaving the paint department. "You could come into the personnel department to be head of employee services," Hanson said. It was the position in charge of employee activities, including men's and women's sports, the Onan Chorus, companywide picnics and events, and a variety of service projects involving employees. It represented a promotion.

That conversation prepared me for what was to come next. A few days later, I sat down with Bud Onan. He said, "Harry, I don't want you to think that we're considering this because you haven't done your job. You've done the job. In fact, you will be hard to replace." But, he said, if I wanted it, the employee-services job was mine. It came with a nice raise and the shirt and tie that I had been wanting to wear to work for a long time. I was the first black employee to move into a white-collar position in the company.

9
Coaching

BY THE EARLY 1940s, boxing had become an integral part of the experience Phyllis Wheatley Settlement House offered the boys of north Minneapolis. That was by Ray Hatcher's design. He believed boxing taught boys discipline, self-control, anger management, confidence, and strength. It prepared boys to defend themselves if necessary. He thought those lessons were especially important for black boys growing up in white Minneapolis. He made boxing a required part of the program for boys ages ten to fourteen and called it the Junior Golden Gloves.

But as important as boxing was to the Wheatley program, it went for several years without an official coach. I started coaching as a part-time assistant while I was still in high school. But as the war depleted the ranks of physically able men in our neighborhood, I found myself with no head coach to report to. University of Minnesota athletes would volunteer as boxing coach for short periods, but they had neither the skill nor the interest to do the job well. Moreover, the Wheatley itself was having leadership problems. Gertrude Brown was succeeded in rapid succession by Louise Bromley and Magnolia Lattimer, neither of whom had Miss Brown's ability or temperament.

Things started to improve in 1942, when Henry Thomas was promoted to director. He had been one of Miss Brown's interns and protégés. He knew her system, and he knew all about the Golden Gloves program and its value. After a bit, he got serious about finding a permanent, salaried boxing coach.

He found me. It was autumn 1943, time for the boxing season to start, and still there was no coach at Phyllis Wheatley. Henry Thomas approached me one day with a proposition: "Harry, would you be willing to coach? The *Star Journal* will pay you thirty-five dollars a month. We've organized the program. You know all the kids." Indeed I did. I had been working as a sometimes-salaried assistant since my senior year in high school. I was also a brand-new father. Volunteering for little or no pay was losing its appeal, but serious coaching, for a paycheck big enough to cover my monthly car payment and gasoline costs, sounded good to me. I accepted Henry's offer.

Golden Gloves at Phyllis Wheatley was part of a network of newspaper-sponsored youth boxing programs that by 1943 stretched around the country. It was especially popular and well organized in our Northwest Division under the sponsorship of the *Star* and the *Tribune,* the sister newspapers in Minneapolis. The division reached into Wisconsin, North Dakota, and South Dakota, just as the newspaper's circulation did in those years. Seasons would begin in the fall and culminate in early February with a city tournament, in mid-February with the Northwest divisional tournament, and in early March with a national tournament. The city and regional events took place in the Minneapolis Auditorium; national tournaments were in Chicago. In its heyday, the Northwest Golden Gloves program involved several thousand boys every year.

At Phyllis Wheatley alone, I had upwards of 125 young boxers at a time to coach. Five days a week, I would come to Phyllis Wheatley at six o'clock and start the evening's round of classes. I had a one-hour class for each group of boxers. There were three groups the first years and four later on. The youngest, ages ten to fourteen, we called the Junior Golden Gloves. Then came the B Class, the sixteen- to twenty-year-olds; that group was later split in two. The Open Class took in experienced young men, ages twenty to twenty-two. All were amateurs, competing for prizes such as trips and trophies, but not for money. The newspapers supplied the prizes.

Though the program was well organized from the top, as a coach I had considerable leeway in how I ran things at Phyllis Wheatley. Before each season started, Ed Haislett, who had been hired as the Golden Gloves organizer from the University of Minnesota athletic department, called on us and conferred with Henry Thomas, the head of the boys' department, and me. Ed would lay out the program's schedule, go over any rules changes, and offer advice about any problem we cared to raise. A few years later, Ed was succeeded by Neil Champagne, a boxer and coach at the College (now University) of St. Thomas in St. Paul. After a visit or two, I think Neil came to learn from us as much as to give us information. I had designed my own system of coaching, one that proved quite effective.

I discovered quickly that I could not give 125 kids the attention it takes to develop unique skills in each individual. So I put together a manual that categorized and described different boxing styles, and I would have small groups of kids practice a particular style for a given period. The groups would rotate so each boy would be exposed to a variety of styles. Further, I assigned each of the Open Class boxers a small group of younger boxers to train. Each of the top fighters would have four or five Junior Golden Gloves and four or five B Class fighters to supervise on a given night. I would supervise the Open Class fighters as they worked with the younger boys in the early part of the evening. Then for the last hour, after the youngsters went home, I would give the top fighters individual instruction. I made sure that each developed the boxing style that was right for him.

My dad used to say, "If you want to become good at what you are doing, watch those who are good already and see what they do." When I started coaching, the coaches at the other settlement houses were all older than I; the one closest in age to me was thirty-five, I think. Some were very good, some were less so; I spotted the difference. The weaker coaches taught only one style, and that was to rush into the ring and try to overpower the opponent. The better coaches taught their kids how to box strategically, how to keep their opponents off balance and take advantage of them. That was more like my own style, aggressive counterpunching. I wanted to train my boxers to beat other fighters to the punch.

I found myself mentally returning to the boxing instruction I had received from my Uncle Dixie when I was eleven or twelve and mimicking it in the lessons I set up. He was patient and methodical with me, more so than he might have been with anyone else, because he had a special feeling for me. He taught me all the basic skills in sequence. We worked a great deal on the stance of a boxer. He would compare a boxer's stances with those of baseball players. Have you ever compared the stance of a long-ball hitter, who places his feet for stability and power, with that of a base-hitter, who needs to sprint quickly down the first-base line? My uncle had me doing that kind of analysis of every move I made in the ring. He also concentrated on leverage in punching. Only a few fighters have naturally heavy hands, the natural ability to be strong punchers. Everybody else has to learn the trick of maximizing a punch through leverage, through throwing one's weight into a punch without losing one's balance. We went over and over these things the summer he trained me. Repetition, I learned, is an important part of teaching.

I remembered those lessons. When I tried them myself as a coach, I discovered anew how effective they were. So I wrote them down, at first in longhand, and assembled them into a coaching manual. It was a book not just for me but for all the Open Class boxers I assigned to work with younger kids. Of course, by teaching, they were learning. So was I.

I had few Open Class fighters in my first years as coach because of the war. But beginning in the fall of 1945, their numbers swelled, until most years I had twenty or twenty-five boxers in the Open Class. In 1945 I was the same age as some of them, just twenty-two. But I had been an assistant coach or head coach for four years already and a successful high-school boxer before that. The Phyllis Wheatley boxers had known me for years. I had no trouble winning their respect.

I came to understand that teaching was my true sports talent—my calling, one might say. I was a much better teacher than boxer. I focused not only on what to teach but how to teach it. I had always admired good teachers—Miss Brown, Ray Hatcher, Miss Quelo, Miss Dorsey, my Uncle Dixie—and I came to realize that what I had actually learned from them was how to teach. My education continued with Ed Haislett and Chet Rowan of the Golden Gloves organization. They gave me pointers on teaching in the context of a network like theirs.

I took coaching seriously, partly because it provided extra income that Charlotte and I needed as our family grew. But more than money was involved. Coaching inspired me. It made me think through what it means to be an adult and to influence young lives. I became a father just as I started coaching. I wanted to give my family something special. I wanted to be the best coach that I possibly could be so that I could teach both my own children and the children I coached how to be winners. What I discovered was that coaching was fathering too. Most of the boys I worked with either had no father or a very busy and distracted father. Families in our neighborhood were large and poor, and fathers often worked a number of jobs. I was well aware that I was supplying some male guidance that my boxers might not receive otherwise. I had a sense that a lot of my boys were looking for someone to tell them what to do and how to live. I had the ability to say to them, "You are somebody."

I adopted the lesson that Ray Hatcher taught: Successful living has three components—body, mind, and spirit. That idea became the cornerstone of my coaching. Your body is your temple, I told the boys, yours to use or abuse. If you abuse it, it won't be in good working order when you need it. They would say, "What do you mean?" I would tell them about matches I had seen involving boxers who had been drunk the night before. They would enter the ring cocksure they could win and would fail miserably. That's what comes from not taking care of one's body, I would say.

My program always began with building physical fitness. We put the boys through a regimen of calisthenics and strength training before we started working on boxing skills. I had them do push-ups on their fingers, not their whole hands, to strengthen their hands against injuries. Exercises that built up the neck muscles were part of the routine to better enable the neck to withstand punches. Balance, footwork, and timing are crucial in boxing, so much so that we included ballet instruction in the program. The lady who taught the arts program at Phyllis Wheatley would bring a few of her ballet students down and have them demonstrate how to do ballet moves. The boys paid close attention to the high kicks! Younger kids would come and laugh at our boys doing ballet moves. I would say, "You join the class and I'll show you how the boys you were laughing at have the advantage over you, just for dancing." Tom Briere, a reporter for the *Minneapolis Tribune,* got wind of our dancing regimen, and he came to the Wheatley to do a feature story: "Why do Negro athletes excel in boxing? Are they hungrier? Do they have more desire? 'No, they're just better dancers,' answered Harry Davis."

When we worked on boxing fundamentals, we gave each punch a number. Later, we taught combinations of punches as sequences of numbers. Only after all those punches were mastered did we begin to work on an individual style for each boxer. I would assess each boxer's ability, body structure, and temperament. I would decide whether I thought he would be better as a counterpuncher, a straightforward boxer, an aggressive counterpuncher, or some other style. Most Golden Gloves gyms did not strive so hard to tailor a program to individual strengths and weaknesses. I did because I remembered what Uncle Dixie used to say to me: "Look at your opponent. If he's short and strong and you're tall and lean, you have to figure out how you're going to handle him and what kind of punches you can throw at him." Every style has its own stance, its own sequence of basic punches, its own use of leverage for best effect.

I taught the boys that their minds controlled their bodies. The mind tells a person what to do. It learns the lessons and acquires the skills that make a person competent. That's where confidence comes from: the mind. Confidence is the by-product of knowing what one needs to know. I tried to give my boxers directions that would make them think about the mental discipline required for good performance. For example, I might say to a boy in the middle of a practice bout, "Here's the combination I want you to throw. Remember we practiced that? Now I'm going to see if you've got confidence in yourself." I was always trying to offer the boys more than a physical challenge, to show them there is more to life than physical ability. I found that if I could get to them psychologically, their heads would take care of the rest.

I also talked about the spirit. I believe that a relationship with God adds a vital dimension to life: meaning. Knowing God and that God loves you is a powerful force for good in a young life. It keeps a boy on the right path. It gives him reason to take care of his mind and his body. He understands them as gifts from God. I wanted my boxers to want to live moral, upright lives and to know they are beloved children of God. That message stuck particularly well with a young boxer named Neil Frazier. He grew up to be a bishop in the Church of God and Christ.

But I also wanted the boys who did not have an internal spiritual compass to know there were some things I would not tolerate. I set simple, straightforward rules they could understand and from which I would not deviate. I had only a few: No drinking. No smoking. No reefers. No skipping practices without a legitimate excuse. Do any of those things and you put yourself out of contention. If you miss a session without an excuse, we will put you "on penalty." That meant you were required to do one of two things. If you were a senior boxer, you would have to box an extra round, without stopping, against a fresh opponent. That may sound easy, but, believe me, it is not. If the offender was too young yet to be boxing, he would have to do an extra series of push-ups or sit-ups or an extra round of rope-skipping. I made my rules stick, even with my champions. In 1955 and 1956, Willie Jemison won championships. He decided the next year that he needed to show up at practice only when it suited him, which was not often enough. When the 1957 tournament began, he needed an entry blank signed by me to compete. I refused to sign. A boxer he used to spar with won that year.

I took one more page from Ray Hatcher's book when I told the boys one night, "We've got something special planned. You are going to put on a boxing exhibition—at Stillwater state penitentiary." Ray had done as much for the Brown Bombers and me when he took us on a Stillwater tour and pointed out the fellows there from our neighborhood who had been smart alecks. That visit had a profound effect on me, and subsequent visits to the prison with my young boxers made a similar impression on them every year we did it. Visiting the prison helped them understand that obeying the rules was important not only in boxing but in life.

It was important to me to teach my boxers to respect themselves, each other, their opponents, and the adults in their lives. That lesson had been drilled into me at Phyllis Wheatley when I was a child, and I knew its value as an adult. So, even when I was not much older than some of the boxers, I asked them to call me Mr. Davis. They called their schoolteachers Mister, and I wanted them to consider me at a teacher's level of authority. I also insisted that they address the referee at a match as Mister. I instructed them to make eye contact as they listened to the referee giving instructions and respond with "Yes, sir" and no back talk. One custom I started has carried over into Olympic boxing: I taught my boxers to bow to the judges after the bout. That caught on as a show of courtesy and respect and is widely practiced today.

I set high standards of conduct for myself too. I used to say to my teams, "Some coaches say, 'Don't do as I do. Do I say.' I say, 'Do as I say, and watch me to make sure that I do as I say too.' I won't smoke. I won't drink. I won't miss training days. I'm going through the same discipline you are." I was not making a big change in my habits. I had never been much of a drinker and only smoked now and then to be sociable with my coworkers during breaks at the Onan plant. I had been coming to Phyllis Wheatley on a daily basis since I was small. The only time I would miss a training day was when Charlotte was giving birth. My teams allowed me that one excuse for an absence.

The boys came to know Charlotte and my mother, both of whom were wonderfully supportive of our team. They organized a club called Phyllis Wheatley Wives, a women's group that put on fund-raising bean feeds for the team and hosted a banquet after the season to celebrate our achievements. Meanwhile, I joined the Men's Club at Phyllis Wheatley. It raised money by sponsoring boxing shows and used the proceeds to buy uniforms, equipment, and year-end trophies for Wheatley youth-sports teams. We also got a group started for young couples called the Royal Twenty Club. Twenty couples were the founding members, hence the name. We were primarily a social group, looking for fun out of harm's way on weekends. The Royal Twenty Club sponsored outings, picnics, and dances, including one black-tie event each year. With some encouragement from me, it also sponsored fund-raising events for the boxing program. The boys were made well aware that a caring community followed their efforts and cheered their accomplishments.

We appreciated the financial support of those Wheatley groups because the annual *Star* and *Tribune* allotment for equipment was never quite large enough to meet our needs. A gymnasium for boxing is expensive, even when Phyllis Wheatley provided the space. A ring at that time cost $600 or $700 to buy or build, twenty times my monthly coaching salary. We did not have that kind of money when I started coaching, so we improvised. A fellow named Mistro, an older man with some home-remodeling skill, used to hang around at Phyllis Wheatley. He was kind enough to build us a ring in the corner of what had been the center's game room, a space that was maybe twenty feet by forty feet. Our ring was less than half the regulation size. Ordinarily a boxing ring is taut canvas over padding over a wood floor. We had a cement floor, which was more hazardous to our boxers but the best we could do. The ring was only a portion of the expense. We also had to have heavy punching bags, small speed bags, boxing gloves, headgear, protection cups, skipping ropes, and so forth. Our space was so crowded that only one boy could use the large bags at a time and only a dozen or so could skip rope simultaneously. When Neil Champagne took over as the regional Golden Gloves organizer, more help from the *Star* and *Tribune* papers began to flow our way. Neil was attuned to equipment needs, yet it took us years to build up the supply of equipment that a program of our size truly needed.

Of course, the best thing I did to persuade my boxers to respect me was to win. We won our first Golden Gloves tournament in 1945, starting a winning tradition that would last all my years as boxing coach at Phyllis Wheatley. Boys who wanted to be winners in boxing gravitated to my program. I discovered that when you've got a product that's in the rough and you start carving it, it doesn't take long to make it look good. Or rather, since our product was young men, it didn't take long to make them feel good about themselves and what they could accomplish.

My first teams in 1943 and 1944 drew boxers from some of the big, established families on the North Side. Those who stand out in memory are Albert Cotton, Charley Cooley, J. D. Carlisle, and Charles James. Those boys did not win city championships, but they worked hard and helped lay the foundation of the success that followed. I am grateful to them.

A scrappy, skinny kid named Eddie Lacy became my program's first Upper Midwest Golden Gloves champion. He was really gifted. He was about thirteen and little and frail when he first started boxing at Phyllis Wheatley in 1943. He did not have much of a father figure in his life other than an older brother. He came from a poor family. We used to have Mrs. Jones, the Wheatley housekeeper, find clothes for him. He and I became close. Right away, he fit into my style. He could box, he could counterpunch, and he was faster than greased lightning. He had what boxers call natural leverage. He could move in any direction without losing his balance. He knew how to move his body to get away from a punch. It's hard to teach that. He was a respectful kid who never used foul language, never smoked, and always tried to help younger kids. He boxed in the flyweight division—that's 112 pounds—in 1945. (In those years there were eight weight divisions in boxing: flyweight, bantamweight, featherweight, lightweight, welterweight, middleweight, light heavyweight, and heavyweight. Now, there are twelve divisions: light flyweight, flyweight, bantamweight, featherweight, lightweight, junior welterweight, welterweight, junior middleweight, middleweight, light heavyweight, heavyweight, and super heavyweight.) The professional boxers who trained at Potts Gym downtown sometimes asked me to bring Eddie there to spar with them, that's how good he was.

In 1948, Eddie and another outstanding fighter, Danny Davis, led us to our first Upper Midwest team championship and put in a strong performance at the Golden Gloves national tournament. Both Eddie and Danny made it to the finals for national Amateur Athletic Union titles. Buddy Bunn and Roland Johnson were also strong fighters that year, as was the 1949 city heavyweight champion, Cozelle Breedlove. He went on to service as executive director at Phyllis Wheatley in the 1980s.

That first Upper Midwest team championship won me the right to accompany our athletes to Chicago for the national Golden Gloves tournament. Also along were *Star* and *Tribune* sportswriters Charlie Johnson and George Barton. They stayed at the Palmer House downtown, while my black boxers and I were relegated to the Parkway Hotel in a seamy part of town. It was so rough that most taxi drivers wouldn't go there. We had to seek out the black-market jitney cabs to get around. We got very little sleep there because there was so much activity all night long. After a couple of nights of this, I had had enough. I announced to Charlie Johnson, "Either we stay at the Palmer House or we go back to Minneapolis on the next train." It was not customary for black people to stay at the Palmer House in those years, but somehow Charlie got us in.

We had a similar scene in Kansas City, Missouri, when Charlie and I accompanied a few of our boxers to the Amateur Athletic Union national tournament in 1948. Our boxers competed there as individuals, not as a team. It was a chance for them to test their skill against others from all over the country and to aim toward competition in the Olympics. Our group included two white boxers, Danny Dillon and Vince Donnelly; two blacks, Danny Davis and Eddie Lacy; and one Latino, Johnny Pacheco. When we arrived at the famous Muehlebach Hotel in Kansas City, the registration clerk refused to provide rooms for Danny, Eddie, Johnny, and me. This time Charlie took the initiative. He complained vociferously, got the hotel manager involved, pointed out that the hotel admitted colored U.S. servicemen, and somehow got us in. We learned afterward that other black boxers in the same tournament had been shunted off to a terrible hotel. We performed well in that tournament, with two national championships and three runners-up. I maintain that getting a good night's sleep helped us.

Charlie took a great interest in Eddie Lacy and often predicted in print that he would be a world champion. But I did not encourage Eddie or any of my fighters to become professional boxers. Through the experience of my uncle, I knew too well the corruption at play in the professional ranks. Eddie did turn pro for a few years, as did a few other Wheatley boxers, but he then chose—wisely, I believe—to enter the building trades.

The Hammond brothers also made an important mark in our boxing program. Matt Hammond was a year or two older than I and a winner of Northwest Golden Gloves tournaments in 1942 and 1943. He had five younger brothers, and all but one of them went on to compete in the Golden Gloves program. Mel Hammond was our 1947 bantamweight city champion and fought professionally for a few years. Matt kept coming around our little gym with his younger brothers, and I enlisted him and other fellows our age—Narvel Brooks and Johnny Bond were two of them—to help me with Junior Golden Gloves. Some of them had not been boxers themselves, but if they were willing to supervise calisthenics or rope-skipping or put on mitts and hold up their hands for a boy to punch, I put them to work.

Wheatley teams started winning the city's team championships consistently in 1951, the year we had three divisional champs—Johnny Bible at lightweight, Wes Hayden at middleweight, and Monroe Gage at light heavyweight—and one runner-up, Dick Hammond at flyweight. We won city team championships through the remainder of the 1950s and won seven team championships at the Upper Midwest division level during that decade. So many outstanding boxers competed on Wheatley teams during those years that I hesitate to begin naming them for fear of offending the deserving boxers I am sure to omit. But, with advance apologies, I have to mention Jimmy Jackson and some of his teammates. He won Upper Midwest championships in the flyweight division consecutively from 1954 to 1959 and won the national Golden Gloves title in 1957. Jimmy was the soft-spoken, mild-mannered star of a team of outstanding athletes that included heavyweight Jerry Bailey, light heavyweight LeRoy Bogar, bantamweights Kenny Rodriguez and Chuck Hales, and welterweight Jimmy Shaw. Each of those young men rose through the Phyllis Wheatley ranks from boyhood except Hales, who grew up in the small, rural-Minnesota town of Staples. As a high-school kid, Hales was one of the Upper Midwest winners I took on our divisional team to national tournaments. He joined the Wheatley team after he graduated from high school. In fact, he moved to the Twin Cities because he wanted to train under my tutelage.

Some of those men and a few others—Asa "Skeets" Grigsby, John Jacobs, Ray Wells, Wes Hayden, Clyde Bellecourt—gathered for a reunion at Phyllis

Wheatley in May 2001. It was gratifying to hear them reminisce with this book's editor, Lori Sturdevant of the *Star Tribune,* about their years on Wheatley boxing teams. Jimmy Jackson said that what motivated him and his teammates to succeed was the sense that "Harry really cared about us—every individual. He really wanted us to succeed and to develop our skills." Chuck Hales said, "He could calm you down when you were boxing in front of ten thousand people. He was someone you could draw strength from." Ken Rodriguez said, "He was like a father to us." Asa Grigsby said, "He didn't just teach me boxing. He shaped the way I live. He shaped my attitude. He cared more about my future than about boxing. He gave us respect and we returned it."

Our success gave me the chance to travel around the region and get to know our state. Along with some of my better boxers, I went several times to Minnesota towns like Hibbing, Staples, and Wadena, and to Wahpeton, North Dakota, to put on boxing clinics. I also made the train trip to Chicago with Upper Midwest champions several times to coach our division's squad at the national tournament. The coach of the team with the most points in the Upper Midwest tournament was automatically designated to travel with the winners to Chicago. I went so often in the 1950s that, by 1958, I began to be a little self-conscious about the honor. So I announced at the start of the 1957–1958 season that, even if Wheatley won the team title again, I would defer to the coach of the second-place team. Sure enough, we won again, and the second-place coach, Danny Dillon of Pillsbury House, went to Chicago.

When my decision was reported in the *Minneapolis Star,* the paper also took note of something I had long been aware of: while Wheatley boxers had enjoyed great success, they also seemed to lose an unusually large number of close decisions. The paper commented, "Many of the verdicts have been downright unfair"—a subtle suggestion, I thought, that racism might have been involved. The item went on: "Through all these disappointing situations, never once has Davis publicly shown his ire. He has boiled inside. He has felt licked and dejected, but never has he put on a demonstration to indicate his feelings. . . . If anyone around here ever gets in the mood to pick the No. 1 sportsman or the most gracious loser, Harry Davis should receive first consideration."

A very nice tribute to my coaching style appeared on the sports pages of the *Minneapolis Tribune* during the Golden Gloves city-championship tournament in 1958. Columnist Dick Cullum described my role with one of my fighters as a "second," the handler in his corner. The first round of this particular match did not go well. I suggested a few changes for the second round; the boxer put my ideas to work and won.

"It is not uncommon for a second to outline a course of action between rounds. It is most uncommon for the outline to take effect," Cullum wrote. "This could only be so because the boxer had been well grounded in fundamentals and had such confidence in his handler that he was willing to take an entirely new plan and execute it positively. Davis' teams have won eight consecutive city championships. They win because they are always in better condition than other teams and because they are firmly grounded in fundamentals. . . . There is probably no coach anywhere in amateur or college boxing who has such a knowing way with kids as Davis."

In 1959, Phyllis Wheatley's gym was host to the city Golden Gloves tournament. That was an honor for us and a lot of responsibility. I was credited in the sports pages again for organizing one hundred Wheatley volunteers to prepare for the tournament and make it run smoothly. We repainted the gym, installed new bleachers, published a special program, and performed many last-minute tasks. I persuaded D. W. Onan to donate the expensive team trophies.

That tournament turned out to be something of a last hurrah for me as a Golden Gloves coach. Neil Champagne informed me that the 1959 season was going to be his last as administrator of Star Tribune Charities, the parent organization of the Upper Midwest Golden Gloves. He would be taking another job at a higher salary. He had been asked by Charlie Johnson and George Barton, the sportswriters who were the program's godfathers, to inquire about my interest in the job. It would be a part-time position that paid a modest salary, but more than I was earning as a coach. Money was an issue for us in those years, with college just ahead for Rita and Butch. Charlotte and I were moonlighting again by cleaning the Flameburger restaurant every night between 10:00 and midnight.

Before long, I was summoned to a meeting at Charlie's office. He made the offer official. I asked for a few days to think it over and talk with my boxers. It wasn't an easy decision—I loved coaching and felt very attached to my kids—but they encouraged me to take the job. I think it was Jimmy Jackson who said, "Harry, then you can quit that cleaning job down there at the Flameburger." I had always prepared a few of the older boxers to be leaders so they could step in and take charge if something happened to me. Several were young adults by 1959, still attached to the program and interested in coaching. Among them was Ray Wells, who came to us as a kid with a record of trouble. In fact, he had been taught to box while he was a resident of Boys Town, the home for boys in Nebraska. When his family moved to Minneapolis, Ray came too and became one of the mainstays of Wheatley boxing. He also married my cousin Rene Jackson. By 1960, he was ready to succeed me as coach. With that in mind, I accepted Charlie's offer.

In 1963, I was the winner of the George Barton Award for making the greatest contribution to boxing in Minnesota, bestowed by an organization of boxing enthusiasts called the Old Guards of the Ring. Dick Cullum covered the award for the *Tribune,* writing, "Nowhere in the country is amateur boxing more intelligently and carefully supervised than in Harry Davis' realm. . . . Moreover, no coach had more respect, admiration and downright affection for his boys." The feeling was mutual, and it lingers to this day.

10
Nurturing

SOME YOUNG PEOPLE MARRY to escape their families. For Charlotte and me, just the opposite happened. Our involvement with our families deepened after we married and had a family of our own.

The apartment on Olson Highway that seemed so perfect for us in 1942 seemed much too small less than a year later, when we were expecting the birth of our first child. We moved into the upper level of a duplex at 1106 Emerson, which was next door to a box factory and across the street from the downstairs duplex at 1107 Emerson where my sister Dooney and her family lived. A few years later, conscious of the fire hazard posed by the box factory, where several small fires had occurred, we moved into the unit above Dooney's apartment. I was once again close to my eldest sister and a playful uncle for her children.

When we moved into that place, it wasn't too inviting, but Charlotte went to work and before long it was quite homey. It had a central stove for heating and wooden floors she would polish until they shined.

It was at 1107 Emerson that we made a home for Charlotte's three younger brothers for a time. Her widowed father could not find the help he needed to care for the boys as they reached their teen years. They were close to Charlotte, who had been their second mother, and to me, through Phyllis Wheatley activities. Her dad trusted us to care for them. We did, under very crowded conditions. Eventually, John NaPue's brother took the boys into his home. The youngest boy, Vern, was with us longer than the others, Delmar and Donald.

Living close to Dooney, and becoming a father, meant that I again saw my own father occasionally. He stayed closer to Dooney than to the rest of his children after he and my mother separated. Like many fathers and eldest daughters, they had a special relationship. Dooney even resembled him more than my other sisters did. He paid her to care for me during my high-school years, and I seldom saw him then, not even at my athletic or musical performances. He called on Dooney during hours when I was at school or at Phyllis Wheatley. He chose not to attend when Charlotte and I were married. He nearly disappeared from my life for several years. But after our children were born, Dad occasionally visited us. Slowly, we began to have a more regular relationship between an aging father and an adult son.

Dad lived a long life, reaching age eighty-three before dying in 1970. But he suffered from low blood pressure in his later years and a form of dementia that then was not well understood by the doctors. He lived in an apartment in the housing project near us. For a spell, he would forget to eat or clean up after himself, or even open the doors to his apartment.

On one occasion when our children were small, he surprised us with an unexpected visit and sat and played with the kids for a long time. It was not usual for him to do that. Maybe two or three days later, Dooney called, saying, "Some people in the project called and said they have not seen Papa for a couple of days." She asked me to go to his apartment and check on him. When I knocked on his door, I could hear somebody inside, but he would not come to the door. I kept knocking, and calling, "Papa, Papa, it's Harry. It's Little Pops." Finally, I heard him say, "Oh, oh, oh." He came to the door, a sorry sight. He had not eaten since he had been at our house, and his place was a terrible mess. I called an ambulance and took him to General Hospital. He came home a few days later with some medication. His condition improved, and for a time he became a more regular visitor in our home.

Then he hooked up with a younger lady, and we did not see him for quite a while. She looked after his health. Sometimes, however, he would pop up suddenly. The Wheatley Wives, Charlotte's club, put on appreciation banquets for my Golden Gloves teams after we won championships. One year when I was sitting at the head table, I looked up and was surprised to see Dad walk in. A few other times, after my name had been in the paper in connection with Golden Gloves, he would appear at a practice or a match, sit down, and talk with me. I knew he was following my achievements and that he was proud of me. He spent his last year at the Willows Nursing Home.

My mother was not blessed with nearly as many years, but I enjoyed a more sustained relationship with her than with my father. She was a great help to Charlotte after the birth of our babies. I think grandchildren attracted her to us and gave us a closer relationship. She was a regular baby-sitter for Rita, whom she called "Peaches" because of her round little cheeks, and for Butchie. She participated often in Phyllis Wheatley activities and followed my boxing teams. She was a cook for the mothers' group at the Wheatley. She maintained her own little apartment and lived quite independently as she grew older. She died in July 1958 at age sixty.

The other kinsman from my parents' generation who made a big difference in my life, Uncle Dixie, was also a recurring presence through my young adulthood. After his professional boxing days were done and his brief first marriage ended, my dad's younger brother settled in Minneapolis. He lived for a time with his mother, my Grandma Molly, before her accidental death. He remained athletic, so much so that he would run downtown and back. We often saw him walking all over downtown. He used to frequent restaurants on Washington Avenue in the years when that street was becoming Skid Row. Because he was a prizefighter, he wasn't afraid of a tough neighborhood. Sure enough, once when he was in his seventies, a couple of fellows jumped him as he came out of a restaurant. They didn't know he was a former boxer, and he just about killed them. Then Uncle Dixie was arrested and had to appear before a judge. The arresting officer testified, "These two young men were beaten up by this man." The judge asked my uncle, "How old are you?" He told them he was seventy-something. The judge asked, "Mr. Davis, what did they do to provoke you?" He said, "They were trying to rob me. They jumped me because I'm an old man. They saw me coming out of this restaurant and they figured that I had some money. I defended myself. I'm a former prizefighter." The judge dismissed the case.

Uncle Dixie was a big fan of my Golden Gloves teams. He would come to the Upper Midwest championships at the Minneapolis Auditorium. If I spotted him, I would invite him to sit with me at ringside. He enjoyed that special treatment, but he would not let me give him a ticket for a reserved seat at a tournament. He always wanted to buy his own, intent on being an independent person who took no charity. He had saved his money and took pride in being able to support himself.

Uncle Dixie had no children, and I became a surrogate son for him. He used to say, "My brother, Lee, got all the benefits. He married Libby. I always wanted to marry Libby." I told him, "Uncle Dixie, if you had married Libby, you'd have been my father." "Yes," he said, "I'd be proud of you." I returned the compliment by adding whenever I introduced him to anyone, "This is the guy who taught me how to fight." In his last years, Uncle Dixie married a Caucasian lady and lived in a high-rise apartment for seniors on

Stevens Avenue. He outlived my dad by only a few years, dying at age seventy-seven.

The other male relative I stayed close to was my brother, Menzy. Nine years older and without any children of his own, Menzy took a great interest in me and, later, my children. He stayed in touch with me when my father did not. He too had an estranged relationship with our father and mother. They didn't approve of his decision to marry a white girl from Wisconsin, an attitude I found baffling given my mother's heritage. Though Menzy didn't graduate from high school himself—none of my siblings did—he encouraged me to get a good education. He also came to Golden Gloves boxing tournaments to support what I was doing. He seemed to like to give me advice, much in the way a father would. He would say, "Pops, if you're going to do something, you're going to have to decide that you will have competence in doing it. You need to think, 'I can do this better than anybody.'" That was the attitude he took to the pitcher's mound and the batter's box when he played baseball. Menzy was a tremendous pitcher, with intimidating size and amazing control. But he was also a great hitter, capable of hitting a baseball out of the ballpark. It was not unusual for a pitcher to intentionally walk him rather than risk pitching to him when runners were on base. I often thought that if he had gone to high school, he would have become a professional athlete.

Unfortunately, Menzy also had a temper that got him in trouble. When we were out together, I would try to steer him away from situations in which somebody might disagree with him or challenge him. If that happened, he would fight and the other guy would get hurt. His temper would flare in protection of me too. Once when we were playing softball, I was playing second base. The ball was hit to the shortstop, and I covered second to make a double play. The base runner came sliding into second and knocked me over. Menzy thought he had done it intentionally. Oh, boy! He took that guy and lifted him right off the ground.

Menzy died at age sixty-seven in 1982, a loss I felt keenly. Not long before, however, I had renewed an old relationship that meant a great deal to me. Ray and Mae Hatcher moved back to Minneapolis to retire. Though they had no children, they told me they wanted to retire near "their children," meaning Charlotte and me and a few of our Phyllis Wheatley contemporaries. It was a great joy to have them back in my life.

Of course, my most important relationships were with Charlotte and our children. Charlotte and I had the great advantage of sharing common values.

Though our home lives as children had been difficult, we both were raised by mothers who cared deeply for their children and adhered to similar principles of moral behavior. We both had been reared under the strong influences of the Minneapolis Public Schools, our neighborhood churches, and Phyllis Wheatley's Gertrude Brown. After our marriage, we worked at developing common interests and activities while at the same time respecting each other's differences. We were both much attached to the Wheatley. It was an important bond between us, and it taught us a great deal about adult responsibility. Charlotte was not much interested in boxing, but she supported what I did there. She would bring the children down to watch practices, but then she and Rita would stray over into the girls' department at Phyllis Wheatley, while Butchie stayed to watch me. That was as it should be, I thought. I tried not to limit what Charlotte could do. She had a number of friendships with other women, and I tried to be available to care for the children on Saturdays so she could shop or have lunch or take in a movie with her friends. That was her chance to have a break from household responsibilities.

Charlotte didn't go back to school after our marriage, but she did go to work, as a retail sales clerk. She worked for Sears briefly before Rita was born. Then, a few years after Butch arrived, she went to work for the city's most prestigious department store, Dayton's. Charlotte was among the first black women to hold such a position; downtown-Minneapolis department stores did not hire their first black employees until 1948. The Daytons were good employers who gave their employees significant discounts on merchandise. That made a Dayton's job a coveted position. Charlotte went to work out of financial need. We hoped to own our own home someday and knew that day would be slow to come on the money I made coaching and working at Broadway Motors. Charlotte was good at her job, and she is still. She still works part-time as a clothing-store clerk.

Becoming parents cemented the love Charlotte and I shared. The day that Charlotte told me she was pregnant for the first time was one of the great days of my life. It started a new chapter for me. Even though we had been behaving like adults, it seemed as though we did not really become adults until we became parents. The day I knew Charlotte was expecting, I began to think of myself as responsible for the welfare of young lives. I thought, it's up to me to put groceries on the table, clothes on their backs, and pillows under their heads. I have to give them love and attention. I have to look after more than just their earthly needs.

Charlotte and I began to think about how we were going to educate Rita when she was barely a toddler. We vowed, "We will never give our children to any school system. We will go to school with them. We will learn along with them." We promised each other that when we took our children to kindergarten, both of us would take them. We would become acquainted with the teacher and know the principal. We would keep up with the work they were doing. We were determined to be active parents.

Rita was a good first child—bright and affectionate, with a strong personality. Even as a tyke, she knew how to speak her mind. When I came home from work, I loved the attention she would give me. She could boss me around and get anything she wanted, or so Charlotte claimed. I always enjoyed talking about Rita with my coworkers at Onan when the conversations would turn to children. She was easy to brag about.

We kept our promise and went with Rita to Grant School, just one block north and two short blocks west of our duplex on Eleventh and Emerson. Three years later, Butchie followed her there. Charlotte had attended Grant and knew the principal, Marshall Kaner. Two decades later, when I was on the Minneapolis School Board, he was one of the district's associate superintendents. We got to know Rita's teachers, all of whom were white. The Minneapolis district did not hire its first black teacher until after the war. Most teachers then were single women who devoted their lives to their work. They were much like the teachers I had at Sumner School as a child. They took a sincere interest in Rita and Butch, both of whom were strong students. Grant School had an active Parent-Teacher Association, which we joined, though I admit that Charlotte took the lead there because of the demands of my Golden Gloves schedule. She became a Grant PTA officer.

Of course, both Rita and Butch attended nursery school at Phyllis Wheatley. When Charlotte was working and Butch was four or five and in nursery school, Rita—who was just three years older—would walk down Eleventh Avenue to Aldrich and then down Aldrich to Eighth Avenue to take Butchie to nursery school in the morning. Then she would come all the way back and go to Grant School. She learned responsibility early and handled it well. In the afternoon, if the children came home before Charlotte's shift ended, they would stay in the lower duplex with my sister and her family or with my mother, who was willing to help out.

We had a dog that we called Poodle, though he was a yellow Lab. He was smart and a valued member of the family. We lived on Emerson, a busy street that always seemed to bustle with children as well as cars. When he was outside with Rita or Butch, Poodle would walk along the curb as if he were patrolling. If any of the kids would head out toward the street, he would walk between them and the street as if he were trying to herd them back. He was a favorite of the neighborhood children. They could do anything to him—pull his ears or his tail or lay on him—and he would never growl or snap. But if any adult came over to the children while they were playing, he would look the person over. If the person did not look familiar and got too close to the kids, he would show his teeth.

The store next door sold fish. The fishmonger would cut off the fish heads and throw them into the garbage. One day, I noticed a terrible smell in the children's bedroom, and we finally uncovered a fish head in Rita's doll buggy under some doll blankets. She assured us she had not brought any such thing into the house. The culprit must have been Poodle.

Our home was important to us, and we worked hard to make it nice, even though we had no chance of owning it. Charlotte managed our finances and planned our purchases of furniture and appliances to keep them manageable on our modest income. We painted the place, upgraded the oil stove that heated it, and bought linoleum for the kitchen floor. We made it cozy, but with just two bedrooms, we were crowded.

After I went back to work for Onan in 1948, we began to think about something our parents could only dream about: buying our own home. The barriers to home ownership that had barred African Americans before World War II began to fall after the war, at least in a few of the city's neighborhoods. We knew if we could save enough for a down payment, we would have a fair chance of persuading a lender to give us a mortgage for a house.

As a junior foreman at Onan in the early 1950s, I made $1.95 an hour. My Golden Gloves coaching job started at $35 a month, but went up to $55 a month, then $75 a month. I also made a little money doing other work for Phyllis Wheatley, and Charlotte's work brought in more money still. And for a number of years, she and I did some real moonlighting. After I came home from Phyllis Wheatley on weekday evenings, we would go together to a downtown restaurant called the Flameburger and clean for several hours. We didn't get much sleep in those years. But we were young and had a dream that energized us.

Our serious house-hunting began in 1953. Charlotte held out hope that we could find a home on the North Side. After all, that neighborhood was home. But the North Side housing stock was deteriorating in those years. Some of the nicer homes, those with hardwood floors and pretty banisters, had been torn down when the first housing project went in. Those remaining that we found acceptable were in the city's northwest corner and beyond our reach financially. Discouraged, we stopped looking for a time and saved more money.

We were more resigned to leaving the North Side when we resumed house-hunting in 1954. We were also increasingly desperate for more room. That summer, Charlotte was pregnant with our third child, Richard Charles (we call him Ricky), who would be born on February 7, 1955. The Central High School neighborhood seemed the right place to look. South of downtown Minneapolis and bounded by Lake Street, Nicollet Avenue, Minnehaha Parkway, and Chicago Avenue, Central was the part of the city most amenable to black home owners. It was where middle-class black people had lived for more than a generation. Pullman porters, postal workers, streetcar drivers, and hotel workers all made their homes in the Central area and sent their children to Central High School. The neighborhood was dominated by small, bungalow-style single-family homes of the sort that sold for under $15,000. That was a lot of money in those years, but it was not an impossible reach.

We found what we were seeking at 3621 Portland Avenue South. It was a three-bedroom bungalow in the middle of the block on a busy street. It was a sound, well-kept stucco house with a fenced yard, front and back. But what we really appreciated was its proximity to three good public schools—Warrington, the elementary school; Bryant, the junior high school; and Central High School. All were considered among the city's best in the 1950s. Sadly, all of those schools are gone today.

We consoled ourselves about leaving the North Side by staying attached to Phyllis Wheatley. By then, Rita was eleven and Butchie was eight. Before long, we considered them old enough to take the bus to the Wheatley. Butch played football there and Rita took classes. We also felt that we were not totally among strangers on the South Side; many friends our age from the old neighborhood had already moved south.

What we did not fully appreciate at the time was that we were part of an exodus that marked the breakup of what had been the Minneapolis ghetto. The North Side of our childhood was home to a mix of people—blacks and Jews, poor and middle-income, old and young, legitimate and illegitimate—all joined by the fact that they were not welcome to live anywhere else in Minneapolis. When that fact changed, the middle-class members of the old community, blacks and Jews alike, moved out. Those of us who moved gained a better standard of living and some welcome distance from the vice with which we had been all too familiar at home. But we lost something too: we would never again experience the neighborhood cohesiveness that we grew up with. The bigger losers, though, were the people left behind in the old neighborhood. The exiles took with them a lot of the resources needed to make a neighborhood strong.

We found our house in Central when some friends told us about it and suggested that we take a look. We piled Rita and Butch into the car and set out to just drive by the place, but when we stopped to give it a long look, the older lady who owned it called to us, "Would you like to come in?" She introduced herself as Mrs. Nanna Estelle and could not have been more gracious. She explained that she was a retired nurse, originally from Sweden, and that she had decided to move back to Sweden to be near family in her declining years. She took a great interest in us and in our children and gave us a chatty tour of the house. We liked its oil-burning furnace, its three-season porch, and—a first for us—its partially finished basement. We also liked Mrs. Estelle, and it was plain that the feeling was mutual. She could see that Charlotte was pregnant, and she treated Charlotte in a motherly way.

We were sold on the house, but we were concerned about being able to get a mortgage to cover the $12,000 asking price. We went to a downtown institution we had heard about when we were kids, Farmers and Mechanics Bank. When we were schoolchildren, we had been given the opportunity to start savings accounts at Farmers and Mechanics. Every Friday, we could bring money to school to deposit in our accounts. The idea was to teach us basic financial concepts, like interest. It also left us with a friendly feeling toward that bank. Our confidence in F & M was rewarded, though it helped that Mrs. Estelle came down a little in her asking price. We got a mortgage for $9,000. We also got a contract for deed to fill a remaining gap in our financing from a local attorney and investor who later became a friend at church, Fred Thorson. When we see him now, he likes to recall that connection we had. He always says, "You never missed a payment."

We became so attached to Mrs. Estelle that she stayed with us for a few days after we moved into the house. She gave us a few knickknacks, and we bought a few other items from her. To this day, we keep a vase that we got from her in our dining room as a reminder of the special relationship we developed with the previous owner of our first house.

Only a few months elapsed between our move and Ricky's arrival. His timing was an early indication of his attention-getting personality. He was born on the night of the semifinal bouts in the 1955 Golden Gloves Upper Midwest tournament. It was a year when we had an outstanding team, led by flyweight star Jimmy Jackson and bantamweight slugger Kenny Rodriguez. I got home from work at four o'clock that afternoon, revved up about the tournament—and there sat Charlotte with a suitcase and a pained expression on her face. She had been in labor for some time already, though somehow she had been able to prepare dinner for me and the kids. She needed to go to the hospital, right now. "We'd better get moving," she said. I called Phyllis Wheatley to tell the boxers what was happening and to ask that someone make sure the team got to the auditorium on time. We also called Charlotte's sister Margaret and arranged for her to come and stay with Rita and Butch. Then we raced to St. Mary's Hospital with little time to spare. Ricky was born at 6:45 p.m. As soon as the obstetrician emerged to tell me everything was well, I shot out of the hospital and headed to the Minneapolis Auditorium.

When I got there, it seemed everyone in the place had heard I was absent because Charlotte was having a baby. The fellow out in front directing parking already knew the news when I pulled up, at about 7:15 p.m. He said, "You leave it there, Harry. Jimmy Jackson is getting ready to go in the ring and he's been hollering for you. I'll park your car." I ran into the auditorium, and they were just getting ready to announce Jimmy's match. Jimmy saw me run in. Boy! He was really pleased to see me. What a night I had! Word of the birth even made it into the *Star* and *Tribune* sports pages the next day. The paper said I came to the auditorium "armed with a box of cigars he passed out, (and) with a smile broader than he sports when one of his fighters wins."

Ricky was a very active toddler, full of energy and potential for mischief. Once when he was about three or four, he ran into our small bedroom and leaped on the bed as kids love to do. It was a warm day, and Charlotte had the bedroom window wide open. Ricky flew in with such momentum that he bounced on the bed and out the window! Charlotte saw it happen and flew out the window right after him to retrieve him. What a sight that must have made for any neighbor who happened to be watching! Luckily, he fell on grass rather than the sidewalk and was more scared than hurt. Charlotte took him to the hospital, just to be sure he was all right. Later, when he was a teenager, I used to tease him by saying, "You're girl crazy now because you fell on your head that time you flew out the window."

Ricky was in grade school in 1960 when I got a call at work one day from a fellow named George Roman, a former Golden Glover who had become a fire-insurance adjuster. I greeted him with an assumption that he wanted to talk boxing. "What do you want to know about the Golden Gloves?" I asked. "Nothing," he said. "I just called to tell you that your house is on fire." I said, "Come on, now. Quit kidding." "No, I'm not kidding," he said. "I just heard it. I chase fire engines and listen to the fire-department radio dispatches. You live at 3621 Portland. Your house is on fire."

Sure enough, it was. The fire started in the basement while Ricky was at school and Charlotte was at home. She smelled something odd, but it didn't occur to her that the scent was smoke. Then she heard the "pop" of glass breaking in the basement, and our family dog came running upstairs. When she peered downstairs, she saw smoke and made a hasty exit out the back door. She called the fire department from the neighbors' house. Firefighters got there in time to confine the damage to the basement.

I dashed home and met George Roman there. He took over, making all the arrangements with the insurance company to repair and remodel the basement and to shelter us while the house was under construction. He got an apartment for us in a motel near Fifty-fourth and Lyndale. Our basement was remodeled from floor to ceiling, and we were well cared for in the process, thanks to George.

11
Border

AFTER OUR MARRIAGE, which church we would attend was a matter of some indecision. Charlotte grew up at Border Methodist Church, and I attended its youth group when the dynamic Reverend Damon Palma Young was its pastor. But I had gone to Wayman African Methodist Episcopal Church as a child and was confirmed there. And while I lived with my sister Dooney, I also often attended Zion Baptist, the church near her house. The Zion pastor, the Reverend Henry Botts, officiated at our wedding. On a few Sunday mornings after we were married, Charlotte went to Border and I went to Zion, or I used the morning to get some rest after a busy week.

Rita's birth settled the matter. Children should go to church with their mother, I reasoned, and Charlotte wanted to go to Border. Rita was baptized there. I joined Border too. It proved to be a fateful choice.

Border had been founded in 1918 as a Sunday school on the city's South Side. It became a full-fledged church a year later, under the name St. John's Methodist Episcopal Church. Not long thereafter, it moved to the North Side and took its permanent name. Along with Camphor Methodist in St. Paul, Border Methodist Church was one of two Twin Cities black congregations in the large national denomination then called the Methodist Episcopal Church. Other black churches had the word Methodist in their names, but they were part of denominations called African Methodist Episcopal or Colored Methodist Episcopal. Eventually, Camphor and Border became part of the Lexington, Kentucky, conference of the Methodist Episcopal Church's all-black Central Jurisdiction. That jurisdiction's very existence told a story about racism and religion in the United States. The Methodist Church in the United States split in two, north and south, over slavery and the Civil War in the mid-nineteenth century. By the 1930s, talks aimed at reunification had begun. The Methodist Episcopal Church–South imposed an ugly condition on reunion: It would not allow black Methodist churches in its conferences.

That was not out of a simple desire to keep its distance. In the Methodist Church, clergy are assigned to conferences and rotated at will by bishops. Create a mixed-race conference and a free-thinking bishop might assign a black clergyman to a white church. That was what the southern Methodists were trying to prevent.

Border's first building stood along the back of the property that contains the Farmers' Market today. It was on Border Avenue (hence the church's name), a short street between Royalston and Highland, and next to the Cedar Lake Ice Company. That was the company that cut large cubes of ice from the lakes in the wintertime and packed them in wood chips and sawdust for sale to home owners with iceboxes. But by the time I joined, the church had been forced by development to relocate to a tiny stucco building at Fourth and Aldrich Avenues. That little building was dedicated in 1937 "to the glory of God and the service of the Negro people of Minneapolis."

When I joined, Border was a small congregation of about 150 members, many of them senior citizens. They included some prominent families in our neighborhood, people who had been active at Phyllis Wheatley and who had tried to keep the neighborhood livable and safe. They established the Border tradition of involvement in neighborhood-building activities. Along with Zion and Wayman, Border was counted among the churches that stood strong against racial injustice, poverty, and other social ills. Despite its small size, it had a good choir, a Sunday school for children, and active Methodist Women's and Methodist Men's clubs. Border took on some of the customs and style of worship of other black denominations. For example, it had female lay leaders—deaconesses—who wore headdresses and white gloves and took a role in worship services. The white Methodist churches in town had nothing similar.

Reverend Damon Young had done a great deal to spread Border's good name outside the church's immediate neighborhood. He was more than a pastor. He was a neighborhood leader, active at Phyllis Wheatley, in the NAACP, and in city politics. He may have been the first Border pastor to come to the attention of people in the big cathedral-style Methodist church a couple of miles south of our neighborhood, Hennepin Avenue Methodist.

In race, income, worship style, and prestige, it is hard to imagine two congregations more opposite than Border and Hennepin. Yet the congregations had a personal connection. Some of the women who were leaders at Hennepin were also board members at Phyllis Wheatley. They became acquainted with Reverend Young there and appreciated the work he did with young people in our neighborhood, walking the Avenue and trying to talk kids away from prostitution and crime. They approved of his efforts to organize all the clergy in our neighborhood into a Black Ministerial Alliance. Reverend Young looked to the Women's Christian Association, the organization that founded Phyllis Wheatley, for financial support for his work. A lot of other ministers in our neighborhood had second jobs; several were barbers whose shops doubled as church offices. But Reverend Young was trying to be a full-time minister and needed support from outside Border Church to do so. When Border needed to relocate to Fourth and Aldrich in 1937, more funds were needed. Hennepin helped then and again later, when Border wanted to supply its pastors with a parsonage. Damon Young left Border in the early 1940s and went on to serve churches in Cincinnati, Detroit, and Chicago. He became a district superintendent in the Lexington Conference before it was dissolved in the 1960s. He died in Columbus, Ohio, in 1980.

In typical Methodist fashion, Border went through a string of pastors in rapid succession during the rest of that decade. In 1949, one came to stay: the Reverend Charles Sexton, an intellectually gifted man from Jamaica. Born in 1894, he had degrees from the University of Kingston in Jamaica, New York City College, Ohio State University, Gammon Theological Seminary in Atlanta, and Rust College in Holly Springs, Mississippi. He worked as a research chemist at the University of Chicago during World War II. While he was a wonderful speaker, he lacked a little of the common touch one expects in a pastor. He stood a little apart from the personal lives of his parishioners and was not much involved in the larger community in the way Damon Young had been. Nevertheless, Reverend Sexton and I got along very well. I admired his scholarly approach to faith; he seemed to have confidence in my abilities. I was pleased when he invited me to deliver the sermon one Sunday when he had to be out of town. I was on pins and needles when I stepped into that pulpit, but I remembered the training I had received from Miss Dorsey at Phyllis Wheatley, and I got the job done. That occasion cemented the relationship between Reverend Sexton and me.

Meanwhile, because of the seeds planted by Reverend Young, a special bond developed between Hennepin and Border. Hennepin was an affluent and socially conscious church in the 1950s. Numbered among its four thousand members in those years were descendants of some of the wealthy families that had founded Minneapolis—the Walkers, the Harrisons—as well as some people whose financial success was more recent, such as Burton Gamble and Curtis Carlson. The Onan family, my employers, were Hennepin members. So was a prominent attorney and member of the city's Fair

Employment Practices Commission, Leonard Lindquist. These people had the means and the desire to make a difference in their community. Hennepin was attuned to the just-developing national civil-rights movement and was eager to advance that cause, as well as to serve the poor and needy of Minneapolis. In 1955, it was among the first churches in the area to adopt a policy that all races were welcome as members. Hennepin's mission-minded members cultivated Border Methodist, thinking our little church could be Hennepin's vehicle for understanding and meeting human needs on the North Side.

Border cultivated Hennepin in return. Beginning during Damon Young's tenure, Border pastors were occasionally invited to preach at Hennepin. Reverend Sexton turned to Hennepin for financial help and advice in 1952, when he initiated an ambitious program for neighborhood and congregational development. Several Hennepin members served on what Reverend Sexton called the Border Advance Committee. Meanwhile, Border's choir occasionally performed at the big church on Lowry Hill. Border's strong choir included Freddie and Rama Estes, members of the family that owned the largest black funeral home in the city. They had beautiful voices, as did June Hawkins, a vocalist in our choir who also sang solos occasionally at Hennepin. Our director was Carrie Williams, a professional music teacher who brought several of her students to our choir. When she found out that I had sung in the North High School choir, she asked me to join and I did. Mrs. Williams soon had us performing ambitious pieces such as "The Seven Last Words" on Easter Sunday.

Laypeople at Border and Hennepin came to know each other through the women's and men's organizations that were strong at both churches in those years. Charlotte was active in the women's group; the Reverend Sexton recruited me for Methodist Men.

Before I knew it, I found myself at a Methodist Men's citywide meeting and was being urged to come to a campground at Old Frontenac, south of Red Wing on the Mississippi River, for a Methodist Men's retreat. This was in the early 1950s, when men's clubs of all sorts were in their heyday. The retreat was a well-organized, inspirational affair with speakers, miniclasses, and sports competitions. I met men from all over the city, including a number from Hennepin Church. My name was familiar to many of them because of the Golden Gloves publicity I had received, so I got to know people quickly. The Methodist Men's leader for all of Minneapolis was Larry Whitely, the owner of a paint shop on Lake Street in south Minneapolis and a Golden Gloves fan. He took me aside and explained that he was looking for someone to play a supervisory role for the organization, working with four congregations to help recruit members and develop strong programs. Ordinarily, they recruited congregational lay leaders for that job, but Border's lay leader, Wendell Jones, had always turned the Methodist Men's club down. Wendell was very active at Phyllis Wheatley, where he had taught me tennis and roller-skating as a child, and he preferred to spend his time there. I allowed that I too was pretty busy at the Wheatley. "Yes, but you are younger," Larry said. I conceded that he had a point. I accepted the assignment and began making twice-yearly visits to Methodist Men's clubs at four Minneapolis-area churches—Richfield, Walker, Simpson, and Hennepin. I would talk with them about their programs for laymen, assist in recruiting, and distribute information about our annual retreat in Old Frontenac. I found myself able to add to the bond between Border and Hennepin churches.

That bridge was put to the test, beginning in 1955, when Border got word that its building was again in the path of urban development. Glenwood-Lyndale, the second big housing project to alter the shape of my neighborhood, was coming.

The first housing project on the North Side was Sumner Field, built in 1937. It reached from Olson Highway to Eleventh Avenue and from Aldrich to Emerson Avenues. It was divided in two by the park that was its namesake, Sumner Field. At the park's north end, the Sumner Field housing project built three-story apartment buildings; otherwise, the housing consisted of two-story townhouses. The project was segregated, with white and Jewish people living west of Sumner Field and black people living east and north.

The next wave of development came only a few years later, when Sixth Avenue was renamed Olson Memorial Highway, after the late Governor Floyd B. Olson, a neighborhood native son. The street was widened and a parkway added down the middle, which had the effect of clearing out the businesses on the south side of the street. The project was popular because it provided jobs and eliminated some trashy businesses. But it made my neighborhood's main street a thoroughfare where pedestrians were no longer comfortable and retail business could no longer thrive. That changed forever the character and livability of the neighborhood.

In about 1955, word came from city hall that urban renewal was coming to the south side of Olson Highway. The plan was to tear down existing structures from Lyndale to Emerson Avenue, between Glenwood Avenue and Olson Highway—hence the name Glenwood-Lyndale. Sumner School's building, no longer in use as a school, would go. So would Border Church.

The news was not as well received as the Sumner Field project had been. Glenwood-Lyndale would destroy much of the neighborhood's history. It would tear down not only dilapidated housing and bootlegging joints but also older, well-tended homes of Jewish families. Several other churches—one Seventh-Day Adventist, one Catholic—were also in Glenwood-Lyndale's path. Those churches put up a fight to stay, won, and are still standing. But few other property owners fought the changes. The Jewish population was deserting the neighborhood for the suburbs in the 1950s. Most of the houses were owned by absentee landlords who would be satisfied with a check from the city for their property.

Border's initial reaction was to stand and fight the city's plan to tear down its building and its parsonage. But the congregation began to weaken when the city offered Border free land for construction of a new church and parsonage. That was an option worth considering seriously, and it started us asking some hard questions about the congregation's future.

Border's membership had been dwindling since the end of World War II. It was down to about eighty-five active members, most of them older people. If we were to build, should we build a tiny church to accommodate the current members, or should we build a bigger place and expect to grow? Would we be wise to go into debt for a big new church? Should we buy an abandoned Jewish synagogue, as the Holiness Church had done a few years earlier? In any event, who would pay off a big mortgage?

By 1955, I had succeeded Wendell Jones as Border's lay leader, which put me in the thick of the deliberations about the church's future. I was also in contact with my friends at Hennepin Church, where I had become well acquainted with some of its members. Among them were the indomitable Miriam Bennett, wife of prominent businessman Russell Bennett and an Urban League board member, and construction contractor Les Parks, who would have a role in building Glenwood-Lyndale. They took an interest in Border's dilemma. "What's going to happen if Border chooses not to build a new church?" they asked me. I recited our options, including the one I feared was becoming most likely: we could dissolve the congregation, and members could scatter to other churches.

I did not like that prospect. It would mean losing contact with people who had become close friends. But as lay leader, I had to be pragmatic. I had to consider the interests of young families like my own, since we would bear the financial burden of whatever decision we made. At the congregational meeting at which the issue came to a head, I said, "I don't think we can do this unless we can greatly increase our membership in a very short time. If you vote tonight to build a new church, we'll go ahead and try to do it. But it's going to cause a financial burden on the next generation. They may not be able to handle it."

The motion to build a new church failed, and the Border congregation faced up to the likelihood that we would disband. Word spread among other churches in the area of our decision, and members began getting invitations to "give us a try." As lay leader, I was still searching for a better alternative and said as much to Miriam Bennett. Her response surprised me: "Why don't we invite all of you to come to Hennepin?"

I could not believe at first that she meant what she had said. Despite all the connections that had been built between Hennepin and Border, it was still a giant leap over a huge social and cultural chasm to think that we could be one congregation. In the 1950s, race was still a rigid dividing line on Sunday morning. But Miriam Bennett was serious. In fact, one might say she was inspired. She took her idea back to Hennepin and set about selling it with a force and determination that made her a wonder to behold. Timing was in her favor. The year was 1956. Only a few months earlier, a bus boycott by black churches in Montgomery, Alabama, led by the young Reverend Martin Luther King Jr., had shaken the nation's complacency about segregation. Liberal Protestant churches were lining up in favor of civil rights; Hennepin was one of them. It put a slogan on its front-lawn sign on Lyndale Avenue: "Welcome to people of all races." Mrs. Bennett asked as she proposed a merger with Border, "Do we mean what we say on our sign?"

We had some selling to do at Border too. I liked her idea. I kept thinking about how good it would be to raise my children in a large, robust church with an established youth program, where we did not have to struggle just to keep operating. I shared those views with others at Border. I also spoke about the fine people I had met at Hennepin and my confidence in their sincerity and goodwill. But we wanted to know more. Mrs. Bennett, Les Parks, and another active Hennepin layperson, Orem Robbins, came to a Border congregational meeting to present the idea. They were not there to offer an official invitation to merge, because that step had not yet been approved at Hennepin. But they wanted to start a conversation with the message that Hennepin wanted to be helpful to Border, no matter how Border decided to handle its building problem.

We ended that meeting with a show-of-hands vote. Most of those present indicated that if Hennepin offered a merger, they would transfer their membership to Hennepin. That put the weight back on Mrs. Bennett's shoulders to open Hennepin's doors to us. She did not have much difficulty: Hennepin's lay leaders were behind the idea, and at Hennepin and most Methodist churches, laypeople make the governing decisions. Hennepin's senior pastor, Dr. Chester Pennington, also approved, but he was not in the forefront on the project. He was quoted in the *Minneapolis Star* sometime later as denying any personal credit for the merger. "From the very beginning, this has been a concern and activity of the laypeople," Dr. Pennington said. He never approved of using the word "merger" to describe our arrangement; he always spoke of Hennepin "extending a personal pastoral invitation" to the Border members. It was a nicety that I thought reflected a certain coolness on his part.

I later heard that Mrs. Bennett had a little quiet lobbying help from a former teacher at Hennepin's University of Life program for young adults, U.S. Senator Hubert Humphrey. He placed a few calls to his old Hennepin students to let them know he supported what Mrs. Bennett was proposing. I also understand that it did not hurt that a number of Hennepin people knew me, either through choir, Methodist Men, Golden Gloves, or Onan. They could vouch for the respectability of Border's lay leader.

The invitation from Hennepin for merger came by unanimous vote of the congregation's 150-member official board in early December 1956. Border voted to accept the invitation December 23. The merger was warmly received but not unanimously accepted. Border members who did not feel comfortable worshipping in a large, mostly white congregation scattered to other black churches. Perhaps four or five families left Hennepin out of similar prejudice. The Methodist Conference bishop, D. Stanley Coors, took some abuse for his enthusiastic support of the merger, receiving anonymous hate mail that promised revenge by the Ku Klux Klan. Nevertheless, the merger went forward with no visible protest or disruption. We heard later that a large Lutheran church in Omaha that had attempted something similar at about the same time was not nearly as fortunate. It was plagued with protesters for some time.

On January 6, 1957, the first joint worship service between Hennepin and Border was conducted. Two weeks later, on January 20, sixty-seven Border Methodists transferred their membership to Hennepin Church. It was a poignant, emotional time for both congregations. We had several meetings to plan the way Border members would be received. It was decided that

Border families would be paired with Hennepin families of similar ages, and those families would sit together that first Sunday. The committee arranged for the paired Hennepin and Border families to meet before the 11:00 a.m. service at the parking-lot door. The Hennepin children would take the Border children to Sunday school. The adults would go together into the sanctuary and sit in the Hennepin families' customary places. That way, Border members would not be bunched together in a few pews but would be sprinkled throughout the large sanctuary. The Hennepin families were asked to introduce us to the people in the adjacent pews.

Dr. Pennington preached a sermon that added to the welcome. But none of us knew then quite how significant the day was. We learned later that we had executed only the second merger of a white and a black congregation in any mainline Protestant denomination in the United States.

Charlotte and I were paired that first Sunday with Orem Robbins and his wife. They are just a little older than we are and their children were close in age to Rita and Butchie. To this day, we attend the 11:00 a.m. service and sit in the same pew that Orem Robbins took us to that first Sunday. Miriam and Russell Bennett always sat nearby. She greeted us warmly that Sunday and nearly every other Sunday thereafter until she died in 1996.

That first Sunday at Hennepin was a huge success, so much so that I think it was the key to making the merger work. Border members went home marveling at the recognition they were given in a congregation of more than four thousand members. Word got back to some of the Border members who had not transferred to Hennepin that those who made the move were welcomed warmly and were quickly at home. A few more Border exiles joined Hennepin later.

Charles Sexton did not join us at Hennepin. For about eight months, he was a "minister of goodwill" attached to the Minnesota Conference, filling pulpits on a substitute basis. One of those was the Champlin Methodist Church near Anoka, then a tiny, all-white parish in the country, so small that it was relegated to sharing a pastor with neighboring churches. In September 1957, little Champlin voted to call the Reverend Sexton as permanent pastor. It was a gutsy move, spearheaded by the youth of the church who had become fond of their substitute minister. The move made headlines. Champlin was the first all-white congregation in the denomination's nine-state jurisdiction to be served by a black pastor.

Sexton finished his career at Afton Methodist Church, retiring in 1964. He died in Chicago in 1985. His abundant talents were not given the exposure they deserved in the little churches he served in Minnesota. But it may have been for the best for him that he did not join the Hennepin staff in 1957. He would not have been welcome to share the pulpit with Chet Pennington, a scholarly homilist whose style was much like Sexton's own. Nevertheless, Border members regretted Sexton's departure as their pastor. Hennepin's official board assured us that Hennepin would ask the bishop to assign a black pastor to the church at the next opportunity. That opportunity was a long time coming. The Reverend Daniel Brewer, a refugee from Liberia, was an associate pastor from 1992 to 1994. In 2000, the Reverend Dennis Oglesby was recruited from Chicago to join the staff. It was a determined move by Hennepin to look outside the Minnesota Conference for black ministerial leadership. I was part of the committee that selected him. We were surprised to discover a historical coincidence: the first pastor of Border Church in 1919 was named D. W. Oglesby.

The Border merger has become a source of pride for Hennepin over the years. It has been celebrated repeatedly in worship services and ceremonies, and with an original dramatic production in 2000. Hennepin's chapel took the name Border Chapel in 1994. Border's baptismal font stands close to the chapel's altar.

I had a call a short time ago from someone wanting information about black Methodist history. He wanted to know how Border Church got "coerced" into joining Hennepin. "What do you mean, coerced?" I said. He was of the mistaken impression that we had been pressured to give up our own church and submerge our identity into that of the larger, richer, white congregation. I set him straight. "We didn't get coerced into anything. We made our own decisions. What would have happened if we had decided to build a new church and not been able to pay for it? Is it being coerced to make a good business decision not to put a load of debt on the next generation?"

We came to Hennepin as pioneers in American church integration. More than forty years later, many of us are still there, as are our children and grandchildren. Other black people have joined in the intervening years. We are no longer pioneers but full participants in the life of a church that has become fully our own.

Charlotte NaPue at about age fourteen, when I met her.

Charlotte NaPue (left) and Lela Taylor at the Phyllis Wheatley operetta, spring 1941. Charlotte, age fifteen, is wearing her first formal gown.

My schoolmate Matt Hammond (right) and I posed after receiving our North High letters for boxing in 1939. Matt was one of seven brothers; I coached many of them at Phyllis Wheatley.

My North High School graduation picture.

Mr. John Vernon NaPue

requests the pleasure of your company

at the marriage of his daughter

Charlotte Jeanne

to

Mr. Harry William Davis

on Saturday evening, October the third

at eight o'clock

1223 Olson Highway

Minneapolis, Minnesota

Our wedding invitation.

Charlotte and I were on our way to celebrate our first wedding anniversary when this photo was taken in our car. Our daughter Rita would be born a few weeks later.

The Onan Company had a party in June 1943 to celebrate winning an E Award (for excellence) from the U.S. Navy. Among the celebrants were (from left) I, Charlotte, and Betty and Jack Strawder.

Leland Davis Jr., "Menzy," in the U.S. Army in 1943.

My brother, Menzy, was the star pitcher on the Onan-Stinson plant softball team before he was called up for military service.

Rita, eight, and Butch, five, visit Santa Claus at Dayton's Department Store in downtown Minneapolis, 1951.

The stars of the Wheatley 1953–1954 boxing team (from left): Ray Wells, Charles Smith, and Neil Frazier. Ray became my kinsman a few years later when he married my first cousin, Rene Jackson; Neil Frazier went on to be a bishop in the Church of God and Christ.

Eddie Lacy was the first Upper Midwest Golden Gloves champion my Phyllis Wheatley team produced. He started winning championships in 1945.

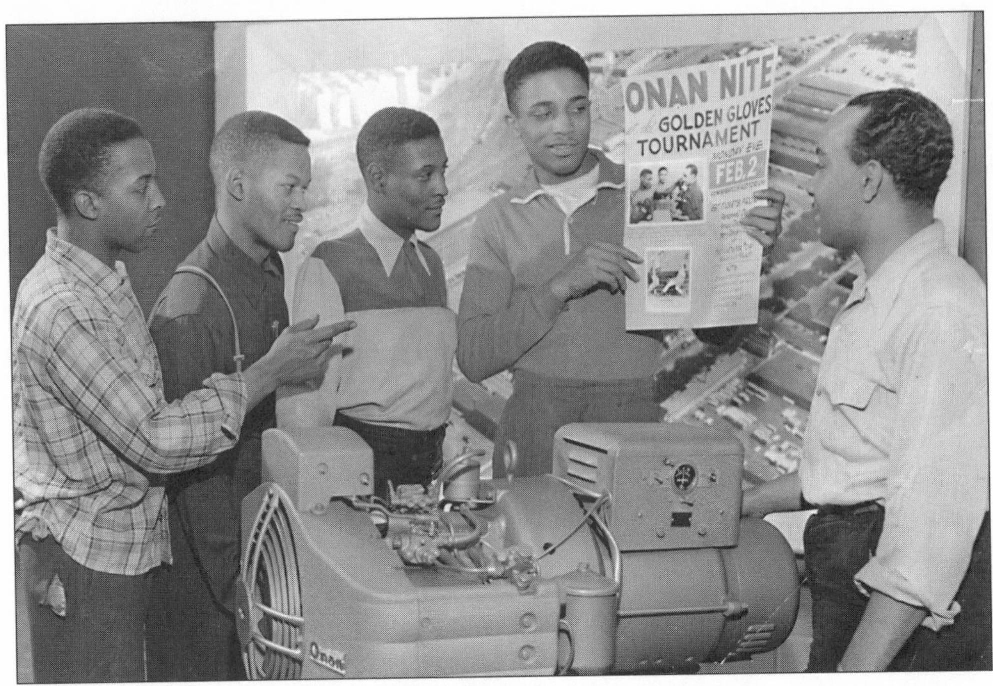

From left: Danny Davis, Wes Hayden, Johnny Bible, and Roger Frazier prepare with me for "Onan Nite" at the Upper Midwest Golden Gloves 1951 tournament. Onan sponsored a night at the tournament every year after my teams became successful. These four boxers all became Onan employees at some point during the 1950s; each went on to fine careers.

In addition to coaching boxing at Phyllis Wheatley, I also coached football for ten-year-olds. The player in the center of the back row was future Minneapolis school superintendent Richard Green.

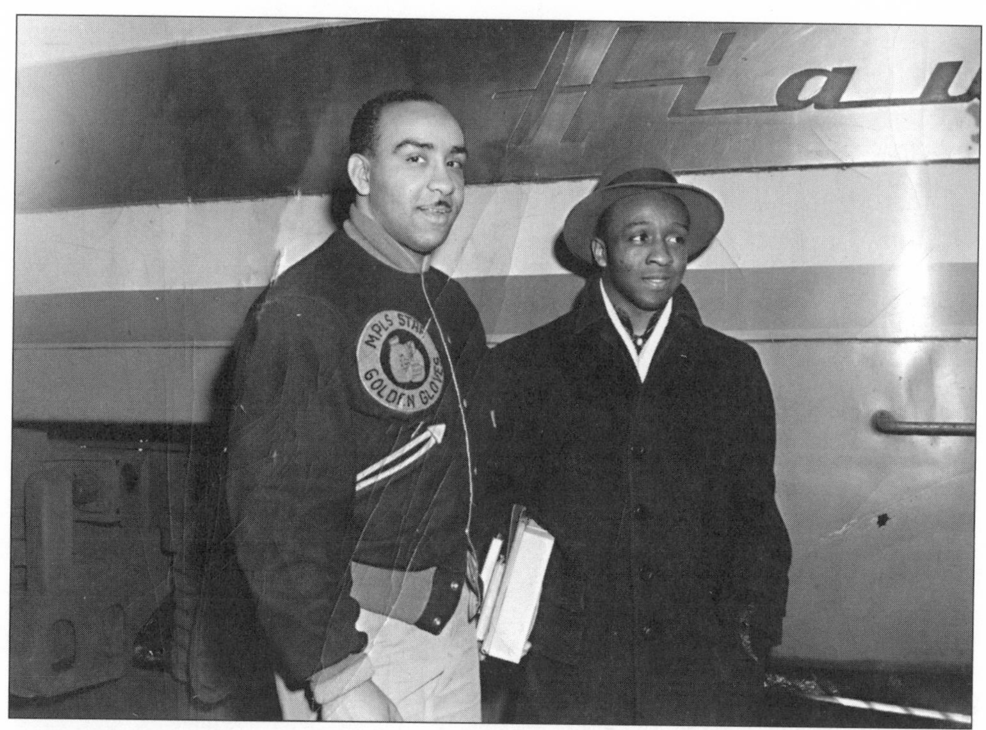

I accompanied Golden Gloves star flyweight Jimmy Jackson on the Hiawatha train to Chicago for the 1957 national Golden Gloves tournament.

The Royal Twenty club, a couples' club based at Phyllis Wheatley, gathers for a photo at its tenth-anniversary party in the late 1950s.

My mother was in poor health when the family gathered for this photo in about 1958. Standing (from left): Joyce, the cousin my mother raised; Leland Jr. "Menzy"; Charlotte "Dooney"; and I. Seated (from left): Eva; my mother, Libby; and Geraldine.

I joined the Onan Chorus in the early 1950s and sang baritone with the group until I left the company in 1968. I am in the first row, on the far left.

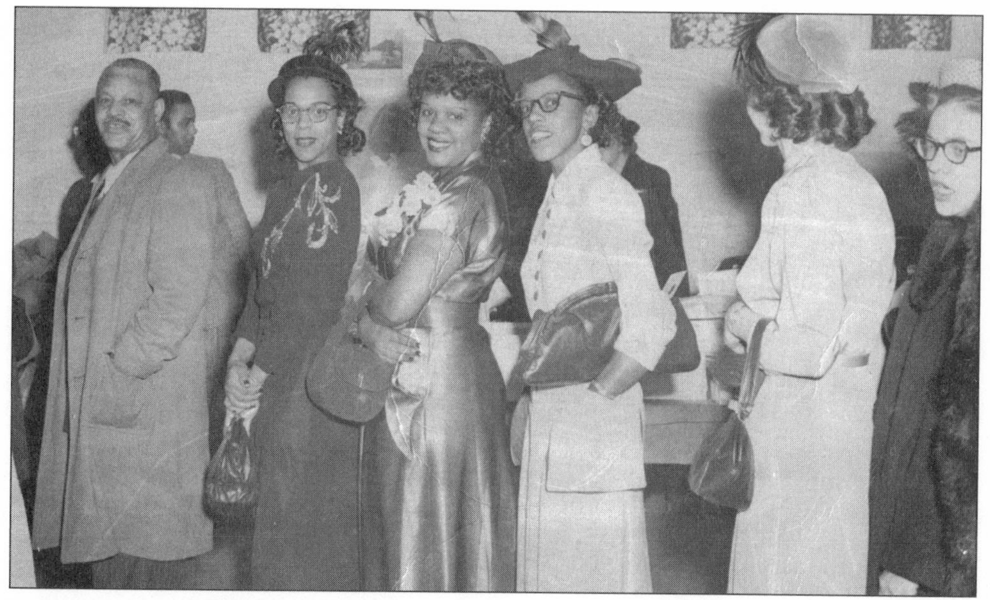

Border Church's Hattie Dryer Circle hosted an annual George Washington tea, often attended by women from Hennepin Avenue Methodist Church. In line facing the camera are Charlotte, her sister Margaret NaPue, and Ruth Majors.

I received my twenty-year watch from the Onan Company in 1965. The man in shirtsleeves is CEO Bud Onan, the son of the company's founder.

This photo marking my promotion at Onan appeared in the company newsletter, *Onan News,* in May 1966. I was given a desk set by my paint-department employees.

Mayor Art Naftalin and Fran Naftalin toasted Charlotte and me as we celebrated our twenty-fifth wedding anniversary in 1967. Charlotte was expecting our fourth child, Evan.

III
CRUSADING

12
Stirring

IT WAS IMPOSSIBLE to be a black man anywhere in America in the 1950s and not be aware of both prevalent racism and a persistent stirring to overcome it. I was a busy husband, father, factory worker, coach, and church layman, and yet the stirring touched me. I followed the news from places like Little Rock, Arkansas, and Montgomery, Alabama. I cheered as Minnesota's Senator Hubert Humphrey became one of the leading voices for equal rights in the nation's government. I looked for a chance to step up my involvement in the organization that had been synonymous with racial equality all my life, the National Association for the Advancement of Colored People, or NAACP.

My chance came in 1960 with a change in my duties in the Golden Gloves program. My years of spending five nights a week in a gymnasium ended. A greater cause was about to fill my calendar.

The NAACP was founded in 1909 in New York and came to Minneapolis in 1914, one year after a branch was founded in St. Paul. But it didn't become a significant force in the community until it became linked with Phyllis Wheatley Settlement House and Gertrude Brown. The Wheatley's first director locked arms with the NAACP as a partner in lifting the sights of downtrodden people, particularly young people. She gave the organization meeting space, recruitment and publicity help, and sound advice. The Junior NAACP was soon melded into the Wheatley's activities for young people like me. I attended NAACP classes at the Wheatley when I was a teenager with my mother's encouragement. She was not involved in politics, but she knew of the NAACP and knew she wanted her son exposed to its lessons. The organization taught a primer in politics. We learned about the precinct, the ward, the district, the caucus. We learned parliamentary procedure, party organization, voter registration, getting out the vote. In election years, we went door-to-door with the organization's senior members, registering people to vote and distributing literature for candidates we supported. The message that was drilled into us, over and over, was the importance of the vote.

I was a young coach at Phyllis Wheatley after World War II, when returning GIs and idealistic young people combined forces with a new, ambitious mayor to ignite greater interest in civil rights in Minneapolis. A potent coalition of leaders took shape. It included W. D. Brown, the physician who had been the Davis family doctor and one of the North Side's leading citizens for decades; Cecil Newman, a journalist, newspaper publisher, and NAACP teacher and leader; Raymond Cannon, an attorney and wonderful speaker; Lena Olive Smith, a human-rights lawyer who was the first black woman to pass the bar in Minnesota; Nellie Stone Johnson, a union organizer and political activist; and the young mayor, Hubert Humphrey. I was acquainted with all of them, including Humphrey, thanks to his friend and my NAACP teacher, Cecil Newman.

Cecil made a point of introducing me to Humphrey in the spring of 1945. It was during the final weeks of Humphrey's successful campaign for mayor. He was the featured speaker at the NAACP annual banquet, held at Phyllis Wheatley. It was a huge affair, elegant and formal. As the Wheatley boxing coach, I was one of the settlement house's staff members, which made me one of the serving crew for the banquet. We flipped a coin and I won the right to serve the head table. It was kind of an honor, but it was also the most work. The head table was situated by the exit door on the west side of the gymnasium. The food would come up by dumbwaiters located on the northeast side, so the waiter for the head table always got a workout, carefully carrying large trays of food. Cecil Newman and Raymond Cannon were seated next to Humphrey, and as I worked, I became aware that they were watching me and appeared to be talking about me. When I got close and began to serve Cecil, he said to Hubert, "This is the former president of our junior chapter, Harry Davis. I'm sure that someday he will be president of the senior chapter. He's our boxing coach here. I'm sure you have read about him in the paper, about the Golden Gloves."

Humphrey stood to greet me. "Yes, I have. Yes, I have," he said, pumping my hand. "You do very well, young man. You know how to treat people. You keep that up and, someday, you may be mayor of Minneapolis." I walked away thinking, "What a dreamer." But I never forgot his words. They raised my sights.

I met other candidates for city office that night and at other NAACP events.

In those years, all of the candidates were white. Few of the delegates to DFL (Democratic-Farmer-Labor) and Republican conventions were people of color. But Cecil was intent on changing that, and he started by recruiting people to work on Hubert's campaign.

I voted for the first time in 1944, for Franklin Delano Roosevelt. There was no question in my mind about whom to support or which party to choose. I had heard since my youth that the policies of Herbert Hoover and the Republicans were especially hard on black people. His refusal to deal with the worsening poverty of the depression in 1931 and 1932 only added to the burdens of the people who were already poor. Roosevelt's aggressive assault on hard times was not always effective, but at least he put men like my father-in-law to work. Our junior NAACP club would gather around the radio when FDR broadcast one of his fireside chats. When Roosevelt ran for reelection in 1940, Cecil had us pass out literature for him. We were taught how to knock on a door and ask the resident if he or she was a Republican or a Democrat. We'd say, "Are you going to vote for Franklin Delano Roosevelt? Here's some material." We were taught how to make a pitch without giving any offense. It was easy and enjoyable work.

One might say that Cecil Newman taught applied political science to more than one generation of young people in Minneapolis. He was publisher and editor of the *Minneapolis Spokesman* and *St. Paul Recorder,* the newspapers he founded in 1934 to serve the black community. He was also an early voice for black people within the new Democratic-Farmer-Labor Party, founded through the merger of the Democratic and Farmer Labor parties in 1944. And he was forever writing editorials for his own newspapers and guest columns for the *Star* and the *Tribune,* decrying discrimination in Minneapolis hotels and restaurants and in housing and employment. He would point out that well-trained black attorneys were denied admission to the state bar and that black doctors weren't allowed to practice in some metro-area hospitals. He kept telling the young people at Phyllis Wheatley that our generation of black Americans had greater potential than any generation before it to end discrimination. He stressed the importance of educating ourselves for that task. Politics provided the means of getting out of the hole, he said.

When as a kid I first met Cecil, I wasn't sure I liked him. He was so serious, strict, and strong-minded. He expected a lot from students in his classes. He associated with some of the biggest names in town. But as I got to know him, I discovered that he was patient, caring, and considerate. He modeled the kind of life he wanted us to live—disciplined and devoted to a lofty purpose. Cecil was out front, all the time, and he would never back off on any issue. He had a great ambition to train youth leaders. He focused on me, talked to me, inspired me. The more I listened to him, the more I thought, "Here's a guy I want to learn from."

Another politically active person who was often at Phyllis Wheatley, inspiring younger people, was Nellie Stone Johnson. Like me, Nellie was a native Minnesotan with a mixed racial heritage—Negro, Native American, and Caucasian. She was a farmer who came to Minneapolis to go to school and wound up becoming a labor organizer of hotel and restaurant employees. She became a crusader for integration of the Twin Cities labor movement with minorities and women. She and her family were staunch members of the Farmer Labor Party. She was in the thick of things with Humphrey when he engineered the merger that created the DFL.

Nellie's emphasis on labor was needed. Unions at that time were just as bad as corporate leaders in excluding people who were not white males. My father was something of an exception to the rule. He became a member of the Local 554 Truck Drivers' Union shortly before the famous truckers strike in Minneapolis in 1934. He was the first colored member of his local—and he had been driving a team, and then a truck, for twenty years in Minneapolis before being allowed to join. I think he was allowed in because he was nearly fifty years old, a quiet sort, and working for a small company. He was not seen as someone likely to try to bring other people of color into the union. That was the way it still was in the 1940s and 1950s, both in labor and in politics. If you insisted on a place, they made room for you, but you weren't urged to join. You would not be successful if you ran for a union office or tried to run for political office. Those were some of the things the NAACP was challenging.

When Humphrey became mayor, he didn't disappoint his NAACP allies. Even though the city's charter provides for a weak mayor, largely beholden to the City Council, he behaved like a strong mayor. He insisted that the police crack down on racketeers. That brought a measure of law and order to my neighborhood that I had never witnessed there before, and the quality of life on the North Side quickly changed for the better. He cleaned house at police headquarters, demoting or firing cops that were shielding gangsters, and he insisted that all parts of the city receive police protection.

Humphrey also decreed, by executive order, that all hotels and restaurants in the city would open their public accommodations to people of color. He backed that up with a threat that their licenses to operate would be in jeopardy if they did not comply. Further, he said, city police would be ordered to help enforce his order. He told black citizens, "If you go into a restaurant and they won't seat you when you see plenty of empty seats, go outside and get a police officer. Be sure to take the badge number of the police officer," he added, knowing that cops on the beat might need a nudge to play their part. Humphrey also leaned hard on the University of Minnesota to integrate its student housing. He announced that he believed that any student who came to the university had a right to be housed in campus housing. Just like that, the university fell into line. He made the same point to the private colleges in Minneapolis and St. Paul, and they too integrated their dormitories. It was the end of college students living at Phyllis Wheatley. Humphrey quickly got a reputation as a politician who promised a lot and then kept his promises. When he ran for reelection in 1947 and for the U.S. Senate in 1948, I was among his enthusiastic volunteers, distributing literature and urging people to vote for him.

Humphrey's actions mobilized the black vote for the DFL, but some in the Minneapolis black community still favored the Republicans in those years. That's because the Minnesota Republican Party then was a large, fairly liberal party with a good record in support of civil rights. Although the Republicans didn't go into black neighborhoods and ask for votes the way the DFL did, they weren't closed to black participation. It was a Republican state senator and future governor, Elmer L. Andersen, who pushed through the state's first civil-rights legislation, the Fair Employment Practices Act, in 1955.

The precursor of that state legislation was a 1947 ordinance in Minneapolis passed at Humphrey's urging. It created the Fair Employment Practices Commission, a panel of five citizens that investigated complaints of discrimination in employment and advised employers about how to comply with the law. An attorney I came to know as a member of Hennepin Church, Leonard Lindquist, was instrumental in developing the commission and became its longtime chair. Leonard is a Republican who thinks like a Democrat. I would eventually serve on that commission, in part by virtue of being president of the Minneapolis branch of the NAACP.

I had maintained my tie to the NAACP during the 1950s, even though I was not able to be active in the organization or in politics generally. I always followed political news and carried a little literature during campaigns. I particularly followed Humphrey as he made Phyllis Wheatley a regular stop when he was back in the city. He always greeted me warmly. He had an amazing capacity to remember people's names and faces—and, I learned, he was an avid reader of the sports pages. I liked to think that I was doing my part politically when I urged my boxers to be aware of events in their communities and, when they were old enough, to vote. The message fell on more receptive ears in the 1950s than it would have ten or twenty years earlier. Young people became more drawn to politics as the opportunity for easy money on the Avenue faded. Young people were more interested in succeeding in legitimate ways. There was a growing sense that what happened in government might make a real difference.

People don't realize it, but sports offer a fine preparation for politics. Often, an athlete moves up to higher levels of competition as much through smart politics as ability. A coach has to know his way around the governing forces in sports competition and know the rules to make sure his athletes get fair treatment. He has to have strong organizational and leadership skills, just like a politician. Golden Gloves taught me a great deal about politics.

During the 1950s at Phyllis Wheatley, I also became acquainted with two Minnesotans who became nationally prominent in the civil-rights movement, Roy Wilkins and Whitney Young. Wilkins was from St. Paul and came up through the St. Paul branch of the NAACP to become the organization's national president. He was among Humphrey's closest civil-rights advisers. By the time I was in the ranks of the junior NAACP, Wilkins was already the head of the St. Paul chapter. Roy was always impeccably dressed. His leadership style was that of a thoughtful, soft-spoken teacher and organizer. He was not one to play to a crowd's emotions. But he was one you wanted on your side for any kind of organized activity. I didn't know Whitney Young as well. He was often at Phyllis Wheatley when he did his graduate work at the University of Minnesota. He then became head of the Urban League in St. Paul and moved up the ranks of the national Urban League.

It was also in the 1950s that I first heard the Reverend Dr. Martin Luther King speak, at an NAACP state meeting. Roy Wilkins brought him here at about the time Dr. King was achieving prominence as a result of the Montgomery bus boycott of 1955. He was a very young man but self-assured and in command of any crowd. What a preacher he was! The meeting that day turned into a preaching contest of sorts, with each speaker trying to outdo the others and the audience replying and reflecting back the message. After Dr. King spoke, you were ready to get out and march and do things. He wasn't a big man, he wasn't muscular or imposing, but he had such confidence. When he would say, "Let's go. Let's get started. Remember to do this," you had to go along with him. I heard him speak on several other occasions, including at the national NAACP convention I attended in Los Angeles in 1965. But I never had the privilege to know him personally.

I stepped up my involvement with the NAACP just as the civil-rights movement was picking up steam nationally. The national organization was much involved in efforts to increase black voter participation, especially in the South. It was funding voter-registration drives in Mississippi, Alabama, South Carolina, and elsewhere. Northern chapters were urged to follow suit in urban areas and to grow and raise money to underwrite the national effort. I was named chair of the ambitious 1964 chapter-membership drive. Our goal was to add one thousand names to our existing roster of fifteen hundred members. I recruited North Side and South Side chairs and in turn helped them recruit other campaign leaders. In all, we had a corps of 320 people working on the membership drive. We had to extend the drive a month past its original deadline, but we made our goal.

Two months later, I was recommended by the chapter's nominating committee to be the next chapter president. In an ordinary year, the backing of the nominating committee would have ensured my election. But 1964 was no ordinary year. A petition was mounted to put another name in nomination, the Reverend Stanley King of Sabathani Baptist Church. Stanley was a critic of the local NAACP chapter, which had a long history of inclusion of both black and white members and which stressed education as a primary tool to eliminate racial injustice. That was too slow for Stan and the people around him. They wanted the Minneapolis chapter to more vigorously demand full integration in both the public and private sectors in the city. Stan faulted the existing NAACP leaders for being "too diplomatic." The NAACP old guard, on the other hand, saw Stan as a troublemaker. I was the old guard's choice, but I tried to be a conciliator between the two camps. I was not opposed to peaceful protest. I had seen the power of demonstration twenty-five years earlier when Marian Anderson was denied admission to Minneapolis's Dyckman Hotel. But I believed protest to be a last resort, and that many steps could be taken short of protest that might produce better results in the long run.

I won the election and took office in January 1965 for a three-year term. Suddenly, I found myself wearing the label "civil rights leader" in articles in the *Star* and the *Tribune*. My opinion on national issues facing our organization, such as whether the NAACP should be connected with people trying to form a pro-equality third political party in the South, became the stuff of headlines. (I told reporter Dick Cunningham of the *Tribune* that I thought we should continue to work with everyone in Mississippi who shared our goals.) To try to bridge the gap the election had caused, I formed a "direct action committee" within our chapter. It would be ready to act quickly by ordering a public protest or a buying boycott of offending businesses whenever we determined that mediation or negotiation could not achieve a particular goal.

But I also continued the NAACP's traditional emphasis on education and job training. Our organization had long maintained that a well-educated black population was key to eliminating racism. Our chapter worked to persuade black families to keep their children in school. We encouraged young men to take the examinations required for employment in the city's police and fire departments.

I was called upon by the local media for comments in August 1965 after several days of some of the worst race-rioting the nation had ever witnessed, in the Watts neighborhood of Los Angeles. I saw the carnage and destruction there as a setback for our movement. "We've come so far now that a Los Angeles (riot) won't stop us," I said. "But it is unfortunate, because the rioters are destroying the very thing we as a people have been fighting for—the right to live in freedom and peace without fear of violence or the destruction of property." I also opined that we would never see such a thing in Minneapolis. Under my breath, I prayed that I was right.

But Minneapolis was no longer the quiet, isolated small city of my youth. It was growing and becoming more like every other urban area in the country. The racial anger that bubbled to the surface in places like Los Angeles and Detroit was present in Minneapolis too. Occasionally, it became visible.

Notably, during and after the school winter break of 1965–1966, several unpleasant incidents involving black youths rattled the city's complacency. There was a shooting at a South Side American Legion post, a melee at a movie theater on Lake Street, and a disturbance in the Seven Corners area near the University of Minnesota campus. Meanwhile, business owners near Pillsbury House complained about shoplifting and misbehavior by young people after evening meetings at the South Side settlement house. I felt the NAACP ought to try calming the concern of both the black and white communities. I summoned NAACP directors to a special meeting in December, after the Vogue movie-theater incident, to discuss how we might be helpful. I then suggested a community meeting of police, educators, social workers, and businesspeople from the area near Pillsbury House to discuss ways to more constructively channel youthful energies. Our meeting on January 13, 1966, made headlines in local newspapers and started some useful cooperation between community agencies that led to more recreational and employment opportunities for young people in that part of the city.

But that spell of trouble was only the start. Early on the morning of August 3, 1966, about fifty young black people walking on Plymouth Avenue, returning from a late-night picnic, began pelting pebbles and stones at cars carrying white people. Things escalated, as they often do when young people are together and probably a little high. The kids went into Silver's Food Market at 1711 Plymouth, and when they were asked to leave, they filled their pockets and overturned display shelves on their way out. Then rocks were thrown at store windows along the avenue, stores owned mainly by Jewish merchants. The kids helped themselves to cigarettes from Hy's Dairy Deli at 1722 Plymouth. Gold's Clothing at 1901 Plymouth reported broken windows but no looting. At Plymouth Hardware Company, owner Bernard Rhode lost a box of hunting knives and gained an aisle full of debris. Koval's Furniture and Appliance at 1601 Plymouth probably got the worst of it; about thirty portable television sets were stolen. A disheartened Ben Koval was only a week away from moving his store to Excelsior Boulevard in St. Louis Park, where it still operates today.

I was one of about fifty people who got word of the disturbance with a phone call at daybreak from the office of Mayor Arthur Naftalin. I was summoned to a meeting at 10:00 a.m. at City Hall to decide what should be done in response. I wasn't surprised to be called; I had supported Art's election campaigns in 1961, 1963, and 1965, and we had developed a good relationship. However, I was surprised to see Governor Karl Rolvaag present when I arrived. Several prominent business leaders were there too. I counseled action to address the root of the problem: idleness and poverty among black teenagers, caused by a refusal of white employers to hire them. For once, Sabathani Church's Stan King and I were in agreement. He was particularly articulate that day when he said, "There are too many young people hanging around on Plymouth Avenue and throughout north Minneapolis and the other low-income areas that don't have a job. . . . What would be a good thing to do, Mayor, is get in touch with the ringleaders of the group that did the damage last night and ask them to meet us at a park. We would guarantee there would be no police in that park. We would meet the leaders and we wouldn't arrest them, but we'd ask them, what did they want? What was the problem?" Stan King offered to find the kids and play the role of mediator. He got the leaders of the rioters to meet us at Oak Park on Knox Avenue North. Stan and I were there, as were Mayor Naftalin and Governor Rolvaag. Rolvaag wanted to be there to show that race relations in Minneapolis were a concern at the highest levels in state government. But, as agreed, no police officers were present. Police chief Cal Hawkinson stayed away. We sat on benches and talked. They said, "What we want is jobs. We want jobs now, and we don't want to wait. We don't want people, when we get there, to harass us." Art said he sympathized with their request and would do something about it.

The next day, we met at Art's office with a large group that included some of the business leaders who were active in the city's antipoverty efforts. Art had a clever idea: he would open the corridor outside his office, which was then on the first floor at City Hall, for a job fair. Several business leaders said they could make a few dozen jobs available on short notice and would be glad to send their personnel officers to City Hall to receive applications. The number of jobs available was not adequate, but it was a start. It was agreed that no one would be subject to arrest as he applied for a job. That kept tempers cool. Art was criticized by some for trying so hard to satisfy lawbreakers. I thought his were the actions of a wise and courageous leader.

I was disheartened that most of the stores that were vandalized on Plymouth Avenue were Jewish-owned. Jews and blacks had lived in cooperative proximity in my old neighborhood for more than half a century, but the passions and events of the 1960s were pulling them apart. The end of housing discrimination opened the rest of the city and its suburbs to the North Siders, both black and Jewish, with the means to move out. Within the span of a few years, shop owners went from being neighbors to semistrangers who lived in comfort someplace else. As the Jewish population assimilated into the larger society, they increasingly became just white folks in the eyes of young black people. For a small but increasingly frustrated and impatient share of the black population that remained on the North Side, the shops became a near-at-hand symbol of what white people had and they did not. The shops were targets of rage, not because they were owned by Jews but because they were not owned by blacks.

I thought the NAACP could bridge the growing gap between blacks and Jews in Minneapolis. Many of the NAACP's white members were Jewish. I called a community meeting two weeks later at Holsey Memorial Christian Methodist Episcopal Church, with the NAACP chapter as the host. It was to be both an airing of grievances and a public attempt to heal the breach between the city's black and Jewish communities. Speakers expressed their disappointment with employers, school counselors, county social workers, police and fire hiring practices—and with the NAACP, which some speakers said had not been active enough in service to unemployed black youth. Then I spoke: "We do not condone the vandalism by Negro youths against the Jewish merchants on Plymouth Avenue. There is no anti-Jewish feeling in the NAACP, and we hope there is no anti-Negro sentiment in the Jewish community now. Our Jewish neighbors have been our oldest allies in the struggle for civil rights. They remain our partners in that struggle." I hoped I was right.

That tense summer ended, and an uneasy truce settled over the North Side. When summer returned, the truce held—until the night after the annual Aquatennial Torchlight Parade in downtown Minneapolis. A black man, Samuel Simmons, was shot at Wayne's Bar shortly before midnight, allegedly by the white bar owner. It was all the spark that was needed. At 2:00 a.m. on July 20, 1967, I was roused from a sound sleep by the telephone. It was Mayor Naftalin, who said, "Harry, I'm up here with the riot squad on Plymouth and Humboldt." I knew the corner; a vacant lot was there. "Almost all of the stores on Plymouth Avenue are burning," he said. "They're on fire. The place is crowded with people in the street. Some of them are in their nightclothes." He paused for a moment for me to take in this bad news, then he said, "We've got to make a decision about what we're going to do. I would appreciate it if you could come up here right away. I've called some other people too. I'm hoping we can prevent a full-scale riot."

I quickly got dressed and drove as fast as I dared to find the mayor. I was distressed by what Naftalin told me but not shocked. I had been worried for weeks about the possibility that one nasty episode would be enough to provoke another eruption. But I was not prepared for the sight of Plymouth Avenue shops burning from Penn Avenue all the way to Humboldt, eight blocks away. There was no fighting. There was no gunfire. There was only fire—fire everywhere, it seemed—and scared, agitated people milling about. It was a case of massive arson.

I understood the frustration that was behind youth violence, but I could not condone the destruction I was witnessing. It was clear that this was too widespread to have been an act of youthful delinquency. This was organized destruction, and an act of great stupidity too. How could people be so foolish as to make a point by destroying their own neighborhood? Would they burn down their own houses to impress someone? Only three grocery stores still operated on all of Plymouth Avenue that summer. Early on July 20, all three were destroyed. For decades afterward, North Side residents would complain that their neighborhood did not have enough grocery stores. It made no sense.

The scene that night on the street was nightmarish. The stench of smoke was oppressive. The heat was intense enough to break display windows, exposing the stores to looting. The streets were blocked. Mayor Naftalin had given my name and car license number to the police with orders that I be allowed to pass the barricade. He had done the same for the other black leaders he had summoned, Stan King and the Urban League's Gleason Glover and Josie Johnson. There sat the riot squad, fifty or sixty officers strong, with a cluster of squad cars, their lights flashing. The police captains leading the squads were standing by, waiting for orders from Chief of Police Cal Hawkinson. He was sitting in the mayor's car. I was directed to join them there.

Naftalin and Hawkinson were discussing the advisability of sending the riot squad down the street en masse with orders to arrest everyone. Gleason, Stan, Josie, and I all urged the mayor and police chief not to do that. "There are too many people on the street, and too many of them are women and children," I argued. "They live here. They are in the street because their homes are in danger. That isn't a reason to arrest people." Further, we said, a sweep of the streets hours after the fires started was not likely to snare the culprits. They weren't going to stick around and get arrested. A sweep would only risk injuring innocent people, and if that happened, we argued, the police might have a real riot on their hands. "When people see kids getting hit, they're going to respond," I said.

Art quickly saw our point. "Yes, we can't put our citizens' lives in danger. The people in the street don't know who started the fires." He refused to order the riot squad to move. That decision disappointed some of the officers on the street, including the vocal head of the Police Federation, a lieutenant named Charlie Stenvig.

Naftalin decided that the riot squad would clear the street only if the crowd interfered in any way with firefighting. It did not. When fire engines arrived, people backed away and gave them room to work. That convinced Naftalin and Hawkinson that the people on the street were not rioters. We then agreed that, after the fire engines did their jobs and extinguished the flames, we would approach people and ask them to get off the street and go home. Only then, if they refused, would the police move in to prevent looting. Their orders were to arrest only those who were caught stealing from the beleaguered stores.

That was how we met the dawn that morning on Plymouth Avenue. There was plenty of sorrow and destruction, but no one was hurt, very few people were arrested, and the streets were comparatively calm. We considered that a major achievement. But Plymouth Avenue remained a hot spot for several more days. Early on July 21, there were episodes of rock throwing and fistfights and reports of gunshots. It was minor stuff compared with the night before. Nevertheless, Art called the new Republican governor, Harold

LeVander, and asked for help from the National Guard. Six hundred guardsmen were on the scene the next evening, a Friday. A dance was held at The Way, a recreational and educational youth center that had opened in response to the disturbances the summer before. Under the watchful eyes of parents and National Guard troops, the dance proceeded without trouble. What came to be called the "Plymouth Avenue riot" was over.

I always suspected that Art called the National Guard not out of concern about escalating violence, but rather to relieve his own police force of the responsibility for keeping the peace. Art was very smart, and he knew his police force well. It was not a contented force. Many cops, including Stenvig and his Police Federation activists, wanted to take a harder line against black militants. Art knew that too much direct contact between cops and black kids was not a good idea just then.

I was soon to come into more direct conflict with Stenvig. The following April 4, the Reverend Dr. Martin Luther King Jr. was assassinated. That horrible news produced a tidal wave of sorrow, anger, and violence that swept through black neighborhoods across the nation. It was a terrible time. But the streets stayed relatively quiet in Minneapolis, and Art and I had an idea that we believed would keep them that way. He asked me to recruit mature black people of goodwill to voluntarily patrol black neighborhoods on weekend evenings. They were simply to move about, be watchful, and radio the police if they observed suspicious activity. They were directed not to carry weapons or to attempt to stop or arrest anyone. We called our little band Citizen Protectors, and I was head of the unit.

Unfortunately, our group included a few young zealots who got carried away and tried to play police officer. I know of at least two volunteers who carried guns against my orders. One group got into an altercation with some Golden Valley police officers on their way home from a downtown bar. Somehow the suburban cops wound up on foot outside of The Way at 1:30 a.m. Exactly what happened was never established, but the police officers complained that they were verbally abused and robbed of more than $100, while the protectors claimed they were shielding three young women from unwelcome advances. Whatever it was, it was all the excuse Charlie Stenvig needed to call a news conference and make a big show of withdrawing the police union's support from the Citizen Protectors program. Art and I had to get busy restoring the program's credibility. I cracked down on some of the hotheaded volunteers; the mayor and Cal Hawkinson issued more detailed instructions for our group; and we renamed it the Citizens Patrol, and set out to incorporate it as an independent nonprofit agency. Art also appointed a Task Force on Police-Community Relations, which made a series of recommendations that amounted to what a future generation would call "community policing." All of the steps we took had merit. Still, I came away wary of Stenvig's capacity to stir up trouble.

For months after the Plymouth Avenue riot, Naftalin and Hawkinson were criticized for what was portrayed as their mild response. It was a bad rap. I'm convinced that their restraint saved lives. I praised Art for his decision the first night of the riot not to unleash the riot squad on Plymouth Avenue. I told him: "If that had been my son on the street and one of the police officers had hurt him, I wouldn't just stand there and let that happen. Either I'm going to get hurt or that police officer is going to get hurt. You acted in the interests of public safety."

That episode sealed a lasting friendship with Naftalin. We had been working together for some time. In August 1965, he tapped me for membership on the Fair Employment Practices Commission. Art had just been reelected to his third term, and I had been a volunteer in each of his campaigns, playing a more vigorous role each time. We began to be more than political acquaintances. He went personally to D. W. Onan to arrange for me to get time off work to serve, a gesture I much appreciated, even though there was no need for any extraordinary persuasion. The Onans were very supportive of my community work.

Art is an impressive person—thorough, organized, and persuasive. He is Jewish, six years older than I, and a native of Fargo, North Dakota. He came to Minneapolis to study at the University of Minnesota, where he received his undergraduate degree in 1939. His classmate was Hubert Humphrey, whom he did not come to know well until 1942, when Art was a graduate student in political science and Humphrey was contemplating his first run for mayor of Minneapolis. Along with Orville Freeman, Miles Lord, Walter Mondale, and Don Fraser, Art became one of the bright young lieutenants in Humphrey's DFL brigade. Humphrey tapped Art as his campaign manager for his mayoral campaigns and made him secretary—the equivalent of chief of staff—when Humphrey was elected in 1945. When Freeman was elected governor in 1954, he chose Art to be his commissioner of administration, which in those years was the top budget officer in state government. Art held that job for all of the six years of the Freeman administration. Elmer Andersen defeated Freeman in 1960, and Art was out of a job. But seven months later, he became the new mayor of Minneapolis.

Along with Cecil Newman, Art was my mentor in politics and government.

He was a magnet. He would draw people to him, not so much with charm, though he could be quite winsome, as with ideas and unflinching integrity. He was an organizer. When he called me into his office, I would usually find myself joining other people he had invited. He would have a plan all laid out and a role for each one of us to play.

One of his assignments for me was a spot on the city's Civil Service Commission, beginning in 1968. I was the first black person to serve on that three-member panel, which reviewed the rules and regulations governing city employment. Art's instructions to me were to find out why the city had hired no black police officers or firefighters and very few other black employees. Years earlier, the city had black police officers, some of whom had climbed the ranks. But that had changed in the 1960s. The 562-person fire department was all white, and the police department had only a handful of black officers. "I understand that a lot of people are taking the examinations, but they aren't getting hired," Art told me. "Find out why."

An attorney with strong union ties, Tom Kachelmacker, chaired the commission. As an old-time union man, he didn't have much sympathy for civil rights. His service on the commission predated Art's term as mayor and, under heavy union pressure, Art reluctantly reappointed him—but then coached me on working around him to accomplish something positive. When I announced, "I would like to review the list of people that take civil-service examinations," Kachelmacker kind of laughed and said, "Yes, you have a right to do that." I said mildly, "Yes, I just want to exercise my rights." So he told the executive director of the Civil Service Commission, "Mr. Davis will be coming down. I want you to get all the tests that were taken in the last three or four years. If you have any identification of the applicants' races, I want you to let him know." He knew perfectly well that the records included race; it was a blank to be filled in on the application.

I got the data and found that the vast majority of people recorded as Negroes had passed the written examination easily, but also saw that they had failed the oral examination. That entailed an interview before a selected panel of police or fire officials or city managers. I examined the names and saw some that I knew from Phyllis Wheatley. For example, there was Larry Brown. I knew he was a college graduate and a veteran, as was his brother. He had passed the fire department's written test in the top ten but failed the oral examination. It was outrageous—Larry was fully capable of serving the city well and would have been impressive in a job interview. If anything, he was overqualified for the job he was seeking. I went to Art and told him what I was finding. Art encouraged me to raise the issue at the next Civil

Service Commission meeting. I warned him, "There are two other people there. I may get outvoted." That possibility did not dissuade Art in the least. "Don't worry about it," he said. "You bring it up."

I did. "It seems to me that there is a pattern of discrimination here," I said, showing the commissioners that a particular mark had been drawn on the application forms of all the black applicants who had passed the written examination. I then showed that all of the candidates whose forms bore that mark failed their oral examination. That mark, I concluded, was in all likelihood a signal to the people administering the oral exams that it was up to them to keep those applicants from being hired. No one admitted that I had guessed the system of discrimination. But from that time on, no more stray marks appeared on application forms. I continued to monitor exam results, and black people began to pass both the written and the oral exams.

Art and I found other ways to work together. For example, in 1966, I helped him fend off a proposal by then City Council member Arne Carlson that the Mayor's Commission on Human Relations be subsumed into the Fair Employment Practices Commission. The Mayor's Commission was Art's way of including in his administration a fact-finding and policy-developing group devoted exclusively to civil-rights issues. Carlson purported to strengthen the employment commission, but he wanted to do so by eliminating staff positions that served the Mayor's Commission. Art and I agreed that the result would hamper the city's overall civil-rights efforts. It was my first political encounter with Arne Carlson, Minnesota's future governor. Carlson and Naftalin were political rivals; Carlson was Art's rival for reelection in 1967. I supported Art, naturally, but Arne and I later became very good friends.

Carlson's idea became tangled in a larger debate over how far the city should go in banning discrimination in housing. Should housing discrimination be forbidden except for private rental rooms in owner-occupied homes? Should that exception extend to owner-occupied duplexes? And who would bear the responsibility to investigate and enforce such a prohibition? I was in the thick of consideration of these questions in 1967 as the chair of an ad hoc Committee on Civil and Human Relations, which represented all of Minneapolis's civil-rights organizations.

By 1967, Art and I had a counterproposal to Carlson's idea. We said we would agree to merging the Mayor's Commission and the Fair Employment Practices Commission if the result were greater, not smaller, than the sum of the two commissions' parts. We wanted a more comprehensive citywide ban on racial discrimination in employment, housing, labor-union membership, and public accommodations and services, and we wanted a vigorous city agency authorized to enforce the ban. Art appointed a strong committee to draft a new ordinance: Leonard Lindquist, State Representative Gary Flakne, Josie Johnson, Stan King, Milt Dunham, Frank Alsup, and me. We did our drafting, then spent many weeks selling the idea to the City Council and staving off weakening amendments. We succeeded in late August 1967. A city antidiscrimination ordinance was passed that went well beyond the state's statutes for fair housing and employment. A new Human Rights Commission was created to make policy recommendations and oversee the investigation of complaints. And a new city Civil Rights Department was created and granted broad enforcement powers backed by the district courts. I was among those who advised Art about the appointment of the first director of the department, Lillian Anthony.

The appointment of the fifteen members of the new Human Rights Commission provided a stormy punctuation mark to my term as president of the Minneapolis NAACP. One controversial name, Ron Edwards, was on the slate of commission members Art Naftalin had sent to the City Council. Ron was twenty-nine years old in 1967, smart, charismatic, and a natural leader. He had the backing of several church and civic groups. But he also had four misdemeanor convictions on his record and a reputation as a radical. The City Council balked at appointing him; the black community strenuously objected to the council's hesitation. The community's reaction brought together old and young, moderate and militant, as they had not been before. But it was also a perilous time. Edwards's rejection came to symbolize whites telling blacks who could speak for them. I knew that unless the City Council changed its mind and somehow accommodated Edwards, Minneapolis was in for more racial trouble. I was asked to be the spokesperson for a number of black groups that came together to push for Ron's appointment.

I decided on a two-pronged strategy. Behind the scenes, I told business leaders about my concern that the Edwards appointment was no minor tiff; it could be a spark to new violence. I asked them to intercede with the City Council. Publicly, I locked arms with Edwards. So did the rest of the black leadership in town, so much so that we all vowed not to serve on the Human Rights Commission unless Edwards was seated too. Two people already on the mayor's old commission, Matthew Little and Nellie Stone Johnson, resigned to make the boycott complete. At a news conference on January 26, 1968, at The Way, I sent a message to City Council president Dan Cohen in unmistakable terms: "Dan Cohen, you are not the master, and we are not your niggers." I looked right into the TV cameras as I said again,

"Dan, we're not your niggers." Cohen could not have missed it. It was all over the news that night and the next day.

It took two months of that kind of public pressure and behind-the-scenes jawboning to get the City Council to back down and put Edwards on the commission. But on March 8, 1968, the council did just that, as part of a face-saving "compromise" that also enlarged the commission to twenty-one members. It was a major victory for a black community that was realizing as never before that it could wield political power.

13
Mobilizing

THE LATE 1960S WERE A TIME of great ferment in the United States, in Minneapolis, and in my life. Great hope and great despair, great victories and great losses, all collided in the span of a few intense years. I was in the thick of it all.

When Lyndon Johnson succeeded the assassinated John Kennedy as president in November 1963, he seized and ran with Kennedy's domestic agenda: a federal guarantee of civil rights, expanded voting rights for all, and a domestic economic-improvement program that became known as the War on Poverty. By 1966, the War on Poverty arrived in Minneapolis and Hennepin County as a series of federal directives and an organizational framework that the city and county were supposed to establish and follow. It involved the creation of a nonprofit community-action program to be headed by a board composed of representatives from underprivileged neighborhoods targeted for improvement, as well as from government, business, nonprofit agencies, and the community at large. Initially, there were to be sixty-six board members in all.

Some of the responsibility to fill those slots fell to my friend, Mayor Arthur Naftalin. He in turn sought the help of the City Council, the Minneapolis United Way, and the NAACP to nominate candidates for the board. Omar Schmitt of the United Way was much involved; so was Tommy Thompson, then the Minneapolis city coordinator, later the county coordinator for Hennepin County. They came up with a slate that had my name on it for the governing board, to be called the Hennepin County Mobilization of Economic Resources Board, or MOER Board for short. It was to function as a nonprofit agency, drawing funds from government and other sources but governed independently.

If our area was to get its rightful share of the federal money that Lyndon

Johnson was dispensing in Washington, it would be up to the MOER Board to get it. War on Poverty funds had already begun flowing to Minnesota in 1966, but the continuation of the initial programs and the start of new ones depended on MOER Board action. The new board was organized in August 1967. It was immediately handed lengthy federal directives for how to approach the various federal agencies, such as Health, Education and Welfare, the Department of Labor, and Housing and Urban Development, with proposals for better education, housing, job training, and health care that could start money flowing our way.

I quickly saw a connection between the MOER Board's assignment and what the NAACP was trying to accomplish. I didn't have to familiarize myself with a new set of issues; I could keep advocating the same measures I had been talking about since becoming president of the NAACP's Minneapolis chapter. But now, with federal money coming our way, I believed I was talking about a vision that could become reality.

The MOER Board was a strong group. It included Urban League official and lobbyist Josie Johnson, attorney Douglas Hall, Honeywell CEO Stephen Keating, *Minneapolis Tribune* publisher Bower Hawthorne, First National Bank vice president Phil Harder, Urban League president Gleason Glover, and union leader Nellie Stone Johnson. Elected as president of our group was Elva Walker, a member of the prominent lumber-industry Walker family. Her husband was a doctor and the grandson of T. B. Walker, the turn-of-the-century patriarch, civic leader, and founding benefactor of the Walker Art Center. Elva was an intelligent, cultured, fine woman. I was elected vice president of the board; Josie Johnson was our treasurer and Doug Hall our legal counsel, secretary, and parliamentarian.

Doug was not initially a member of the MOER Board, but he was added to the board at the first meeting at the request of several organizations that knew him as an important ally. I was pleased with the addition. A white attorney who specialized in discrimination law, Hall looked nothing like a regular lawyer who would walk in wearing a shirt and tie and carrying a briefcase. Doug wore his collars open and his hair long, and at times he had a beard. He generally showed up in some old tweed sport coat, jeans, and tennis shoes, but his appearance was deceiving. He was an outstanding legal mind who could quickly gain the respect of business leaders and community activists when he started talking.

Josie was every bit as bright and even more engaging. She was then as she is now: poised, calm, witty, a glutton for hard work, and as shrewd as they come. Though she was still a young woman in the mid-1960s, Josie was already a veteran civil-rights campaigner and a seasoned lobbyist for fair housing and employment laws at the State Capitol. She was known and respected by legislators, governors, and business leaders. She eventually became a vice president and a regent at the University of Minnesota. The financial structure Josie put together for the MOER Board was the envy of War on Poverty programs around the country.

Art Naftalin made sure that labor-union leaders were on the board too. Dave Roe, the head of the Central Labor Union in Minneapolis and the future president of the state AFL-CIO, was among them. That provided an important connection, one that I believe became a turning point in the relationship between organized labor and the black community in Minneapolis. I knew Dave because of a Golden Gloves link. He was a boxing fan, and 1948 Golden Gloves champ Eddie Lacy was one of his favorite fighters. Eddie went to Minneapolis Vocational High School while he was boxing. In those years, the Sheet Metal Workers Union put on a boxing show as a fundraiser, and they asked Eddie to headline for them. They took a liking to Eddie and Eddie did to them, so much so that he decided to start sheet-metal-worker training. The union arranged for one of the members of its boxing committee to be Eddie's mentor. He supplemented Eddie's academic training with real-world experience and contacts that paved the way for Eddie to get a job in the building trades when he graduated. He became the first black member of the Sheet Metal Workers Union.

Dave and I hit it off on the MOER Board. He's a good man, honest, loyal, and true to his word, though he can be quite bullheaded. He and I talked about the way blacks had been made to feel unwelcome in union ranks. I think I opened his eyes to the extent of the discrimination that had been at play. He set about to change that. He would say, "Harry, you can bet money on it," as he would pledge to take some step or another to change union behavior. When the next meeting came around, Dave would have it done. We became very good friends.

The MOER Board's executive director was an able fellow named Edgar Pillow, who was also director of the Hennepin County Office of Economic Opportunity. He was a St. Paul native, a University of Minnesota graduate, involved at Hallie Q. Brown Settlement House, and associated with the NAACP and the Urban League. He was well qualified and a great help to us.

The business leaders on the MOER Board proposed making the board the fiscal agent for all that would come later. We would develop programming agencies, but they would be financially accountable to us. We were conscious of the fact that the money we were dispensing had come from taxpayers' pockets, and we wanted to be sure it would be spent wisely. Moreover, we were under federal orders not to mingle War on Poverty funds. If we received money for early-childhood development, it could not be unilaterally transferred to job training. We needed a system to carefully track the flow of funds. The business community donated the talent needed to do the job right.

The first thing we tackled was an expansion of Head Start, the program for preschool children that started as a six-week summer program in 1966. I think it was one of our proudest accomplishments. Larry Harris of the Minneapolis Public Schools was instrumental in getting our proposal for federal funds for a year-round Head Start written and approved and then in implementing our plan. I knew Larry well; he had been involved with Pillsbury House and Unity House when I was at Phyllis Wheatley, competing against athletes from those other settlement houses. Larry counseled that, instead of operating Head Start independently, we should make it a joint project of the MOER Board and the Minneapolis School District. We took that idea to Superintendent John B. Davis and the school board. They agreed to co-ownership and co-promotion of the year-round preschool. MOER had to be involved as the receiving agent of federal funds. But we trusted the school district's expertise and commitment to serving all children equally and wanted it to build a program that would mesh well with the summertime Head Start that the district was already offering. We quickly got together, and by 1968 Head Start was a year-round program, serving about one thousand four-year-olds.

We also immediately responded to the need for good-paying jobs for young people of color, particularly young parents. A lot of young fathers in the black community were unemployed—or, more often, underemployed—and in need of more education to secure a higher-wage job. A successful program started by the Reverend Dr. Leon Sullivan to train inmates in a Philadelphia jail for work was being copied all over the country. Minneapolis fell in line in August 1966 with the start of the Twin Cities Opportunity Industrialization Center, or TCOIC. We turned for help to the Urban League, which had been working on better employment for black Minneapolitans for three decades. I also asked my old mentor, Cecil Newman, to get involved. When he headed the Junior NAACP program, he added a fair amount of job counseling to the curriculum. I could personally attest that his lessons worked. Cecil agreed to chair the OIC board.

Each member of the MOER Board served on task forces. We assigned a number of businesspeople to the OIC task force; they in turn recruited other business owners and executives to take part. The task force's goal was to establish an agency, serve as its channel for federal funds, and control its finances, but also to train the agency leaders to become independent of the MOER Board. When one of our agencies was up and running, we wanted to spin it off as a freestanding nonprofit agency.

My NAACP rival, the Reverend Stanley King, was hired as the first executive director of TCOIC. Stan was a clergyman whose career was a bit unconventional. He was bright and an inspirational speaker but a bit of a loose cannon, independent, and headstrong. He liked the finer things and always dressed immaculately—shirt and tie, boutonniere, everything perfect. He had been an assistant pastor at Zion Baptist, serving with my old friend Reverend Henry Botts. But when Stan did not get the senior pastor's assignment when Botts retired, he bolted from Zion and started a small congregation on the South Side called Sabathani Baptist. He was something of a risky choice to head the OIC. He did not have a high regard for following federal rules and regulations. He wanted to operate the agency the way he saw fit. For example, he didn't want a regular board of directors. He proposed having a community group serve as advisers and no more. But as long as Cecil chaired the OIC, Stan's idea did not go far. Cecil believed in control, and he had a lot of control over Stan.

TCOIC grew rapidly, receiving more applications for training than it could handle. The program started by emphasizing the training of young women for office and clerical jobs. Those first graduates had jobs waiting for them, courtesy of some of the business members of the MOER Board. Steve Keating at Honeywell would offer to hire some number of the graduates, and soon Judson "Sandy" Bemis of the Bemis Company and Earl Ewald of Northern States Power were chiming in, matching Keating's offer. It was a far cry from the attitudes I remembered prevailing only a few years earlier.

It was a few years later, after Cecil retired from the board, that Stan did some things the MOER Board did not like. For example, federal rules would allow a budget item for a rental car for an agency executive director. Stan seized on that, and the next thing we knew, he had rented a chauffeur-driven Cadillac! He also used his OIC job as a springboard for developing his own little business in telephone repair. Though he had a good staff to backstop him, his distraction took a toll at the OIC.

My relationship with Stan was respectful but never warm. He always seemed to want to challenge me. He felt that he was spokesperson for the black disadvantaged, even though I came from more humble circumstances in north Minneapolis than he did. He liked to snidely suggest that I was kowtowing to the desires of the white majority and looking for my own personal gain. I would take only so much of that before I would respond. At one MOER Board meeting, Stan complained, "I don't expect to get too much done because we've got a bunch of Uncle Toms running this." I replied, "You know, Stan, I didn't come from a wealthy family. I don't know whether you did or not. I don't drive a Cadillac. I don't see anybody that you represent that drives one. I don't have a chauffeur. I don't see anybody that you represent that has one. I don't have a leased car. You do. I don't have a church. You do. You have a family; I do too. I hope you take care of your kids and your family the way I take care of mine." I wouldn't back away from him, and he would only push me so far.

TCOIC started operating in cramped quarters in the old First National Bank building downtown. Not long afterward, it moved to the North Side, to Lyndale Avenue North and Seventh Street. Much later, Ramsey County established its own OIC, and the Minneapolis-based program merged with Summit Academy. Today Summit Academy OIC sits at 935 Olson Memorial Highway, though, as has happened so often on the North Side, its current location is slated for redevelopment. It appears that the school will soon be on the move.

We also talked about health problems, about kids not getting vaccinations or the health care they ought to have before they start attending school. Phyllis Wheatley provided those services for the North Side when I was a boy, but that part of the settlement-house program had lapsed by the 1960s. The NAACP chapter had been looking for a way to reestablish free or low-cost public-health services in the neighborhood. So the MOER Board applied to the federal Department of Health, Education, and Welfare for funds to establish a branch facility of Minneapolis General Hospital, the big downtown public hospital that was soon to change its name to Hennepin County Medical Center. We got the funds we asked for, both from HEW and from the federal Office of Economic Opportunity—a source we had not expected. The result was the establishment of Pilot City Health Services on Penn Avenue, right off Plymouth. It occupies the former Beth El Synagogue, which I always thought was the best built of the North Side synagogues. The Beth El congregation was on its way to St. Louis Park. It took only a small investment to convert the space into the examining rooms and offices that were needed for a good-sized clinic. It still operates at the same site, as an extension of Hennepin County Medical Center.

Pilot City was structured a bit differently than other MOER Board agencies. A funding clause indicated that it was to be independent of the MOER Board from the start. With other agencies, the MOER Board task force functioned as a board of directors for a period of usually several years. But we were able to run Pilot City financially until its own board of directors was fully functioning. The initial organizing board, called the tactics board, was headed by soon-to-be Phyllis Wheatley director Cozelle Breedlove. He had been one of my boxers twenty years earlier.

The MOER Board wasn't done yet. We attacked the problem of inadequate housing for the city's low-income and minority populations. The problem is still with us today, but it was exacerbated in the 1960s by the fact that parts of the city still were effectively closed to minority home owners. A state Fair Housing Practices law had been on the books since 1961, outlawing most housing discrimination, but proving blatant discrimination in the financing of home mortgages was not easy. Our approach was to encourage the formation of neighborhood residents' councils throughout the city and make low-interest housing money available through those groups. The program was called Model Neighborhoods. One might consider it a forerunner of the Neighborhood Redevelopment Program that has been at work solving neighborhood problems in Minneapolis for the past decade. Model Neighborhoods organized the city's neighborhoods, encouraging the establishment of neighborhood councils that would establish priorities for public improvements and communicate them to city, state, and federal funding agencies. The MOER Board also encouraged the establishment of neighborhood centers where people could gather and get information about city services. Some city neighborhoods already were clearly defined, while others did not have a clear sense of place and identity. The Model Neighborhoods program gave an identity to every block, often appropriating the name of a school or a park where a name was lacking.

The very active MOER Board was hailed as one of the most successful local arms of the War on Poverty in the nation. The War on Poverty never became synonymous with fiscal mismanagement in Minneapolis as it did in other parts of the country. Its structure of fiscal control was part of the reason. MOER Board programs were never criticized for improper use of funds or for extravagant boondoggles that produced no results. We had the business community, the larger community, and the government all pulling together, and we had firm control over the purse strings. When that happens, tremendous things can be done.

Yet I was frustrated by the government red tape, constant fear of congressional budget cuts, and restrictions on the scope of our activities—and by the controversy that perpetually swirled around our large and unwieldy board. Some elements in the black community saw the ease with which Head Start and TCOIC were established as evidence that the War on Poverty could work all kinds of miracles. They wanted more, they wanted it now, and they wanted a personal share in the action.

Perhaps it was to be expected that controversy was a constant for the MOER Board, beginning only a few weeks after the worst race-related violence on Minneapolis streets in the city's history. At the first meeting of the full board, on September 25, 1967, a group with complaints about the board's composition was so disruptive that Elva Walker closed the meeting about halfway through the agenda. Matt Eubanks of the East Side Citizens Community Center was particularly vocal in demanding more community representation and fewer business and at-large members on the board. He claimed that the community representatives already on the board, including me, did not represent the neediest people in the neighborhoods we were trying to serve. The problem was that the people chosen to represent the community often rise to visibility through organizations, such as the NAACP or the Urban League, and the very poor were not involved in organizations. Of course, his real goal was not representation. It was to get his hands on federal money.

Matt represented a more militant mind-set that was coming to the fore among younger black people, in Minneapolis and around the country. They doubted that verbal or legal action would ever produce justice for people of color. They put their faith in physical action instead. The Black Panther organization sprang from that mind-set. Locally, it was associated with the new youth center on Plymouth Avenue called The Way. It was founded after the 1966 Plymouth Avenue disturbance to serve young black people who said they didn't think Phyllis Wheatley met their needs. They wanted a place of their own, they said. It went into an abandoned storefront that had been a tropical-fish store. The Way had charismatic leadership from Syl Davis (no relation to me); his wife, Gwen Jones-Davis; Ron Edwards; and a young Harry "Spike" Moss.

A fissure developed in the black community between the more militant voices and those who preferred to work for civil rights within organized channels, such as the NAACP. I was plainly in the latter camp, so much so that more than once I was publicly called an Uncle Tom. But my coaching days had given me a personal connection with some of the younger people who thought more like Eubanks. I tried to stay on good terms with all of them.

With Eubanks himself, that was difficult. He did not believe in peaceful work.

Eubanks was a native of Kansas City, Missouri. I knew him and his family, some of whom wound up on the wrong side of the law. Matt was a well-educated man who had spent many years as a student at the University of Minnesota. He landed a job as a community organizer and drew to himself a cadre of like-minded young men who were attracted to his intellect, his idealism, and, most likely, his impatience with the status quo. He traveled around the country to participate in civil-justice demonstrations in the 1960s and tried to organize a Minnesota chapter of the national Poor People's Campaign in 1968.

Matt and about a dozen of his allies would enter the MOER Board meetings as if they were an invading military force. They would even be dressed in army camouflage clothing, which always looked as if it had been worn for weeks. They would loudly assemble outside the meeting room, conduct an angry pep rally, then march in and circle around the room until they had blocked every door and surrounded the audience. Then one of them would shout, "We want this meeting stopped. If you don't stop the meeting, we're going to stop the meeting." Then they pulled back their jackets to show that they were wearing guns on their sides. People squealed in fear.

MOER Board meetings were much like those of a school board or city council. We sat on a little stage before a public audience and asked that people who wanted to address us notify us twenty-four hours in advance. Those who wanted to present a proposal were asked to give it in writing to the secretary. That arrangement ordinarily worked quite well, but it did not suit Eubanks and his followers. His real goal was not to convey a coherent message to the board. It was to intimidate us—and he was good at it. He could scare you half to death.

At our second meeting, Matt made a dramatic entrance and demanded more money for the Citizen Community Centers. Minneapolis had three of them. They were small neighborhood storefront agencies that could refer people to services outside of their own neighborhood, such as OIC, that they might not otherwise know about. Matt argued that, on that basis, some TCOIC funds should flow to the little center on the East Side, where he was a staff member. "That can't be done," Elva Walker said. "We are not allowed to mix the money." They said, "If we don't get it, you don't get out these doors." It was like a holdup.

Elva decided she had had enough. She had chaired many a formal meeting in her time, but she had never dealt with anything like this. As the vice chair, I was sitting next to her and tried to help her. I recognized some of the guys in Matt's group as my kids from Phyllis Wheatley. I knew them well enough to feel confident that they had no intention of pulling those guns. "Let's just get through this meeting. Then we'll make sure that they don't come in with guns anymore," I whispered to her. So she tried to mollify Matt's group by pledging that the board would make a special request of the federal agencies to see if the rules could be broken in this case. We knew that wasn't going to be. But Matt said, "So, at the next meeting you'll come back with a response from them?" We said, "Yes, we will do that." Then Elva excused herself to go to the bathroom and asked me to take over the remainder of the meeting. She didn't come back—ever. Suddenly, I was MOER Board chair.

When that meeting was over, I asked a few board members to linger a moment and discuss what had happened that night. I said, "Look, I don't know what happened to Elva. I'm sure that she got scared, as I'm sure everyone here was." Tommy Thompson said, "The next time we have a meeting, we'll have police officers here." I suggested that as many of us as possible meet the next morning at 9:00 at City Hall. "We've got to tell the City Council that they need to pass an ordinance about carrying guns with live ammunition in holsters," I said. Carrying concealed weapons was against the law in Minneapolis then, but visibly carrying a loaded gun was not. Matt knew that full well. He had looked it up. He was no dummy.

Thompson got busy the next morning. Never had I seen such immediate response from city hall. Before the day was over, the City Council had passed a ban on carrying a loaded gun without a permit. Moreover, Tommy arranged for two uniformed police officers to be present at all future MOER Board meetings. At our next meeting, when Matt came in with his gang, he made a point of showing that they were not carrying guns. They had a shouting match in mind. They said, "You made it illegal for us to carry weapons here. But we'll stop this meeting anyway. We don't want the cops in here." Some members of Matt's group were wearing holsters containing toy guns, just as a test of the new law. The police would not let them in. That produced a disturbance outside the meeting.

That was my first full meeting as chair. I was trying hard to keep order and to get the board to concentrate on its work. Suddenly, in walked Dr. Herman B. Dilliard. He was a surgeon at the University of Minnesota, one of the first black men to hold that position. He was also a large man, the largest brother from a family of big people—one of whom, his brother George, had come to the meeting with Eubanks. Herman weighed about 350 pounds, stood about six-foot-six, and had great big hands. I knew him well. He had been one of my kids at Phyllis Wheatley. When he didn't have decent clothes as a young kid, I took him to the housekeeper at Phyllis Wheatley, Mrs. Jones, and helped him find some clothes that would fit him. By 1967, he was "into the Sixties." He sported a large Afro and often wore bib overalls. The effect was to make him seem about the size of a small house. He walked into our meeting carrying a carbine and two .45s with pearl handles, and these were no toys. He looked at the police and said, "Which one of you SOBs will stop me?" The officers gave no response other than to back away. He walked right down the center aisle and sat in the front row, right in front of me. The meeting came to a halt, as everyone watched to see what would happen next.

Herman addressed me. "Harry, you're the chair?" I said, "Yes." He said, "I understand that there are some people walking in here with guns and threatening you guys." I tried to keep things cool. I said, "I think we've got it straightened out, Herman. Those fellows that are lined up around the back there came in, and we had a disagreement." He said, "I just want them to know that if anybody is here to interfere, if anybody threatened you . . ." He paused and stood, and displayed his carbine and two guns. He took the pistols and flipped them around, gunslinger-style. You should have seen those cops look. You should have seen his brother and the rest of them. He announced to the room, "If any of you sons of bitches puts a hand on him," meaning me, "expect to see this." He stood and stared at them for a long moment. Then he walked out, got into his car, and drove away. I remember thinking, "That Phyllis Wheatley coaching is sure paying off!"

I did not back away from Eubanks. One day after we turned down another of his demands for money, he asked to meet privately with me at a storefront on Plymouth Avenue. I wasn't born yesterday. I knew what was likely to happen there. He was planning another little intimidation exercise, with no police or Dr. Dilliard around to protect me. I agreed to the meeting but arranged for some intimidation of my own. I brought along two of my Golden Gloves boxers—heavyweights. I took Don Riley, who weighed about 250, and Charlie Smith, who was the Upper Midwest champion. Matt hesitated to let me in when I showed up with my two companions. "If they can't come in, I don't come in either," I said. While we talked, Matt had some guys walk through the room and glare menacingly at us, then the meeting ended and we left. Nothing was resolved, except perhaps Matt's ideas about how to get his way with the MOER chair.

Even though Matt and his thugs stopped carrying guns into our meetings, they continued to harass the board. Finally, with help from the business community and Tommy Thompson, we stepped up security. We arranged to move from small meeting halls, where they could easily surround us, to a big room in the Minneapolis Auditorium. We also beefed up the police presence. I hated to ask people to come to a meeting that was supposed to be about community improvement under such conditions, but I could not ask volunteer board members to put themselves in harm's way. It was a stressful situation.

Eubanks seemed to thrive on creating stressful situations for others. He had the entire University of Minnesota on edge in January 1969, when he met with black students and convinced them to occupy Morrill Hall, the administration building, to demand the creation of a black-studies program. The arguments for black studies had legitimacy. A student could take just about any European language at the university but no African languages. A student could learn about every aspect of European history and culture but find very few courses about Africa's past or present. Contemporary black authors were also given short shrift. Matt used his Citizen Community Centers as a sort of school for protest, convincing unhappy black students to take over the administration building and block the doors to make their point. I am not opposed to nonviolent protest, but I was not happy with Matt. He was putting young students right out in front and possibly in harm's way. Who would be hurt if the university called in the National Guard or directed the police to clear the building? Not Matt.

Fortunately, the university president then was Malcolm Moos, a wise, peace-loving man who acted with restraint. The building takeover began the afternoon of January 14. That evening, Moos summoned several African American MOER Board members to a meeting to discuss ways to end the siege at Morrill Hall without violence. One of those at the meeting was Oscar Howard, a friend of Cecil Newman, who owned a restaurant and catering business. He was with us because he was present at a meeting at his restaurant when Moos tracked us down, and we invited him to come along. We made an agreement with President Moos: He would not call in the National Guard for at least a few days, and we would go to Morrill Hall in small groups the next day and attempt to reason with the students and negotiate an end to the standoff.

I said I would make the first foray to Morrill Hall and Oscar agreed to be my partner. We were allowed to enter and encountered Matt Eubanks coming out the door as we were coming in. He laughed when he saw me. He had been expecting me, he said, and had been telling the students that I was an Uncle Tom whom they could ignore. He was a terrific speaker, the kind who could get you to walk a tightrope even if you were scared to death. I steeled myself for a big challenge. But the students seemed willing to listen to me, so I told them about my background, about my life in north Minneapolis, what I planned to do when I was a youngster, how I had been inspired by Cecil Newman and Gertrude Brown and others to live my life trying to make a difference. I told them about Hubert Humphrey and how he changed the housing practices at the university. I told them that I considered the reasons for their protest legitimate. "But the last thing in the world that I would do is encourage you to take over this place and fight an opponent that you are not equipped to fight," I said. "The police can come in here and beat you and kill you. You're disrupting a great university. You're doing damage to this building. You're destroying property, and maybe you'll even destroy someone's life. You would be responsible for that. I would never put you in that position. I don't know who talked to you. Whatever they told you about making changes, you can't make them by trying to hurt somebody else."

By then it was about 9:00 a.m., and I saw no evidence that anyone had had any breakfast. I asked, "Are you hungry?" The kids said, "Yes, we haven't eaten since yesterday." It was a great thing that Oscar was there. I suggested that he call his catering service and bring the students breakfast. He called, and in a short while, trucks bearing a lot of food pulled up to Morrill Hall. We called Malcolm Moos and he directed the university police to let the trucks pass. All the kids were fed. We had a very interesting conversation after that because the kids were full and they were willing to open up and do some serious negotiating. At about noon the students agreed to end their takeover, and Moos announced that he was willing to take the first steps in creating a black-studies department. It was a good resolution.

Eubanks's harassment of the MOER Board and other community organizations and businesses eventually came to the attention of the Office of Economic Opportunity in Chicago, which was, in essence, our parent organization. Eubanks was turning the Citizens Community Centers into a base of operations for staging anti-establishment demonstrations and protests, something that was not allowed under the guidelines for the program's receipt of federal funds. OEO threatened to yank the funds from all CCC programs in Minneapolis. More than $400,000 a year was on the line—real money, in those pre-inflation years. Much as the MOER Board disliked what Eubanks was doing, we thought that killing all community centers in the city went too far.

We found ourselves in an awkward alliance with Eubanks for a few tense weeks in the late summer of 1969 as we fought—successfully—to keep the CCCs alive. Some CCC officials called news conferences to blast me for not doing enough to keep them funded, even as I was going to Chicago for meetings to find some compromise that would keep the funds flowing. I knew that a resolution had to involve Matt's departure from the CCC, but I also knew that I would cause an uprising among his followers if I were to publicly call for him to step down. Matt finally figured out for himself that he had to go. But he did not go quietly. He fought the compromise I had reached that kept the Minneapolis CCCs funded, which involved the creation of a temporary monitoring board to oversee CCC operations. At one MOER Board meeting at which Matt and I did some verbal sparring, one of his young lieutenants tried to do some real sparring. Matt himself had to restrain the young man.

Minneapolis Star columnist Jim Klobuchar put his finger on the spot I found myself in with the MOER Board. Klobuchar said I was becoming "a guy caught in the middle . . . who right now has the militants' distrust and the establishment's sympathy and doesn't want either." Much as I believed in what the MOER Board was trying to accomplish, I wanted to find another way.

14
Urban Coalition

I RESIGNED FROM THE MOER BOARD on February 1, 1970. I said at the time that I was leaving because I was involved in so many organizations and activities that my effectiveness was at risk. But I had also found a vehicle I considered more effective than the MOER Board for tackling problems such as unemployment, inadequate job training, and limited economic resources. I had become executive director of the Minneapolis chapter of the Urban Coalition.

Thanks to Art Naftalin, Minneapolis was party to the founding of the nation's Urban Coalition movement in August 1967. Art was among a handful of big-city mayors who were determined to set race relations right in their cities. They wanted no more "long, hot summers" of tension and violence in black neighborhoods. They wanted to take quick, decisive action to improve the lives of minority citizens in their communities. They were intrigued by the idea of John W. Gardner, a Republican serving Democrat Lyndon Johnson as secretary of Health, Education, and Welfare, for a new kind of public-private partnership with the power and flexibility to truly improve life in urban neighborhoods.

That August, Gardner convened an "emergency" founding conference in Washington. Art recruited a delegation of forty Minneapolis business, government, and community leaders to attend. I was among them. Art was on the conference steering committee, which quickly became the national Urban Coalition steering committee. He tapped several Minneapolis people for prominent roles at that meeting. For example, John Cowles Jr., then editor of the *Minneapolis Tribune* and the *Minneapolis Star,* led a workshop, as did Atherton Bean, the board chair of International Milling Company (later International Multifoods.) City Council member Gladys Brooks was there in that capacity and also as a vice president of the National Council of Churches. Four other council members—Dan Cohen, Richard Erdall,

Robert MacGregor, and Donald Risk—were also there.

It was another of Art's brilliantly organized stratagems to get something done. The national-conference delegation was soon the planning committee for the new Minneapolis chapter of the Urban Coalition. Art put the arm on fourteen business leaders to contribute $1,000 apiece to launch the coalition. He recruited Earl Ewald, CEO of Northern States Power, as the chair of the planning effort, and Honeywell CEO Stephen Keating as the first chair of the board. Keating was a fortuitous choice. He was energetic, smart, friendly, and, in my view, an organizational genius. When he started putting together the coalition's structure, he was in his element. He knew every business in town, it seemed, and was masterful at tapping talent. He would say, "At Pillsbury, you've got so-and-so, who is tremendous in the area of personnel, and we need him on our employment task force." Keating was a magnet for other business leaders. Not only was he committed personally to the ideal of racial equality, he also understood race relations as a matter of his company's self-interest. Honeywell's headquarters stood about a mile from my house, in the heart of a racially mixed neighborhood.

The planning effort was headed jointly by T. (short for Theatrice) Williams, executive director of Phyllis Wheatley, and Larry Harris, director of urban affairs for Minneapolis Public Schools. Both took leaves of absence to get the Urban Coalition launched. By February 1968, it was on its way. The board was in place. It consisted of sixty people, a mix of leaders from business, labor, religious groups, civic organizations, and public and private social-service agencies. They vowed to create an organization that would only rarely deliver services directly. Rather, the Urban Coalition would serve as a catalyst and a resource for other public and private agencies. It would provide money, strategic planning, advice, and a platform for constructive dialogue. It would spot needs, propose solutions, and finance their implementation. Funds would come from the business community via the Minneapolis Foundation. Task forces were planned to tackle each of the problem areas on the coalition's agenda. The board began hiring or otherwise acquiring the staff for five initial task forces: education, housing, employment and training, economic development, and law and justice. Someone whose corporate rank was no less than vice president would chair each task force. The board itself would elect no chair whose corporate rank was below CEO or executive vice president. Anyone of lesser position need not apply.

Many people on the Urban Coalition board had also been involved in the MOER Board. In addition to Keating and Cowles, the coalition included Phil Harder from First National Bank, Judson "Sandy" Bemis from the

Bemis Company, Donald Dayton from the Dayton's retailing company, Fran Van Konynenburg of Midwest Radio/Television (WCCO), Bill Mullins of Minnegasco, and Bill Humphrey of General Mills. All were getting a good education about their city's minority neighborhoods. Bonds of personal acquaintance were being established, often for the first time.

The young organization was less than two months old when it was put to a severe test. On April 4, 1968, the nation's leading voice for civil rights, the Reverend Dr. Martin Luther King Jr., was gunned down in Memphis, Tennessee. It was a devastating loss. I heard the news on the radio, having just come home for dinner after an Urban Coalition task-force meeting. I immediately turned on the television and heard a local newscaster saying, "It looks like there's going to be another riot in north Minneapolis. Young men are running up and down Olson Highway." Without waiting to be summoned, I jumped back into my car and headed to my old neighborhood. I knew that was where I needed to be.

I spotted a cluster of squad cars around Sumner Library and was not surprised to find Art Naftalin and several other Urban Coalition board members already there. The streets were also full of distraught and fearful neighborhood residents. I was a bit fearful myself. When you wade into a crowd like that, you never know what is going to happen. But I was reassured to see that there were no police decked out in riot gear and no sign of anyone doing anything obviously criminal.

We decided that the Urban Coalition should issue a statement immediately. Fran Van Konynenburg was there, and he offered the resources of WCCO radio and television to broadcast anything we wanted the community to hear. Some of us got busy drafting. This is part of what our statement said: "Racism killed Dr. Martin Luther King. In recognition that such racism exists here in Minneapolis, though hopefully in less violent form, the Urban Coalition of Minneapolis will organize immediately an anti-racism program to deal in our area with this basic root of tragic violence in America." We also sent telegrams to the president, the governor, and the members of the Minnesota delegation to Congress, asking that the state and federal governments respond not just with resolve to apprehend Dr. King's murderer, but also with promises to root out racism.

The presence of the mayor and the squad cars made the library lawn a focal point for residents, and a good-sized crowd gathered. We decided to use a police loudspeaker to address the people. A number of us took our turn with the loudspeaker, starting with Art. When it was my turn, I said, "Let's not make this look like Los Angeles or Detroit. Let's not tear up our own neighborhood. Dr. Martin Luther King was shot and killed. Our leader is lost, but this does not end our march for freedom."

Our impromptu outdoor rally had its desired effect. People stayed in the street for a long time, but they were calm. After a public tragedy, people just want to be together, it seems. They want to hear someone saying something reassuring like, "Look, Martin Luther King is gone, but he would expect us to carry on. What we're doing here in Minneapolis is trying to get jobs, better housing, better education. We've got the Urban Coalition. We've got the MOER Board. We've got a chance to make things better." I said as much; so did other speakers. We also worked to quell rumors. One was that anti-black white people were coming into the neighborhood to fight. Word spread that there was a car of skinheads on Plymouth and Oliver. Some from our audience wanted to go have it out with them. We said, "No, don't do that. We don't want a confrontation with them. Let the police do their job." It worked. There were riots in many American cities that night and over the next few days but not in Minneapolis.

During that tense evening, Fran Van Konynenburg's eyes were opened to the racial reality of law enforcement in Minneapolis in the 1960s. There were very few black cops. Fran said to Art and me, "The only way we're going to give some security to north Minneapolis, because of its large black population, is to find enough black police officers to patrol here. We don't have that many." After that night, Fran was determined to do something about it. His resolve led to the formation of the Urban Coalition's police/community-relations task force, on which he and I served.

The next morning, Art and I appeared together at a news conference in his office to announce our intention to form the volunteer Citizens Patrol. I also pleaded with white residents of the city not to cruise through black neighborhoods that weekend just to "see what's going on." The potential for violence was simply too great. "We cannot swallow the bitter pill of hatred with a glass of revenge," I said.

Later, Steve Keating told a newspaper reporter that the assassination of Dr. King galvanized the young Urban Coalition for decisive action in the months that followed. At a time when people desperately wanted to believe there was still hope that America could be one country, the Urban Coalition was the shiny new apostle of hope in town. "It was almost as if they were waiting for a signal" to move, Keating said of the city's business leaders. Martin's death was that signal.

But in the first days after the assassination, it was the militant wing of the black community that came to us. Syl Davis, head of The Way, came to the Urban Coalition on April 6 with a list of fourteen proposals from a "steering committee of the black community." They were presented as "demands," not recommendations, illustrating the intensity of the moment. But while the rhetoric was strong, the ideas on the list were, by and large, sound. I was asked to be the coalition's liaison to Syl and his group. After only a few days of negotiations, the coalition was able to respond with fourteen points of its own that embraced most of Syl's demands. I called an all-city meeting at Phyllis Wheatley on April 15 and presented the coalition's response. The reaction was overwhelmingly positive from both blacks and whites in attendance. Not only did those at the meeting indicate their support, but many also volunteered to serve on committees and help make our plan a reality. My mailbox at home was flooded with letters from average citizens, most also offering their help.

The fourteen points became guideposts for action for the Urban Coalition in the years that followed. Among them: Pressure for aggressive enforcement of antidiscrimination laws. Greater representation for minorities in government, on nongovernment organization boards, and on the city's police and firefighting forces. Expansion of job training and hiring of minorities. A quick end to the war in Vietnam. Park and recreation improvements in black neighborhoods. Gun control. Elimination of racism in the judicial system. More college financial aid for minorities. More minority teachers in public schools and better diversity training for all teachers. These were things the whole city could embrace. The coalition was formally commended by the city's Council of Churches for taking so much of the black community's agenda and pledging to run with it.

Still lacking as the weather warmed that tumultuous spring was a full-time, permanent executive director for the Urban Coalition, a position that later was renamed president. Larry Harris had been serving on an interim basis and wanted to get back to his public-school position. The board advertised for applications and received quite a few. I did not apply for the job; I thought I was busy enough. I was chair of the MOER Board, director of Star Tribune Charities (the Golden Gloves), a new member of the city Civil Service Commission, and still employee-services director at the Onan Company, which had been sold and was by then the Onan division of the Studebaker-Worthington Corporation. As soon as my term as president of the local NAACP chapter ended, I accepted the presidency of the new Sabathani Community Center at Thirty-eighth Street and Third Avenue South, not far from my home. It was going to be the first Wheatley-like community center on the South Side.

I was also, once again, a new father. Evan Wesley, our fourth child, was born on January 16, 1968. He was a very happy but rather surprising addition to our family, born more than twenty-four years after our eldest child, Rita. In fact, not long after Evan was born, Rita, who had married Joseph Lyell, announced that she was expecting her first child. Corey Lyell arrived fifteen months after Evan's birth. When Rita went back to her Northwestern National Bank career after maternity leave, Corey came to our house for day care. Charlotte had her hands full with babies once more. Corey and Evan were raised almost as brothers—and what a lively pair they were!

Ricky was in junior high when Evan was born, and Butchie was in college at the University of Minnesota–Duluth. Both were very good athletes who kept us running to football games and track meets. Ricky kept our household lively in one other way. At Bryant Junior High School, he connected with a young musician named Roger Nelson. We had known Roger's mother, Mattie Del Shaw, and his aunt, Mattie's twin sister, Edna Mae, at Phyllis Wheatley. Roger started a rock band and Ricky played drums for him. They practiced in our basement until Charlotte said she could not stand the noise and moved them to the garage. Pretty soon our garage was the hangout of every kid in the neighborhood. Ricky eventually gave up the drums, but Roger Nelson stayed with his music and changed his name—to Prince.

With all that going on at home and in the community, I was not looking for a new job. But Art called. "Harry, I've been talking with a lot of people, a lot of businesspeople and a lot of community people. I've been talking to some of the people on the MOER Board, including the government people, Tommy Thompson, and some others. Harry, we would all like you to apply for the Urban Coalition job." He said they wanted someone who was respected by all the stakeholders in the project. I think they also wanted someone who was already aware of the coalition's work and could hit the ground running. Art was persuasive, offering to intercede with the Onans on my behalf if I became the board's choice. He even spoke with the Onans before I applied to prepare them for what could be coming. I could not say no. I applied. I went through interviews and a screening process, as did quite a few other good candidates. I personally didn't think that I would get the job. After all, I was already an Urban Coalition board member, and a board does not usually hire one of its own. But a few days after the interview, I had a visit from Steve Keating of Honeywell and Dean McNeal of the Pillsbury Company. If I would take it, the top staff job was mine.

Take it I did, and gladly, in July 1968. My arrangement was a leave of absence from Onan to last no longer than five years. The Onans were very accommodating. I think they were proud that a kid they had hired for one of the rock-bottom jobs in their plant had come so far. I was pleased I didn't have to fully sever my tie to Onan to take the Urban Coalition job. I enjoyed my Onan career and the people I knew so well there, and I was proud to be the first black employee to rise into management ranks. Moreover, I learned a great many lessons at Onan about management. It was there that I came to understand the importance of interdependency. I learned that I could take orders as well as give them, and that I could put together a complex work plan involving many people and tasks. I learned the importance of establishing relationships with people to get the job done efficiently and well. I always appreciated the fact that I worked for a family-owned company, for people who valued their employees. I still treasure a photo of Bud Onan presenting me with a twenty-year watch. Still, my salary at Onan was none too generous. Becoming executive director of the Urban Coalition raised my income 50 percent.

The more I considered the potential of the Urban Coalition, the more I knew I wanted to make it a focus of my activity. All the things that got in the way at the MOER Board—the federal red tape, the congressional budget cuts, the sniping from people like Matt Eubanks—were not a problem for an organization less bound up with government. The Urban Coalition was going to have what it took to get action: money, talent, modern equipment, and, most important, power. We used to say that politicians think they are powerful, but they come and go with every election. If you've got the head of General Mills and the millions that corporate foundations give away on your side, that's real power. The Urban Coalition involved a broad swath of the community, but the business community was the controlling factor.

The heavy hand of business might raise a great deal of suspicion in the black community today. It had its critics then too. But the business community in Minneapolis was seen in a more benign light in the 1960s than it is today. One reason is that nearly every large corporation then was locally owned and controlled. The same people, year in and year out, filled the Minneapolis Club. Some businesses, such as Dayton's, had been in the same family's hands for generations. They were not much affected by Wall Street pressure to maximize their bottom line. Business owners prided themselves and judged their peers on their community involvement, charitable giving, and commitment to their employees. They felt personally stung by the Plymouth Avenue violence of 1966 and 1967 and had a personal stake in restoring harmony. The next riot, if there was one, might happen downtown.

Politics was not such a point of division between the black community and the business community as it is today. Black Republicans and DFL business owners were not as rare then. Both major Minnesota parties championed civil rights. Republicans in Minnesota were in that party's liberal wing. They favored Nelson Rockefeller over Barry Goldwater and were less than enamored of Richard Nixon. It was a less polarized time.

I was aware that there were some very low-income minority people whose voices were never heard by the Urban Coalition. Their circumstances isolated and alienated them from the community. It was the same problem the MOER Board faced, one that opened the MOER Board to protest and disruption. I wondered and worried about how to reach the very poor. I still do. But I distinguish between the truly poor, whose voices should be amplified, and those who purport to speak for the poor but whose real interest is in drawing attention to themselves. Those are the ones with the loudest voices and who often don't bother to inform themselves before they start talking. Their real aim is to get top billing. In every new community activity, one has to deal with people like that, often by doing the work and moving on.

It was crucial to the early success of the Urban Coalition that top people from the member corporations were personally at the board meetings and personally heading task forces. That meant when they said at an Urban Coalition meeting that a loaned executive could be provided, or a certain number of job trainees could be employed, they were speaking for their companies. When they said government help should be enlisted, they were saying they would personally place a call to the governor or the senator. The power was sitting right there. For me, that was very appealing. I could recommend, "Here's what we need to do, and here's how much it's going to cost," with considerable confidence that I would soon be authorized to spend the money to do just that.

That's not to say we were not careful with money. We were so careful that we had separate funds for operations—for staff salaries, office rent and equipment, and the like—and for task-force expenditures. When a task force brought forth an idea for development, it also brought its financial request to the board of directors. Board approval was always needed before the staff could spend money on task-force proposals.

We had a fine staff of about fifteen people, a mixture of people I recruited and others that businesses loaned to us for particular tasks and tenures. They were a diverse group—white, black, American Indian, Chicano. Minneapolis had very few Asian Americans then, or I am sure they would have been represented on my staff too. I interviewed and approved them all, even the loaned executives. My years in employee services at Onan served me well. I knew that almost more important than an applicant's background and education was his or her commitment to community service. When possible, I tried to hire people with a personal connection to the community they would be serving. That created an immediate confidence and trust that helped the coalition act quickly.

Hennepin County District Judge Franklin Knoll, who also served in the state Senate, headed our legal staff. He was instrumental in putting together a de novo program, which provided a way for expunging the criminal records of men who led law-abiding lives after serving jail or prison time. My vice president was Larry Brown, a good friend who had a background in finance and tax law and who worked for several years in East Africa helping young governments with tax policies. He had been one of my boxers at Phyllis Wheatley. I asked him to receive and analyze all requests for funds and let me know which requests were worthy of board action. He was a tremendous help to me. Because I trusted him so fully with financial matters, I was free to meet with organizations around the community, like the Urban League and Phyllis Wheatley, and make sure they were connected to the coalition's work.

A couple of our loaned executives made history while they were in that capacity. I was well acquainted with Clyde Bellecourt, who worked in those years for Northern States Power. He and his brothers had been in the Golden Gloves program. They were very good boxers. There was a degree of trust between Clyde and me. Clyde made me acquainted with Dennis Banks, who worked for Honeywell. They had a dream: to extend the benefits of the civil-rights movement to Native Americans. They wanted to organize AIM, the American Indian Movement. They needed time away from their jobs to do it. Together we approached Steve Keating at Honeywell and Don McCarthy at NSP and persuaded them to make Clyde and Dennis loaned executives of the Urban Coalition. They had a variety of jobs, but their main assignment was to create an organization that would advocate for full civil rights for Native Americans.

All the talent on loan to the Urban Coalition from the corporate world made us a very orderly operation. Every task force had clearly stated, measurable goals and objectives. The senior staff member for each task force was not a member of the Urban Coalition's permanent staff, but a loaned executive. That was my idea. I didn't want to spend a lot of time recruiting and hiring staff for the task forces, nor run the risk of choosing someone who would not perform. I wanted the task forces to move quickly, with staff that the business members already knew. And in the event that someone was not meeting our needs, I wanted the ease of being able to tell a CEO, "This fellow you sent over is not doing the job. Send me somebody else."

I soon saw, however, that the secret to the coalition's effectiveness wasn't the structure or the staff; it was the willingness of some of the most powerful people in the city to personally confront the needs of some of the poorest. Task forces sat down and truly listened to the black community. When the law-and-justice task force heard complaints about police brutality, for example, the leading lawyers in town were there to hear them. Peter Dorsey and Leonard Lindquist were on that task force. They could assign junior lawyers at their firms to research complaints. They could talk with the judges. They knew the juvenile system and could make solid recommendations for improving it. That task force proved important in changing the way the whole justice system responded to the black community.

Similarly, it made a big difference that WCCO's Fran Van Konynenburg was on our employment task force. An important goal of the black community was to integrate the news media. If more black people were reporters, editors, and producers, it was thought, news coverage would more fully and accurately reflect the black experience. Fran picked up on that idea and contacted his fellow CEOs at the other three local television stations at that time. With that kind of connection, things moved smoothly. The task force created what was called the Broadcasters' Skills Bank. We understood that it was unlikely that any new minority applicant would land in an anchor's chair right away. But there were a hundred other jobs in a news organization and good technical schools and journalism schools in the Twin Cities to train people. The Broadcasters' Skills Bank sought minority applicants for broadcast news jobs and shepherded them into the proper training. If applicants successfully completed the training, they had good assurance of a job. All four stations agreed that it was a good thing to do, though Stan Hubbard at KSTP, a notoriously independent operator, started his own minority-hiring program instead of joining ours. Rather quickly, the race barrier in local television journalism was broken.

Our education task force was a big focus of our efforts. John B. Davis, the very able superintendent of Minneapolis Public Schools, served on the coalition board and on the task force. We recruited the head of the teachers' federation and the principals' organization as well. We were careful not to try to usurp the schools' responsibility, but we arranged for certain businesses to "adopt" schools in poorer neighborhoods and to bring added financial resources, tutors, and mentors to those schools. We saw these as demonstration projects, with the idea that if we could show positive results, more cooperation between city schools and the business community would follow. General Mills adopted the North Side Learning Center. Honeywell had the Bryant Junior High "Yes" Center, right in its building. Several businesses helped with a building program at Clinton School. These ties came together quickly. That's what can happen when CEOs and the school superintendent sit around the same meeting table, month after month.

Our aim was for our task forces to be spawning grounds for new or improved programs and agencies that would do the hands-on work of fighting poverty and racism. It was gratifying to see that begin to happen in the early 1970s. Our economic-development task force led to the creation of MEDA, the Metropolitan Economic Development Association. It provided venture capital for small-business start-ups. The housing task force was the godparent of the Greater Minneapolis Housing Corporation, which provided grants and loans for affordable housing. The loaned executive from General Mills who worked with that task force, Chuck Krusell, went on to become head of GMHC and later the Greater Minneapolis Chamber of Commerce. The Urban Coalition was involved in the foundation of two education organizations that are still thriving today. They are the Urban Concerns Workshop, which exposes city high-school students to the workings of state government, and the Minnesota Council on Economic Education, which brings innovative programs for teaching economics into the state's high schools. I served on the boards of both.

There was a great, positive reaction to the Urban Coalition. It overcame some of the mistrust of government that tainted the work of the MOER Board. It also was able to pursue a broad agenda all at once so that many people's interests were simultaneously served. As a result, Minneapolis was a more hopeful place than it had been just a year earlier. Still, the whole city was jittery about what would happen during the long, hot summer of 1968. It was still an agonizing time for the whole nation. Robert Kennedy was killed in June; Hubert Humphrey's nomination for president was spoiled by police brutality in the streets of Chicago; anger and despair over the loss of Martin Luther King darkened the outlook of black Americans.

That summer, as young people gathered at the city's premier lakes for relief from the heat, there were several near disasters. If a number of black youths arrived at Lake Calhoun and stood together in the parking lot or on the beach, some busybody would call the police and say that black youths were getting ready to create a riot. That would trigger a message to Art Naftalin, to the chief of police, and to me. I was still head of the Citizens Patrol, the volunteer neighborhood watchdogs we assembled after the King assassination. I was also on the list to call because Gleason Glover, Josie Johnson, and I had been leading a racial-sensitivity training program with the rookies in the Minneapolis police force.

I was called the hot evening of July 9 at about 9:00 while I was at a meeting at Phyllis Wheatley. I was told there was trouble across the street from the Calhoun Beach Club and the police chief wanted my help. I drove there quickly and found about twenty members of the riot squad, under the command of Sergeant Jack McCarthy, assembled on one end of the beach. On the other side were about two dozen black teenagers and young adults. They were casting noisy remarks back and forth, but I saw no evidence that the kids had been doing anything wrong. Luckily, I had arrived before either side began advancing on the other. Syl Davis was there, as were Matt Eubanks and William English, director of the Sabathani Community Center. Gleason had been called and was on his way. I sought out Sergeant McCarthy and asked for time to talk to the crowd and get them to disperse voluntarily. "Now, let's not create a riot," I said to him. "If you advance, these youngsters are not going to run. They are going to stand and fight. You're going to hurt them, and some of you are going to get hurt too. If you don't want your people hurt, let's try to talk this thing out." So we talked and talked, back and forth. The two sides stayed apart. I stood right in front of the kids. They were still taunting the cops, but I had the impression they were not itching for a fight. I asked the kids to pipe down and stay calm. Meanwhile, the situation was drawing a crowd of onlookers. Suddenly, a Coke bottle came flying from the crowd, right into the middle of the police cluster. It landed hard on the shoulder of one of the officers, Thomas Halsey. The reaction was quick. The police started moving toward the kids—and me. I thought, here I am, foolishly standing right in the line of fire. I yelled for them to stop. Somewhat to my surprise, as the police got near me, they did just that. And when they halted, so did the kids. Just about then, Gleason arrived and he helped me disperse both crowds.

Moments like those jarred the city's serenity. There were more of them that summer and fall, including a clash between militants and police officers at Central High School in September. But there was no race riot in Minneapolis in 1968, nor has there been one since. For that, I think great credit is due the Urban Coalition. In every area we tackled, we made positive changes. By 1969, the Minneapolis Urban Coalition was being hailed as a model for coalitions in other cities. I traveled to Milwaukee and St. Louis to speak to young Urban Coalitions there about what we were doing. I would tell audiences about how the work of all of our task forces fit together. I would describe the first house we bought in our scattered-site housing program, a big, dilapidated three-bedroom crate on Irving Avenue near Plymouth. We hired a black subcontractor from the neighborhood to remodel that house, which we then sold to a neighborhood family with four children. The family's father had been unemployed a short time before, but he was referred to TCOIC (now Summit Academy OIC) for training and then landed one of the jobs opened through the efforts of the Urban Coalition. He was able to get a mortgage for the house through the new bank that the Urban Coalition had launched. We referred him to places where he could get low-cost furnishings for the house. We ushered that family from joblessness to home ownership, improved the neighborhood, and added to our city's security to boot.

One of our projects caused a turn in my own life that I could not have predicted. It was the establishment of the first truly local bank to serve my old neighborhood, First Plymouth Bank. I was one of the bank's three founding trustees.

The Urban Coalition's economic-development task force recognized early on that a community bank was needed on the near North Side. We approached the two big downtown banks, then called First National and Northwestern National, about putting a bank on Plymouth Avenue. They declined, saying that they thought the North Side black community was adequately served by their banks on Broadway Avenue. But I knew better. Low-income people who lacked cars and lived near Glenwood Avenue or Olson Highway had a hard time getting up to Broadway. Moreover, they considered the area around Broadway Avenue a neighborhood where they did not always feel welcome.

A local bank would also better provide the particular services my old neighborhood needed. Merely providing savings accounts and checking accounts and mortgages would not be enough. A local bank would have to educate its customers about each of those services. It was not that North Side people were ignorant. You don't learn to speak English unless it is spoken to you. Many low-income people had never been bank customers, nor had their parents before them. We wanted a bank that would conduct weekly consumer-education classes.

Our bank plan really took fire. A bank charter was available; our board of bank trustees and First National Bank made a joint application and got it. Phil Harder arranged for First National Bank to acquire property on Plymouth Avenue and build a bank there, with the idea it might eventually become a First Bank branch. Meanwhile, the bank would be in Urban Coalition hands. We would rent a storefront and work with Phyllis Wheatley and Pillsbury House to start the consumer-education program so people could learn what that bank could do for them. We also began a children's education component, modeled after a program the old Farmers and Mechanics Bank had years before.

The task force came up with a unique way to capitalize the new bank. When our member corporations withheld payroll taxes, they did not send that money directly to the state and federal treasuries. They deposited that money in a bank, which in turn paid the government but also collected a few days' interest before it did. All of the major banks in town agreed that a portion of that interest would accrue to our new bank for a period of time until it was adequately capitalized. It was a rare act of cooperative generosity among rival financial institutions.

The new bank was popular with North Side residents. We had a unique demonstration of just how popular after the bank had been open a short time. Two guys came in and held up the bank. The robbers were from the neighborhood. What they did not bargain for was that the bank employees were also neighborhood residents who would recognize them. When the police came, identifying the culprits was not a problem. Neither did the police have to spend much time looking for the fugitives. The next day, community people brought the two robbers back into the bank and made them return the money. The Urban Coalition board was impressed by that show of community support.

It was at the very next economic-development task-force meeting that First Plymouth presented the design of the new building it would build at Newton and Plymouth Avenues. The building included a large community meeting room in the basement that I knew would be well used. At about the same time that the bank was built, a shopping center went in across Plymouth Avenue, replacing some of the buildings damaged during the 1967 riot. The face of the North Side was rapidly changing.

The charter required that the bank have three trustees who were not bank owners. The three the coalition appointed were John Warder, Luther Prince, and me. One of us had to be the bank's president. John, who owned a printing company, had a degree in finance; Luther was a Honeywell computer engineer; and I had the Urban Coalition to run. We thought John was the natural choice to be our president, but his background did not include any real training in banking. So First National Bank asked the president of its

Broadway Avenue bank to take the title chair of the board of First Plymouth Bank and to serve as acting president while John was trained through the First Bank system. Likewise, First National and Northwestern both loaned the new bank other staff on a temporary basis until employees from the neighborhood could be trained.

On that basis, John Warder agreed to take the First Plymouth Bank presidency. To give the new job the attention it deserved, he also decided to resign the seat he held on the Minneapolis School Board. It was a decision that opened a new chapter in my life.

15
School Board

JOHN WARDER'S DECISION TO LEAVE the school board in January 1969 created a situation that Superintendent John B. Davis Jr. regarded with some urgency. The tension between blacks and whites in Minneapolis was spilling into the public schools. Harmony depended in no small part on school leadership's ability to reflect both the black and the white faces of the community. John Warder was the only black member of the school board; he was only the second black person ever to serve. It was crucial that his replacement also be black.

The matter came up at one of the Urban Coalition executive committee's Tuesday-morning breakfast sessions at the Minneapolis Club. I became aware that Dean McNeal and Phil Harder had already been in conversation with John Davis, and that school-board members Viola Hymes, Lawrence (Duke) Johnson, and the Reverend David Preus had also been consulted. They already had in mind a replacement, someone whom they said would be respected not only by the school board and administration, but also by business and government leaders in the city. I was the replacement they wanted.

I was flattered, naturally, but also very much aware of my already jam-packed calendar. I had more obligations than John Warder did. If I agreed to serve on the school board, something would have to give. That something was the Civil Service Commission, on which I had served for less than a year. In that year, I had made a dent in the color barrier to police and firefighter hiring. I decided it was worth the sacrifice of leaving that commission to take my work for racial equality to the schools.

I exacted the promise of more staff help for my work at the Urban Coalition and the MOER Board. With that pledge from Dean McNeal, who had succeeded Steve Keating as the coalition chair, I accepted the school-board seat.

The board was independent and had the authority to fill its own vacancies between elections. I was the unanimous choice of the remaining six board members. I was sworn in on March 11, 1969. My term would expire in a little more than three months. If I wanted to keep the seat—and I did—I needed to start campaigning immediately.

Daunting as that prospect was, I felt prepared for it. I came to the school board with a lifetime of experience with the Minneapolis Public Schools, much of it positive. Growing up, I never had a black teacher, from kindergarten through high school. For black role models, I looked to Phyllis Wheatley, not the schools. Yet with but a few exceptions at North High, my teachers gave me the same interest and attention that any other student received. At Sumner School, where I spent grades four through nine, great effort was made to give adequate attention to students of color and to involve their parents if the students were not performing well. I was able to know my teachers at Sumner well, and I was impressed with each one's kindness and character. They were the best people.

By and large, I felt good about the education my children received in the Minneapolis Public Schools as well. But my concern was that some teachers did not encourage children of color as they did white children. I had seen some of that myself at North High. I was on guard against that sort of subtle discrimination in my children's classrooms. It is so important that kids understand that they are somebody, and that they come to school to learn to be somebody. That's where they learn to achieve, so that they can be successful, responsible adults. Too often, at that time, teachers did not encourage black children to set their sights on college and careers of leadership.

Charlotte and I were active in the PTA, particularly in the years when we had three children in three public schools: Ricky at Warrington Elementary, Butchie at Bryant Junior High, and Rita at Central High School. Central was the focus of some race-related protests and demonstrations in the years when our children were there and shortly thereafter. That was in part because, in those years, Central shared a building with Minneapolis Community College, attended by older and more politically aware students. The building was wide open to anyone who wanted to come in and stir up a demonstration. We PTA parents became concerned about our children's security. In those years, the fire code required that school doors must be open both ways all day. As a result, protesters were free to walk down halls and disrupt classes. During one period when protesters were coming to the school with some frequency, we recruited a group of PTA parents to patrol the school corridors during the day. We then appealed to the fire chief: "We want to be able to lock the doors from the inside. We have a select group of parents that will be walking the halls. If there is ever any fire or any trouble, we'll have people there to open the doors." The fire chief allowed us to try a lock-in at Central. It worked; the disruption of classes by protesters stopped. When there was similar trouble later at Bryant, Charlotte and I told of our experience at Central. The same approach worked at Bryant. The parents in the neighborhood got to know each other better as a result. Those parents became a core group of support for my first school-board campaign.

Integration was coming to the teaching and administrative ranks in those years. Two friends from my youth, Bill McMoore and Earl Bowman, were promoted to principals. Earl had been Butch and Ricky's coach at Central and a terrific mentor and role model for both. They helped expand my acquaintance with teachers in the district. Also climbing the ranks was one of my Golden Gloves boxers, Richard Green. He would soon become principal at North High. Butch's wonderful English and social-studies teacher at Bryant, Gail Dahlstrom, was very active in my campaign and became a good friend. She is the most beautiful lady inside and outside that you ever want to meet. She loved those kids and they responded with good behavior. Whatever Mrs. Dahlstrom said, they did. I am sure that positive experiences with Gail and so many other teachers through the years are what made me something of a voice for teachers on the school board. During my first campaign, I often said I thought that a stronger connection was needed between teachers and the board. I proposed regular joint meetings as a starting point.

My involvement with the NAACP prepared me well for school politics. The NAACP had been a leading force in the 1950s, in Minneapolis and around the country, for ending school segregation, hiring black teachers, and promoting administrators. The Minneapolis School Board did not resist the organization's efforts, but neither did it eagerly embrace them. In those years, most school-board members came right out of the Minneapolis Club. They were fine, upper-class, well-motivated people, but they did not represent the community they served. When John Davis became superintendent in 1967, he stepped up the pace of integration. He aggressively recruited people of color, not just for teaching jobs but also for every position in the district, from janitor to his own administrative cabinet. He took on the unions as necessary to make that happen. He singled out promising young black teachers and groomed them for leadership positions.

He also was keenly aware that Minneapolis students were not being educated in an integrated racial environment. In one sense, Minneapolis schools had always been integrated: all students attended the schools nearest their home. But because the neighborhoods had been divided by rigid color lines for decades, the schools reflected de facto segregation. When I was a kid, people of color could live in only about five of the thirteen wards; people of color couldn't buy or rent there. That kind of discrimination was outlawed in the 1960s, but the established residential pattern prevailed. John Davis knew that if the right kind of legal suit were brought, Minneapolis schools would likely face a court order to do something about segregation. From the start of his tenure, he began talking privately with school-board members and other trusted advisers about how best to desegregate. Among the people he conferred with were the first black member of the school board, Judge L. Howard Bennett, and John Warder. I became privy to those talks as John Davis and I got to know each other on the Urban Coalition board.

By 1969, John's desegregation idea had grown into an application for a federal grant for a pilot project called the Southeast Alternative Program. When funded a year later, it encompassed all the schools in the southeast part of the city, including Marshall-University High School. It was the city's first experiment in public-school choice. Children who lived in that area had a choice of public schools to attend, and each elementary school adopted a different curricular style. Montessori, continuous progress, open, fundamental—all those were available. Parents were not assured that their children would be admitted to their first-choice program, though most were, and virtually every family was accepted at either their first or second choice. The program also involved an experiment in limiting classroom size to fifteen to determine how smaller classes affected student progress. All this was imminent as I came on the school board. I quickly got up to speed and became an enthusiastic backer of the idea in my campaign. John and the board were ready to go to community groups and sell the idea, and I was happy to do my part.

I was well received by the other members of the school board. The quickest bond I made was with the board chair, the Reverend David Preus. We became very good friends. David came from a long line of Norwegian Lutheran clergy, though one of his kinsmen had also been governor of Minnesota in the 1920s. He was pastor of University Lutheran Church of Hope in Minneapolis, an American Lutheran Church congregation known for its intellectual bent and social activism. That church is in southeast Minneapolis, which made David a neighbor and friend of both Art Naftalin and DFL U.S. Representative Don Fraser, whom I had come to know. David is tall, gregarious, and commanding. He's down-to-earth and understanding, but he projects great strength. He's probably one of the most humane people I have ever met. He had an outstanding career before him: he became president of the American Lutheran Church and a leading force behind the merger of several Lutheran denominations into the Evangelical Lutheran Church in America in 1987.

Three of the seven school-board seats were up for election on June 10, 1969: David's, one being vacated by Viola Hymes, and mine. David said, "Harry, why don't you and I run together, as a team? Why don't we go out and get endorsements together? Maybe some of the endorsements that you may not be able to get alone I can get for you, and vice versa." I thought it was a great idea and generous on his part. His own reelection was never in doubt. He had won handily in 1965. But I was new to city politics and my vote-getting ability was untested. David had in mind joint lawn signs, joint advertisements, joint appearances, and joint appeals for endorsements. That last part would be tricky. I was a DFLer. David was a Republican.

I had been involved only at the edges of party politics, and then only through the NAACP, the MOER Board, and Art Naftalin's campaigns. I had not been going regularly to the party's precinct caucuses, which elect delegates to party conventions. A DFL incumbent running for reelection can generally count on both party and labor support; for me, however, none of that was automatic. Though he was a Republican, David was actually in better standing with the Minneapolis Central Labor Union than I was. He ran with labor endorsement in 1965. When I first went with David to screen before the Central Labor Union, some fellows there were a little reluctant to back me. The building trades had few minority members then, and they were not rushing to admit more. But at the head of the Central Labor Union was Dave Roe. He had become a loyal friend. And because of Eddie Lacy, who helped us win the 1948 Upper Midwest Golden Gloves championship, the sheet-metal workers knew me. They came through with endorsements for both David and me.

We went together to the Republican and DFL endorsing conventions. School-board races are technically nonpartisan. But the parties have long considered it their prerogative to endorse candidates for school board—and candidates willingly line up for party backing because of the campaign money and assistance that goes with it. Running for school board is not cheap. It is a citywide election that requires the full gamut of advertising to build name recognition. The Republican convention was first in line. I was not at all sure how I would be received, but David was reassuring. He said, "Harry, I don't know if this will help you, but it can't hurt you." I found that I knew quite a few people at the Republican convention. A number of businesspeople I had met through the Urban Coalition were there. I knew some of the party's officials, including legislators Lyall Schwarzkopf, Gary Flakne, and Wayne Popham. David and I had our names placed in nomination for endorsement. No other names were submitted, and in a quick voice vote we were endorsed. It was a snap.

The DFL convention was a different matter. A number of active black DFLers—Nellie Stone Johnson, Matthew Little, my old friend Cecil Newman—had been busy greasing the skids for my endorsement. They thought it was crucial that at least one seat on the seven-member school board stay in the hands of a black person. But the idea of teaming with a known Republican was more than some of those fierce DFL partisans could take. I think it also bothered them that we were incumbents setting our own agenda. We were not answerable to the party in the way that someone who had risen through party ranks would have been. Several other candidates were nominated. We fought through several ballots until finally I crossed the crucial 60-percent threshold for endorsement, but David did not. The delegates cast only one more ballot, and again David's vote was shy of 60 percent. We were disappointed but determined not to let that setback alter our plan. We told the DFL delegates that we planned to continue to run together. Our literature would simply say that I was DFL-endorsed and David was Republican-endorsed.

David coached me on how to handle candidates' meetings. He gave me pointers on how to set up the line of discussion and control the topics being presented. I tended to fear being asked to speak first, but David showed me how to use that position to my advantage. He would say, "When you speak first, you speak to the issues that you want to address. The last statement you make is the question you leave behind you. You can set the agenda for the candidates that follow." I took that insight to heart. At forums when I spoke first, I would end my remarks by asking the others, "What do you think about the Alternative Program?" Candidates who were not already on the board knew very little about that proposal and its potential to end segregation. I was able to put them on the defensive and show that David and I were far more knowledgeable than the others.

Our teamwork paid off on election day. David was the top vote-getter out of six candidates with 69,519 votes; I came in second with 63,475. That victory said a lot to the black community, which previously had had only a smattering of success in electing people of color. Also elected that day was Richard Allen, an executive for the Bemis Company. The chairmanship of the board rotated every year. Replacing David after the 1969 election was

Stuart Rider Jr., an attorney who had been chair twice before. I was elected clerk of the board.

The board keenly felt two stress points as I began my first full term. Relations between the district and its two teachers unions were worsening and heading for a breaking point. And the need to find a politically acceptable way to desegregate city schools was rapidly becoming more urgent. I tried to be a conciliator in the first instance and a prod to action in the second.

Salaries were the central issue between teachers and the district. They were simply too low, unconscionably so. In 1969–1970, teachers' salaries in the city ranged between $6,760 and $15,555 a year. For years I had considered the teachers in Minneapolis schools underpaid. They were people of such talent and were so deserving of a decent standard of living. Through the 1960s, hard feelings had developed between the teachers unions' negotiating teams and the district's administration. But there was also mistrust between rank-and-file teachers and their unions, the Minnesota Federation of Teachers and the Minnesota Education Association. The reason for two unions claiming members in the Minneapolis schools is lost in the mists of history to me. What was clear was that the MFT was much closer to the city's Central Labor Union and the rest of organized labor. The MEA teachers saw themselves less as union members and more as members of a professional association. Nevertheless, at contract time, the MEA behaved like a union. The district insisted that the larger of the two, the MFT, bargain for both of them—a situation that left MEA teachers feeling excluded and insecure.

Negotiations went poorly in the winter and early spring of 1970. The MFT sought a strike authorization. In most years, that was a routine, saber-rattling step, but I sensed that this year was different. For one thing, the school board felt it had little financial wiggle room. In those years, public education was funded primarily through local property taxes. Significant state aid for public education did not begin to flow until 1972, after the so-called "Minnesota Miracle" was enacted in October 1971. Voters in Minneapolis were already up in arms about high property taxes. Mayor Charles Stenvig was elected in 1969 in part on an anti-property-tax platform. We were convinced that the voters would not stand for any more.

Being the board's clerk made me part of its negotiating team with the teachers. I worked to assemble an offer that went as far as I thought we dared go in salaries and sought to make up deficiencies in cash compensation with adjustments in benefits. That was acceptable to the MEA members, but not to the MFT. A strike began April 9, 1970. It would last fourteen days, long enough to create considerable inconvenience for families throughout the city and considerable stress on the seven members of the school board. We kept school doors open for two days after the strike began, hoping to give families extra time to find child-care arrangements. We couldn't afford to offer that service any longer, and we got no credit for doing that much. My home phone rang so often during the strike that I had to take it off the hook to get any sleep at night.

It was an arduous time for the whole board but particularly for Frank Adams. He was a Central Labor Union officer and had been a lifelong union member. Never did he expect to land on the management side of the table during contract negotiations, let alone a strike. But he was also a school-board veteran, having served from 1953 to 1962 and again since 1967. Rather than duck out of the firing line, Frank stood right with us in public; in private, he became our go-between to the unions. He made sure our messages got across to the right people. Frank had become my good friend during the 1969 campaign, when he helped David and me get union backing in my first school-board election. He was a fine public servant.

Many of our meetings during the strike occurred in the Minneapolis Public Schools administration building, which was being heavily picketed. We had to cross the picket line every time we went inside. It was not something I did lightly. My Teamster father had taught me to always respect a picket line. Besides, I was a labor-endorsed elected official. That meant something to me. So every time I entered that building, I felt I had to apologize to the picketers. "Look, we're getting close," I would say. "Don't feel insulted because we're walking across the picket line. We have to do that to settle the strike."

The state had not yet passed an open-meeting law, which left us free to meet at undisclosed places and times as well. We made the Minneapolis Club our private headquarters for hammering out offers to be presented to MFT negotiators. Stu Rider was much involved as chair of the board. So were David and I, as the board's designated negotiating team. Florence Lehmann and Richard Allen were also party to the bargaining. David and I were considered "pro-teacher" board members who were eager to assemble a package that would satisfy the MFT and end the strike. The offer that finally settled the strike was a financial reach, so much so that it mustered only a four-to-three vote by the board. But it put strife with our teachers behind us as we headed into a most challenging time.

The circumstances of that vote were a bit unusual. One morning during the strike, after an early-morning meeting with our negotiating team and legal people, I went to my office at the Urban Coalition. I had what I thought was a cold, but I could not think of taking a day off. I called my secretary into my office and began dictating a letter to the coalition board of directors. Suddenly, I passed out. My secretary yelled for other staff members to help revive me. I came to all of a sudden, but I had difficulty breathing. They called my doctor, Thomas Johnson at Mount Sinai Hospital, and he said, "Bring him in." I went to the Mount Sinai emergency room. There, I was almost the victim of a strange mix-up. On that day, methadone treatments were being administered to drug addicts at Mount Sinai. All that separated them from the emergency room was a drape. My cubicle was right next to the area where the methadone patients were served. My doctor examined me, and then he called a Dr. Cohn, a lung specialist from Glen Lake Hospital, a tuberculosis sanitarium. Together, they diagnosed my illness as a type of pneumonia and asked the nurse to get me some hospital clothing. I was to be admitted to the hospital. They left me alone to take off my street clothes. Just then, a nurse came in, then another. They had a little tray. I said, "Hi, how are you?" "Fine," they said. "Why are you taking off your clothing?" I said, "I'm going to be admitted to the hospital." The nurse said, "You mean to tell me you're not a methadone patient?" I said, "No." We laughed about their near mistake. But when I told Dr. Cohn what had happened, he became really upset. They could have had me higher than a kite. He made sure that the nurses apologized before I went upstairs.

The next thing I remember is being in a room, surrounded by an oxygen tent. I was pretty sick and not fully alert. The phone rang. It was David Preus. He said, "Harry, we've got a pretty close agreement on our offer." He had called my office and my staff had told him that I was in the hospital. He asked, "What are you doing in the hospital?" I said, "The doctor said I have pneumonia." He said, "What do you want me to do?" It occurred to me to ask him for a good Lutheran prayer. Instead, I said I would talk with my doctor about whether I could meet with my school-board colleagues and call David back. My doctor said, "We don't want all this strain on you. What we will allow is to have Bernie Kaye [the administration's representative on the negotiating team] and David Preus come here and explain to you what the deal is." That is what happened. We were indeed getting close to a deal. I suggested a response to the MFT offer that they took back to the teachers. I was in the hospital for four or five days. During that time, a steady parade to my bedside continued the negotiations. And that's where the final board vote took place, with all the board members in my hospital room as we agreed to a wage package that would boost average salaries by about $1,000 in the next year.

That vote ended the strike, but it did not put all of the hard feelings to rest. Some MEA members remained dissatisfied and did not immediately return to work with the rest of the teachers. They eventually filed a lawsuit challenging the MFT's authority to bargain on their behalf. It took almost five years to settle the suit and a generation to end the conflict once and for all. The MFT and MEA merged in 1998, becoming Education Minnesota.

Tense as the teachers strike had been, it was but a prelude to the real excitement soon to hit the city's schools. Now that the Southeast Alternative Program had been launched with federal funds, it was time for the next step. On November 24, 1970, we unveiled a proposal that the *Minneapolis Star* later called "an educational Pearl Harbor for the Minneapolis School Board." We presented what we hoped would be seen as a modest start to citywide school desegregation. Among other things, it would "pair," or merge, almost all-white Hale School with predominantly black Field School, both elementary schools on the city's South Side. Grades kindergarten through three would attend Hale; grades four through six would be at Field. The neighborhoods surrounding the two schools were much alike aside from race. On the economic ladder, they were the same. The parents had the same aspirations for their children. The vast majority of families expected to send their kids to college. We thought starting with such similar schools so closely situated would be reasonably well received. Instead, the reaction was explosive. That November 24 meeting lasted five stormy hours. Afterward, police followed both John B. Davis and me to our homes and guarded us through the night. Once again, the phone had to be taken off the hook. As David Preus told a reporter later, none of us board members was particularly eager for "noble martyrdom."

But we knew what the citizens who opposed us did not: a federal judge was soon going to insist that Minneapolis schools be integrated. That was the pattern that had been started in 1954 with the U.S. Supreme Court's landmark ruling on a school-segregation lawsuit in Topeka, Kansas, *Brown v. Board of Education.* In the intervening years, the courts had stuck to their guns. Segregated schools violated the equal-protection clause of the U.S. Constitution and would not be allowed to stand.

The lawsuit that led to a court order was filed by the Minneapolis NAACP in 1970. Sam Richardson succeeded me as president; he was followed by A. Matthew Little. Both made integration of Minneapolis schools a top priority. They knew, as I did, that it was not the policy of Minneapolis schools to enroll students in particular schools because of the color of their skin. There was no Governor Orval Faubus in Minnesota standing in the school doorway, keeping black students out. But the schools clung to a geographic enrollment model, and the geography of Minneapolis was highly segregated. Schools in affluent parts of the city had no black students because the neighborhoods they served had no black residents. It was prima facie segregation, and John B. Davis and the school board knew it. I supported the NAACP's suit, even though being a school-board member made me one of the defendants. I agreed that it was time to force the issue of race in Minneapolis schools and only a lawsuit would make that happen. I said as much at NAACP meetings. I also advised my chapter that it need not stage demonstrations and protests to pressure the school board into action. I assured them that the board was already moving in the right direction and that we would comply with any reasonable court order.

Shortly after the suit was filed, the district's attorneys received a quiet word from the federal courthouse that we would be allowed to express a preference for which of the state's three federal judges would decide the suit and oversee the implementation of any ordered change. I was involved in a conversation at the Minneapolis Club about which of the judges we would rather have, Edward Devitt, Miles Lord, or Earl Larson. Of the three, Larson was the only native of Minneapolis and graduate of Minneapolis schools. His parents still lived in the Minneapolis area. He had not been a rich kid. He was known to be very interested in education. We thought he would give us sympathetic oversight. Through channels, we asked that the case be assigned to Judge Larson.

The first meeting of the school board, district administrators, representatives of the teachers federation, and Judge Larson confirmed our opinion that we had the right judge. We met in his chambers in the old Federal Building on Fourth Street downtown. His manner was friendly and informal. He came in smiling, sat down, and said, "Good morning. How are ya? We're going to be together for a while. I'm sure that we can make things happen in Minneapolis. I'm an old Minneapolis public-school kid. Everything I am, the position I have, is because I had some good teachers in the Minneapolis schools. We're not going to have a hard time getting along."

Superintendent Davis explained the Southeast Alternative Program and his idea for desegregating the schools by implementing a similar plan citywide. The judge reacted positively. He then told us, "I'm not here to run the school board. I'm here to make sure you desegregate and integrate that system with an educational program that will benefit our kids. I'll keep your foot to the fire on that. When you come in with a plan that does that for those kids, you're not going to have any problems with me. I don't want to be the superintendent of the schools. I do want to make sure that you get your job done." Referring to the Southeast Alternative Program, he said, "It looks like you've started already."

We knew that implementing something like the Southeast menu of curricular choices citywide was going to be difficult. Where would we find all the Montessori teachers we would need, and who would license them to teach in public schools? How would we train enough teachers to meet parent demand for the "open" and continuous-progress curricula? How would we put the various curricula within the geographic reach of every family in the city? How would we handle families with several children, who wanted all of them in the same school? John had answers. He proposed to divide the city into three zones—north, east, and west—and put a superintendent in each zone, which would have the full gamut of curricular choices included within its boundaries. Secondary students would have the choice of a traditional curriculum, an open curriculum, and magnet programs emphasizing particular aspects of the curriculum, such as fine arts or math and science. Each school would have a program designed to attract students who lived outside that school's traditional geographic boundaries. The old boundaries would no longer rigidly determine attendance. Funding to implement the change would come in part from business sponsors.

Logistically, we knew we had a challenge on our hands. We also saw that we had before us a big public education job. What none of us fully appreciated was the extent to which we had a political challenge before us as well. If I had gauged public opinion more accurately at the start of 1971, I might not have announced my candidacy for mayor.

16
Candidate

MY WORK WITH THE MOER BOARD, the Urban Coalition, the school board, and Golden Gloves gave me definite ideas about city leadership. I became quite familiar with the issues that were dividing people in Minneapolis and developed a sense of what it would take to bring them together. The various camps were not that far apart, it seemed to me. Despite the hostile rhetoric and the violence on Plymouth Avenue, most people in the city had the common goal of a decent, prosperous life for everybody of all races. They were all talking about the same things: high-quality education, affordable housing, plentiful living-wage jobs. I learned that the people disrupting meetings and threatening the peace often acted that way because they did not really understand the other side's position. Similarly, those who were so critical of militant blacks did not see that the protesters' goals were reasonable, even if their methods were not. I thought it should be quite possible for Minneapolis people to get along and achieve their mutual goals, especially if they had a mayor who understood that conciliation is a big part of leadership.

Unfortunately, the 1969 election had not given Minneapolis such a mayor. Art Naftalin had stepped down because of ill health. He discussed his decision with me and said he hoped that people he had put in visible positions in the city, people like me, would consider running to take his place. I noticed that, as his health failed, he consulted with me more often. I had the sense he was grooming me to climb the next rung. But circumstances landed me on the school board in 1969 and on the ballot to keep that seat in the 1969 election. I decided that school-board membership was my rightful role in city leadership—that year, anyway.

But I could not help but be disheartened as I watched the 1969 mayoral race unfold. The one DFLer in the race, City Council member Gerard Hegstrom, was knocked out in the primary. The two candidates on the June ballot were Dan Cohen, the Republican president of the City Council, and Charlie Stenvig, a political independent and the vocal president of the Minneapolis Police Federation. I did not hold either of them in high regard. Cohen and I had tangled over the appointment of Ron Edwards to the Minneapolis Human Rights Commission in 1968. And Stenvig and I had clashed over the handling of the Plymouth Avenue disturbances and the use of civilian watchdogs to keep the peace in black neighborhoods in the spring and summer of 1968. Both were loose cannons. Neither had been an ally of Naftalin. Neither made achieving equal opportunity a top priority. But I considered Cohen the more intelligent and responsible candidate. While I did not publicly take sides in the race, I cast my own vote for Cohen. The campaign turned on Stenvig's tough-talking calls for law and order in the streets and lower property taxes. The city's blue-collar neighborhoods—traditional DFL territory—pushed Stenvig over the top.

For the people who favored Art Naftalin's kind of leadership, Stenvig was a disappointment. He initiated virtually no programs or new policies and stood in the way of much of what the City Council initiated. He made liberal use of the mayoral veto. He made no overtures toward either the business community or the city's minorities. Politically, he was something of a loner. Nevertheless, Stenvig was popular. Like another popular Minnesota political figure a generation later, Governor Jesse Ventura, Stenvig was admired for his plain talk and his independence. But in contrast to Ventura, Stenvig based his appeal on a defense of the status quo at a time when many people were fearful of change.

Of course, my business was change—positive change for the poor and minority communities of the city. That is what the MOER Board and the Urban Coalition were all about. That is what drove the school board to a policy of racial integration. The people pushing for change fell into two camps: one might call them conservative and liberal. The business community, which was on the conservative side, wanted change to come through regular channels. The more liberal side, most evident in the black community, agitated for immediate action.

As different as the two camps were, I recognized that they were talking about the same things. I was close to both camps, and I believed it should be possible to bring them together. Many times I found myself in conversations that would go like this: "Here are our goals. They're your goals and the other side's goals too. There may be a little different route that you'll want to take than the other side, but the result is the same. Now, how do you want to get that done? Do you want to get that done ten years from now, or in three or four years?" The black community's answer was always, "We want it right now." That was not realistic. But neither was inaction. Initiatives had to be started to end the segregation of public schools and other injustices. Much of the political discussion in Minneapolis in those years boiled down to a question of how soon progress could come. I worked to find an answer both near-term and realistic. I became increasingly aware I was in a unique position. I believed I was there for a reason. That sense was at the root of my desire to run for mayor.

Another attraction of the mayor's office was the chance it afforded to improve relations between the Minneapolis police force and the black community. For generations, cops ignored the North Side and vigilante justice ruled. That changed when Hubert Humphrey was mayor, and by the late 1960s the police had discovered my old neighborhood at Sixth and Lyndale Avenues North with a vengeance. Complaints of police harassment and brutality toward black people were commonplace and on the rise during Stenvig's term. Meanwhile, some blacks noted that when skinheads or aggressive white kids came to the North Side to make trouble, cops looked the other way. Stenvig was allied with an element in the city police force that was viewed with suspicion and hostility by many in the black community. His rhetoric in his 1969 campaign was telling. He kept saying he was going to go into north Minneapolis and make sure there would be no more riots by putting lawbreakers behind bars. He implied that the only place harboring criminals was north Minneapolis.

After Stenvig's election, he and I publicly clashed over his approval of new police policies for the discharge of firearms. The change gave the police more latitude in their gun use. I thought just the opposite was needed. I had been working closely with the police force, along with Gleason Glover and Josie Johnson of the Urban League, to teach race-sensitive policing to rookie cops, many of whom were recruited from all-white rural Minnesota. Our training sessions were arranged by police chief Don Dwyer, a very good chief, and were tolerated by the police federation. While Stenvig did not publicly object to our classes, he did not attend them either, as he might have while he was still in the police force. My sense was that he was less than fully committed to fair policing in the city's black neighborhoods.

By the late fall of 1970, one other issue—school desegregation—put Stenvig and me at odds. I strongly supported Superintendent John B. Davis's plan for using school pairing and curricular choice to desegregate the city's schools. I was offended when Stenvig's campaign started playing the demagogue with the issue. He and his wife, Audrey, and their vocal ally, WLOL Radio talk-show host Paul Helm, were outspoken opponents of the plan. They said things like, "Minneapolis is no Little Rock. There isn't going to be any integration here." That was stupid. The NAACP was about to file a desegregation suit in federal court. Once a federal judge issued an order, the school board would be in no position to resist, no matter what the mayor said. Stenvig's camp wanted people to believe that the district's plans would force the long-distance busing of children, deprive regular instruction of financial support, and send property taxes soaring. None of those charges was true. Classroom and transportation funding came from separate sources and could not be mingled. But when the mayor made a claim, it was hard to refute.

Stenvig remained unaligned with the major political parties in 1971, but his supporters had coalesced into something they called the T Party. T stood for "taxpayers," they said, but it was also supposed to be reminiscent of the Boston Tea Party of 1773, when rebellious colonists dumped tea into the Boston harbor rather than pay a despised British tax. The T Party claimed opposition to high property taxes as a key issue, which I found curious, since Stenvig had done little about property taxation as mayor. In the winter and spring of 1971, property-tax policy was the marquee issue at the state legislature. DFL governor Wendell Anderson had put forward a bold plan for state taxes to replace a large share of the local property taxes that paid for school costs. I supported his idea. In fact, I was willing to go one step further and seek legislative authority to place a city surtax on the state income tax to allow for an even bigger reduction in property taxes. For months, Stenvig made no public comment on either Anderson's idea or mine. When he did take up the issue, it was with an incoherent proposal for eliminating property taxes altogether. It was plain to me that Charlie didn't know what he was talking about. I thought voters would see his ignorance too.

Stenvig's third party seemed much more interested in blocking school integration than in changing tax policy. Only two of the seven school-board seats were up for election that year. The T Party candidates for the seats were Marilyn Borea and Phil Olson, both serious contenders. They did a lot of Charlie's dirty work for him. When the school board held open meetings to allow the public a chance to testify, T Party people would pack the auditorium. One of those meetings, at the old Vocational High School, lasted twelve hours, from 5:00 p.m. until 5:00 a.m., as we tried to accommodate all those who demanded to speak. Our only restriction was a three-minute limit per speaker. We heard the same speech, over and over again. Some speakers made a point of walking close to me and muttering obscenities. At one point, a man sneaked along the side of the room and ran up on stage. As he got close to me, he spit. He missed me, and to his surprise, a plainclothes police officer came out from behind a curtain and hauled him away. The police then warned the audience that anyone else who tried to climb onto the stage would be arrested. That was indicative of the quality of public discourse that the T Party brought to the city.

Stenvig himself seldom spoke directly on the school issue—or on any issue, for that matter. For all his popular appeal, he was not much of a public speaker. He seldom gave interviews to reporters. He operated with news releases and surrogates. But his allies kept the school issue at the center of the mayoral campaign. I didn't run away from the issue; after all, it was among my reasons for opposing Stenvig. But I also knew that if the election turned on the school issue alone, I would lose. To fearful white people, school integration meant black people moving next door, dating their children, exposing them to crime. Fear was the hallmark of city politics in 1971. It put me on the defensive.

I could not run away from my race, either. But in the first interview I gave in November 1970 as a potential mayoral candidate, I made clear my desire to be defined in terms other than the color of my skin. "If I do run, I'm not running as a 'black candidate.' I want that to be well understood. I'm going to be identified with my qualifications and my record," I told the *Tribune*'s Dean Rebuffoni, in the hope that I could make it so.

Most of my early backers were people in the business community whom I had come to know through the Urban Coalition. Almost from the start of Stenvig's term in 1969, business leaders said they wanted to find someone to run against him in 1971, someone they trusted and who had proven voter appeal. They were aware that in my run for the school board, I had received both DFL and Republican endorsement and had come in second behind David Preus in votes. I also had labor's backing in 1969. My backers thought I could put together that coalition again. If I could, it would be a formidable array against an independent, even if he were the incumbent. Several times, members of the Urban Coalition board said to me, "Harry, you're the one who ought to challenge Charlie Stenvig." I had encouragement from business leaders Steve Keating, Dean McNeal, Sandy Bemis, Fran Van Konynenburg, Bower Hawthorne, and Les Parks, my old friend from Hennepin Church who had become head of Baker Properties. They gave me seed money and a leave of absence from the coalition presidency at half salary. With that evidence of support in hand, I announced my candidacy on January 19, 1971. As I did, however, I could not help but notice that many of my more prominent supporters lived in the suburbs, not the city, and would not be voting in the June 8 city election.

The most important encouragement I received came from Charlotte. She was always in my corner, as committed as I was to advancing racial equality. But she was also a busy mother and grandmother. Evan turned three in 1971, and Ricky was in high school. Charlotte was used to managing the home front and she was good at it, but for the children's sake, she would often say, "Harry, you've got to spend some time at home." One night, Evan was drowsing on her lap as they watched the local TV news. I had not yet come home because of one of our protracted school-board meetings. The news included a sound bite of me speaking. She roused him and said, "Look, there's your daddy. That's probably the only time you'll see him today."

My work was spilling into our home in some unpleasant ways. Even before I became a candidate for mayor, I would get hateful anonymous phone calls at home at all hours. They were more annoying than frightening. The opposition to school desegregation here was never as violent as it had been in other parts of the country. None of our meetings got as ugly as the MOER Board meetings had. We always had police officers present at the school-board meetings should anything ugly arise. I was pretty confident that the police would be able to control any disturbance and that Charlie Stenvig, who ran on a promise of law and order, was not going to incite anybody to lawlessness.

The hateful calls stepped up when I became a candidate for mayor and were more threatening. I began to worry about my family's safety. I asked for police protection. Starting several months before the election, I had squad cars around my house at all hours of the day and night. I had a bodyguard who followed me wherever I went. The police asked Ricky to ride in a squad car to school, even though we lived within walking distance of Central High. He hated the idea, but he did it. When Charlotte took Evan to Montessori school in a church on Forty-second Street and Lyndale Avenue, a squad car followed her there and back. The fact that the police seemed to be taking the threatening calls so seriously made us nervous. Officers warned us about crazy people who could strike against us at any time. They offered me a permit to carry a gun, but I resisted the idea. "There's no use of me carrying a gun if I don't know who is going to be shooting at me," I said. "I don't have an equal chance. I'd just be a dead man with a gun in my hand or in my pocket. I can be dead without it." Then I added, "If you think I'm in such danger that I need a gun, you need to get me more protection."

Not long after that, an FBI agent, a black man, was assigned to guard us. The local police said they invited the FBI to take over because I was receiving hate mail from out-of-state places like Racine and Eau Claire, Wisconsin.

But I also suspected that the police lost interest in protecting me after I issued a campaign statement saying that if I became mayor, I would make the police department look more like the citizens of Minneapolis. It would be an integrated department. That didn't sit well with certain local men in blue. It was right after I made those statements that I was given an FBI bodyguard. The FBI's involvement gave us some reassurance. The agent was very kind. He would say, "Don't worry, we're here. You may not see us, but we're here." We would look out our window every night toward Thirty-sixth Street and Portland Avenue, on the west side of the street, and see one or more cars with their parking lights on. We liked knowing that car was there for us.

For a time, I got a menacing phone call every morning before I went to work. My pattern was to drive east on Thirty-seventh Street and north on Chicago Avenue to downtown Minneapolis. On the corner of Thirty-sixth and Chicago stood a pizza place with a big billboard on its roof. The voice on the phone generally said something like, "Good morning, Nigger Mayor, which you're never going to be, because when you go by Thirty-sixth and Chicago today, we're going to shoot you through the head. We're going to kill you and your wife is going to be a widow." Needless to say, those calls were upsetting.

My FBI bodyguard was soothing. He said, "Mr. Davis, don't worry. We'll take care of that. There won't be anyone in a recognizable uniform, but we'll be there." The police and FBI who arranged to stake out the corner met with me and laid out a plan: "Mr. Davis, when he calls tomorrow, say to him, 'Now that you're going to kill me, let's see how brave you are. Yesterday, the police permitted me to get a gun, and I bought a .45 automatic. You've got a high-powered rifle. Let's see if you've got guts enough to stand from behind that billboard and face me.'" The FBI agent said, "Now, don't worry," as he gave me a bulletproof vest to wear. "If he is there, we'll get him before he raises his hand." I delivered the message the next day as I was told. Sure enough, no one called my bluff. No bullets flew at Thirty-sixth and Chicago that morning or any other morning during the campaign.

But the calls continued for weeks thereafter. The tactic changed, with the callers threatening to blow up my house. In response, the FBI installed a security system and also brought two guard dogs to the house, a female German shepherd and a male half-German shepherd and half-husky. The female dog would stay inside the house and the male would sleep outside, even in the snow and cold. The idea was that if anyone approached the house from the outside, the male dog would warn the dog on the inside. She would in turn get our attention, so we could trigger the alarm and summon the police. The callers were quickly aware of the dogs' presence. "You've got two dogs," the voice said one morning. "You'll soon have two dead dogs. We're going to shoot those dogs." Other callers would say, "The police that are walking around your house are not your friends. The guard you've got is not your friend." The most frightening call came the day Ricky was representing Central High School in a regional track meet at Macalester College in St. Paul. The caller said, "I understand Central High School won the city track meet and you're going over to Macalester to watch your kid run. That's a wide-open place there. What if we shoot Ricky as he wins the track meet? Don't you think it's time that you just give up?"

Miserable as the calls made all of us, they were particularly hard on Charlotte. At home all day, she took some of the worst of them. She also was more affected by the measures we had to take to protect ourselves. The dogs were her daily companions and a huge attraction for Evan and our grandson, Corey. Fortunately, the dogs loved kids. Those little boys could do anything to those dogs and the dogs would happily take it. There was never a growl or a snap. Still, the boys were only two and three years old and the dogs were large. They could mow the boys down. One day, when the boys were in the backyard with the dogs, Evan suddenly ran in to the house, calling, "Mama, Mama, where's the paper?" Charlotte said, "It's right over there. What do you want the newspaper for?" Evan said, "Shep's got Corey down and I've got to whip her with the paper!" Shep, the female dog, had knocked Corey flat and was still playfully licking him as Charlotte raced outside.

People often asked me during the campaign what it was like to be the first black person to run with major-party backing for mayor. I always answered in positive terms, reflecting on the fact that running for city office seemed an impossible dream when I was a child, and recalling Hubert Humphrey's offhand remark in 1945 encouraging me to be politically active. I could also have mentioned that a bodyguard was at my side and the reason he was there, but I never did.

I was the choice of the DFL Party's nominating committee, headed that year by attorney Ellis Olkon. He helped persuade other possible candidates to stand aside. It was his judgment that only a united DFL front had any chance of defeating Stenvig. By the time of the February 20 endorsing convention, the only opponents I had were a political gadfly named Hal Krieger—and Stenvig himself. Though still an independent, Stenvig was popular among blue-collar DFLers. His presidency of the police officers' union gave him an edge with labor. Though he didn't offer himself as a candidate for DFL endorsement, he got 16 percent of the vote on the first ballot. That, combined with Krieger's vote, was enough to keep me from being endorsed until the second ballot. Still, I had substantial backing from the party. Even labor activist Nellie Stone Johnson, who had always considered me too conservative, worked for my endorsement and election.

I flirted with the idea of trying again to have Republican endorsement too, as I had for the school-board election in 1969. But the only way the leaders of that party would have me is if I shunned the DFL, which I would not do. So the Republicans backed Bruce Rasmussen, a young attorney and electrical engineer who was executive secretary of the Minnesota Municipal Commission. He was not well known in city politics.

In most city elections, DFL and labor endorsement go hand in hand, but that was not the case for me. Even before the party's convention, the city's Teamsters Union—my dad's union—endorsed Stenvig. That hurt. Less than a week after the convention, the city's Central Labor Union Council also went with Stenvig. I was told afterward that my friend Dave Roe had tried to block the endorsement, but that Danny Gustafson, who eventually would succeed Roe as president of the state AFL-CIO, was firm for Stenvig. That the city's building trades were cool to minority membership likely had something to do with the endorsement. The *Minneapolis Star*'s Jim Shoop quoted an anonymous labor leader saying as much: "Let's face it. The color thing had a lot to do with it."

The loss of labor support was a major blow to my campaign. Still, I persevered. I told reporters I was an old boxer and had learned in the squared ring that it's staying power that wins matches. With good advice from my campaign manager, Steve Keefe, soon to be a state senator, and my steering committee—Mary Ann Scroggins, Bea Doerr, and many others—I set out to make the most of the advantages I did have. I knew that the black community, even the militant wing that had been critical of me, was behind my candidacy. But I also knew that too many black people were not registered to vote. Those were the years before election-day registration. No one could vote unless his or her name was on the rolls as of a date several weeks before the election. So a big voter-registration push was launched by some of the organizations that knew me well—the NAACP, the Urban League, and Phyllis Wheatley and Sabathani Community Centers. I headed the boards of directors of both Phyllis Wheatley and Sabathani in those years. Scores of people helped with our registration campaign. I like to think that my campaign made voters out of nonvoters for many elections to come.

I was popular among young people within the DFL, and that inspired my campaign committee to recruit college students as volunteers. The civil-rights movement and the Vietnam War had attuned many students to politics and inspired a willingness to get involved. I visited campuses in both Minneapolis and St. Paul—Macalester, Augsburg, Hamline, Concordia, the University of Minnesota—to introduce myself and ask for help. Often I spoke to political-science classes. My pitch seemed particularly effective at Macalester. Students from that St. Paul college started showing up regularly at my campaign headquarters in the old Produce Bank Building in downtown Minneapolis. They would be available to distribute signs and literature, stuff envelopes, make phone calls, and do whatever else needed doing. We had little stickers reading "I'm just wild about Harry" that they plastered all over town. Some nights we had more students than we could fit into our cramped headquarters.

I was still Upper Midwest director of the Golden Gloves boxing program and had just completed a term as the organization's national president. My boxers, past and present, were in my corner. They put on a couple of boxing shows to benefit my campaign.

I had the advantage of some national publicity. Not many big northern cities had black mayors yet in 1971, a fact that was to change in the decade ahead. The novelty of my bid caught the attention of the civil-rights movement nationally and helped me snare the inestimable singer Mahalia Jackson for a benefit concert organized by the musicians' union, which supported me for mayor. The union included members who were Minneapolis public-school music teachers and who had seen me as an ally in the 1970 teachers strike. It was a thrill meeting Mahalia Jackson, who was the headliner at what was called the Weekend Jazz Festival for Harry Davis. It started Friday night at the old Labor Temple building downtown and lasted through Sunday. The school food-service workers' union supplied the festival's food, which was great. The music was incredible. We had all of the big entertainers in the city and Mahalia Jackson to boot. It was the biggest single fund-raising event for my campaign and a lot of fun.

My campaign did not lack for money. In all, I raised $52,000—a fair amount by 1971 standards. My friends in the business community were generous supporters.

Another advantage I thought I had was in public speaking. Stenvig seldom gave speeches and repeatedly refused to debate. I was no Hubert Humphrey, but I was willing and able to address a crowd. Mary Ann Scroggins, who was married to the *Tribune*'s fine-arts writer, Will Jones, and my Urban Coalition allies arranged special training for me to improve my effectiveness. Business leaders Phil Harder and Dean McNeal took me to the Old Log Theatre in Dean's car one day for a coaching session with the theater's founder and legendary director, Don Stolz, who said, "Harry, I'm going to give you some issues, and I want you to get up on the stage and speak to those issues. We're going to sit in the audience, and we're going to say whether you impressed us or not." We spent several hours with that kind of back and forth. They critiqued both my speaking style and the substance of my arguments. For example, they encouraged me to point out that the only way the mayor can control property taxes is through his influence with the state legislature and the city council. You have to have a mayor who has the confidence of the legislature and can work with the city council. Stenvig was failing on both counts. They liked my comments about the opportunity Minneapolis had to lead the nation with a new model for school integration. The Minneapolis School Board plan would keep busing to a minimum and improve educational opportunities for all children. Don encouraged me not to speak standing still, but to move as I spoke. He had me talk directly to first this individual, then that one, to look them right in the eye, point to them, and make as many personal connections as I could. I knew just what he was saying. It's the technique black preachers use to get people in a congregation to respond "Amen!" I discovered that it's fun to speak that way. When that day ended, I was a more confident speaker.

I accepted every possible invitation to appear at candidate forums and meetings. Sometimes I wound up debating an empty chair. Stenvig and I had five joint appearances over a five-month campaign but only two were genuine debates. The first, on May 16, was a fairly tame exchange before 150 people at St. Helena's Catholic Church, at East Forty-third Street and Thirty-third Avenue South, a Stenvig-friendly working-class neighborhood. The livelier second debate, sponsored by the League of Women Voters in south-central Minneapolis, at Mayflower Church, drew more than 250 people. Charlie came armed with a large three-ring notebook and accompanied by Paul Helm of WLOL, who claimed he was there as a journalist. A lot of other people were part of Stenvig's entourage. We began with brief prepared presentations, then took questions from the audience. Many questions came from Charlie's supporters, all wanting to talk about school busing. He had his lines memorized about that. But when he got a question he didn't expect, he would start fumbling through his big notebook for an answer. More than once, a kid sent by Paul Helm would run up behind us and whisper something in Charlie's ear. I thought it was a sorry display of ignorance by a man who already had been mayor for two years.

The central question that night, as it was throughout the campaign, was,

"What would you do if the federal courts ordered the Minneapolis school system to bus children for school desegregation?" Stenvig boasted, "I would override the court's order. There is some doubt that the law says you have to have mandatory busing to have integration." It was a ridiculous answer, but the crowd loved it. A great roar went up. When I was asked for my response, I said, "You must understand that the Minneapolis school district may be an independent district, but it is a part of government. Our federal government has preemptive authority over the fifty states. The United States Supreme Court has ordered the federal courts to make sure that schools around the country be racially balanced. If it takes busing to get racial balance, that has to be done. We have the option: we either desegregate our school system or the court will order it. We would rather not wait to be directed. My concern is the children of the city of Minneapolis. I know, as a member of the school board, that we have plans that will give parents choices and that will not require that busing be done all over the city. I would say this: If you had been discriminated against and the federal government says that it's time to end that, if the shoe was on the other foot, you wouldn't be making these statements. The mayor of Minneapolis must understand that he's the mayor of all the people, all the children, regardless of the color of their skin. He has to carry out a federal court order. If I'm elected mayor, that's what I will do."

The response? A few hisses and only a smattering of applause. The room was warm and crowded, and the tension between Stenvig supporters and my supporters was palpable. It suddenly occurred to me that this debate could have an ugly ending and that I ought to say something to defuse the situation. So at my next opportunity to speak, I said, "I hope that we don't allow this campaign to get into a confrontation. Whoever you elect as the mayor is going to be the mayor of all of us, whether we like it or not. If you don't like me and I'm elected mayor, I'm going to be your mayor. The same goes for Charlie Stenvig. This debate is not intended to be a contest of power or strength. It's just a chance for you to hear each of us answer the questions you have and for you to see which person you want to be mayor." On my way out of the room that night, a couple of Stenvig supporters spit at me.

I had plenty of chances to repeat my speech. My leave of absence from the Urban Coalition gave me time to speak to various groups and to campaign door-to-door in city neighborhoods. I enjoyed door-knocking. It was especially fun in my old North Side neighborhood. People were so happy to see me. Fathers and mothers would call their children to the doors. "This is the man on the school board who is running for mayor," they would say. They wanted their children to know that someone whose color matched theirs could do such a thing.

The controversy surrounding the pairing of the Hale and Field schools made my reception in south Minneapolis more unpredictable. Because of all the meetings that proposal produced, I had met a lot of people in the south-central area of the city. I never knew when I approached a doorstep whether I would get a warm or a hostile reception. But when the response was negative, I used the moment to do a little educating. I tried to counter some of the widely circulated misinformation about what we were trying to do with the schools. I considered those valuable stops, even if they did not win me votes.

As the campaign progressed, my campaign committee urged me to spend more time in northeast Minneapolis. We were running way behind there, in an area that DFLers could usually count on for support. My committee arranged for a candidates' meeting at a junior high school. I went expecting the worst, but it went surprisingly well. My school-board colleague Frank Adams, a union official, introduced me. Stenvig did not appear. I let myself hope that my committee was wrong and that not all the DFLers in "Nordeast" had abandoned me.

But the accuracy of the committee's assessment became apparent as I knocked on doors in that part of the city and had many slammed in my face. I was called plenty of impolite names. But I was not bereft of all support. After only a few days of that treatment, I was called by one of the city's prominent DFLers, Bob Short. The big Irishman owned several hotels, including the Leamington and the Nicollet. Bob said, "I'd like to have you come down to the Nicollet Hotel. I'm going to have some people there to talk to you." I appeared as requested, and found Senator Hubert Humphrey waiting for me. He said, "Harry, I heard that you've had some problems in northeast Minneapolis. Don't let that upset you. You're going to find some people in Northeast who are going to really get behind you." After a moment, Don Fraser, the city's DFL congressman, also joined us. He was very supportive of what the school board was trying to do. He too gave me pointers and encouragement.

Later that day, I was back on the streets of northeast Minneapolis. My reception was cool, but not as hostile as it had been in previous days. I had stopped at only a few houses when a car pulled up alongside me. Out of it jumped Hubert Humphrey and Don Fraser, who said, "Harry, we're coming to give you some help." They offered to go with me and introduce me at each door as their choice for mayor. They spent the rest of that afternoon with me and the next day too, doing just that. Hubert then had to go back to Washington, but Don stayed with me several more days. It may have been the nicest gesture I ever witnessed in political life.

Don and Hubert made several other joint appearances with me that spring, and Don and Governor Anderson taped radio commercials on my behalf. They gave me a big boost at a time when I was smarting from the refusal of some city DFL candidates to support me. Alderman Sam Sivanich of the First Ward was openly backing Stenvig. One of the kids I had coached, John Derus, seeking to unseat incumbent Mark Anderson in the Fourth Ward, kept his distance while giving me tacit backing. That was their privilege, of course. But it bothered me that my campaign was paying for the city DFL sample ballot that helped all of them, including those who didn't support me. It also bothered me that well-informed public officials, people who knew how bogus was the rhetoric coming from the Stenvig campaign, would still support him.

The April 27 primary was a harbinger of what was to come. It narrowed the field of seven candidates to two, Stenvig and me. But the numbers weren't close. Stenvig got more than forty-nine thousand votes; my total was just under twenty thousand. Charlie carried every ward in the city. A cold rain on election day dampened turnout, or so I said to explain my poor showing. Rasmussen, the Republican candidate, divided the pro-integration vote with me, but he got only about eight thousand votes. I knew that my general-election prospects were not good.

A few weeks later, a *Minneapolis Star* Metro Poll predicted that I would lose by a devastating three-to-one margin. The same poll found that, despite all the talk about school desegregation, the issue most important to voters was the same one that catapulted Stenvig into office in the first place: law and order. I was hearing it as I knocked on doors around the city. One elderly lady in a senior citizens high-rise asked, "How are you going to protect us if you're not in charge of the police?" Many people did not understand that the police force is answerable to the mayor, no matter who that mayor may be. They had been led to believe by Charlie's campaign that only he, as a former police officer, could provide adequate public safety. In response, I stepped up my attacks on Stenvig's administration of the police. While he was concentrating on Plymouth Avenue, I charged, the illegal drug trade in Minneapolis was burgeoning. Moreover, I said, Stenvig was lax in responding to legitimate citizen complaints about police brutality.

Despite my gloomy prospects, both the *Minneapolis Star* and the *Minneapolis Tribune* editorially urged voters to elect me. The *Tribune*'s endorsement said, in part, "Through a lifetime of work in community affairs, Davis has obtained a broad knowledge of city problems that could help him become an effective mayor. Davis would take a more aggressive leadership role in helping Minneapolis solve its problems." The *Star*'s endorsement editorial used a boxing analogy. It said I had "employed an aggressive, sometimes daring attack on Mayor Charles Stenvig, trying to draw the incumbent into a free-swinging exchange on the issues. . . . The betting at ringside is overwhelming that Stenvig will unleash his knockout punch at the polls Tuesday. Yet Davis has managed to accumulate enough points, according to the recent Star Metro Poll, to convince 61 percent of the voters that he would be a good mayor. We urge those who think so to give Davis their vote in Tuesday's election, so the better man may win."

In so many ways, it was a wonderful campaign. We did so many things right and rallied so many fine people to our side. We struck down a racial barrier and helped assuage people's fear about school integration. We brought white and black people together in a way that no previous citywide campaign had. I felt like a fighter, in good shape and pumped up for the next round, when the family gathered in their Sunday best at the Nicollet Hotel on election night. We had dinner there before the usual election party. In addition to Charlotte and the children, my brother, Menzy, and sister Dooney were there. There were also two empty seats at the table. That was Charlotte's surprise. Just as I began to wonder who was missing, in walked Ray and Mae Hatcher. My old Phyllis Wheatley coach and mentor had come all the way from Detroit to be with me that night. It was wonderful to share the evening with them. The mood was festive. "Harry Davis for Mayor" signs were everywhere. I had both a victory and a concession speech written and in my pocket. It was hard to believe this was the end.

But the evidence was in hand soon enough. Stenvig was reelected with more than 70 percent of the vote. He had carried every ward. The contest was closest in the affluent Seventh Ward, the university-dominated Second Ward, and the Fifth Ward, my old North Side neighborhood. But I got clobbered in the blue-collar neighborhoods. The polls had been closed for less than two hours when I decided it was time to pull the concession speech out of my pocket. Charlotte stood beside me and the family stood behind me as I spoke. Ray and Mae took their places with the family, as was fitting. In front of me, sitting on the floor in a tight semicircle, were perhaps a hundred of the students who had been volunteers in my campaign. I had a great feeling of gratitude to those students for the time and effort they donated. I know that a good speaker looks right at his audience, but I could not look for long at those dejected students. I was aware that some of the girls were crying. After I was through speaking and the TV lights were off, one tearstained girl came up to me and said, "Oh, Mr. Davis, I so wish that you could have been mayor. You would have been a great mayor." I replied, "One of the things that you have to remember is that you never know unless you try. When you try, you've got to be able to accept the disappointment of losing. Who knows? This may be the part of your life that sets the stage for you. Who knows? Someday you may be mayor."

That girl's name was Sharon Sayles. Twenty-two years later, as Sharon Sayles Belton, she was elected mayor of Minneapolis—the first African American mayor in the city's history. During her 1993 election-night victory speech, she called me to the podium and told her supporters about our exchange on June 8, 1971.

For a while afterward, I felt that Minneapolis showed its true colors in the 1971 mayoral election—and those colors were unattractive. But in time I came to understand that my campaign caught the crest of a wave of fear that would rapidly subside. All the turmoil surrounding the civil-rights movement and the opposition to the war in Vietnam in the late 1960s had produced a full-blown backlash by the spring of 1971. The nation had come to the brink of revolution, many people felt, and had to be pulled back, even if it meant failing to educate our children in a way consistent with the U.S. Constitution. I tried to say in the campaign that Minnesotans had no reason to be afraid. We are intelligent enough to understand that the Constitution means equal protection for every American citizen, not just the citizens of one color. We are creative enough to find a way to extend equality of opportunity to all, without doing a disservice to the majority. It did not happen in time for me to be elected mayor. But within a relatively short time, that message got through.

I came to believe that more came out of my campaign through losing than would have come from winning. If I had won, there would have been such high expectations that I would have had difficulty satisfying everybody. In losing, I became something of a martyr, especially to the young people who supported me. For years afterward, those young people wondered what role race played in my defeat. They wondered what we could have done differently to ease people's fears and inspire their support. They took lessons from what happened to me that they have applied in ways I will never fully know.

In later years, people have occasionally approached me to voice regret about the outcome of the 1971 campaign and even about their own role in it. Ironically, one who did just that about ten years ago was Charles Stenvig himself. Charlotte and I ran into him and his new wife at the Decathlon Club in Bloomington after lunch one day. I said, "Gosh, Charlotte, that looks like Charlie Stenvig." Charlotte looked up and said, "It is." He looked at us too and approached us with a big smile. "Harry Davis! I haven't seen you in a long time," he said. We shook hands, he introduced us to his wife, and, after we talked for several minutes, he said, "You know, Harry, I really should apologize to you." I said, "What for?" He said, "I should never have been mayor. Really, I didn't want to be mayor. I didn't know anything about anything. You would have been a much better mayor than I was." I said, "Charlie, people voted for you. That's the way you settle elections." He said, "You really don't have any resentment?" I said, "After the election was over, I was kind of upset, but I got over that. You became mayor and that's the way it was." He said, "I shouldn't even have run for mayor." Then he told how his disagreement with Art Naftalin's handling of the 1967 Plymouth Avenue disturbance, and his first wife's interest in politics, inspired him to run. "But the more I thought about that, as I got older, the more I realized that you and Art were right that night [on Plymouth Avenue]. If we [the police] had gone down that street, we would have hurt a lot of innocent people." We talked about a few other things, then shook hands and parted. He said, "I hope we see each other again sometime." I hope so too.

RETURN TWO GOOD MEN TO THE SCHOOL BOARD

W. Harry Davis

Executive Director of the Urban Coalition. Appointed to the School Board to replace John Warder. Endorsed by Republican Party, DFL, and Labor.

David W. Preus

Chairman of the Minneapolis Board of Education, Pastor of the University Lutheran Church of Hope. Endorsed by the Republican Party and Labor.

Vote For Two Able Citizens Dedicated To Serving Our Community—and Our Children.

[X] VOTE TOMORROW

Minneapolis Primary Election

If You Would Like To Help, Please Mail This Coupon:

MAIL TO: Bi-Partisan Committee for Davis and Preus
657 Northwestern Bank Building, Minneapolis, 55402

Yes, I Would Like To Offer The Following Assistance:

☐ Volunteer Work ☐ Enclosed is my check or money order

☐ You may use my name as a supporter of Harry Davis and David Preus

NAME: . . . .

ADDRESS: . . . .

CITY & ZIP CODE . . . . **PHONE** . . . .

PAID ADV.: Prepared, inserted and paid for at regular advertising rates by the Bi-Partisan Committee for Davis and Preus; Leslie C. Park, chairman; Atherton Bean, financial director; C. Stanley Rude, treasurer; Mary Ann Scroggins, coordinator, 657 Northwestern Bank Building, Minneapolis, Minn. 55402.

The Reverend David Preus and I ran as a team when I made my first bid for the school board in 1969. I had been appointed to the board earlier that year.

With Evan, 1971.

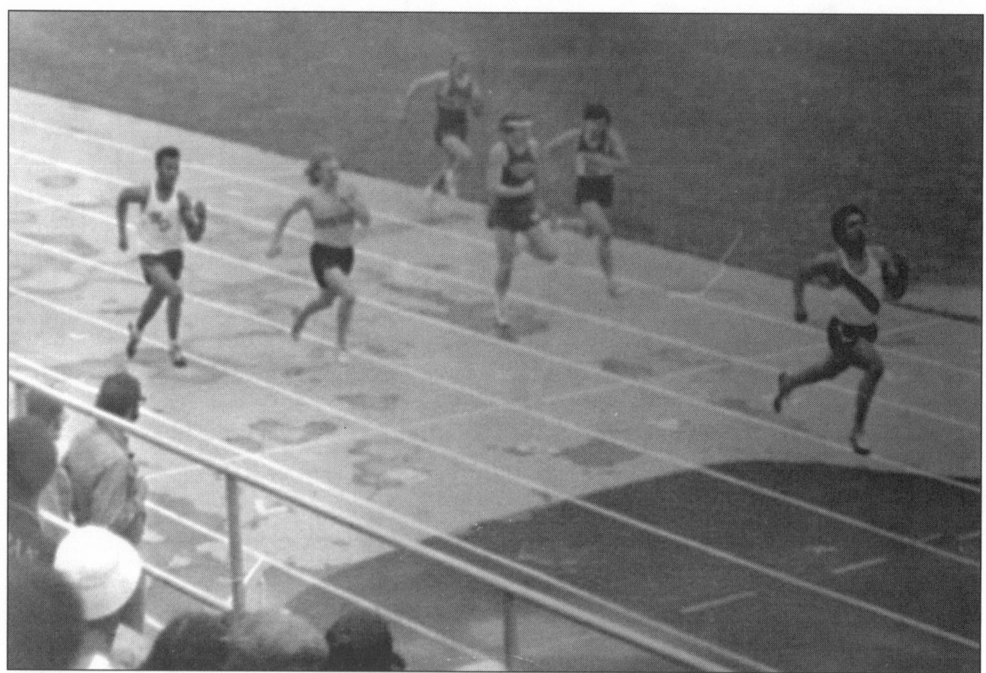

Ricky leads the way, easily winning the 220-yard dash at the regional high-school track meet in 1971 at Macalester College. He ran knowing that I had received an anonymous telephone call earlier that day threatening his life.

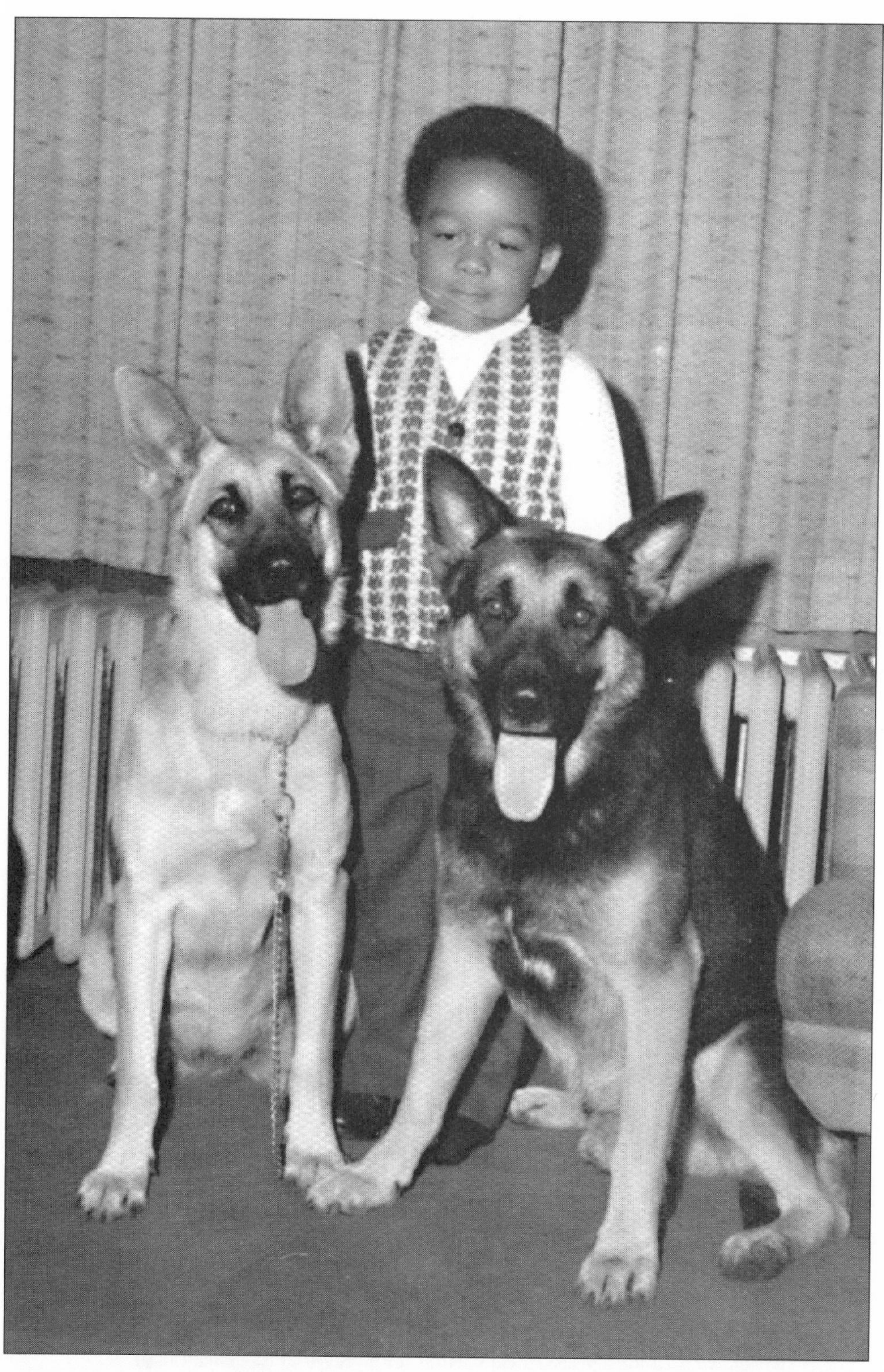

Grandson Corey with guard dogs Shep and Brute, our watchdogs during my 1971 mayoral campaign.

Art and Fran Naftalin looked on as I filed my candidacy for mayor of Minneapolis in 1971. Fran filed that day for the Minneapolis Library Board, a position she won and held for many years. To the right of me is Ralph Forester of the library board.

The family posed for a professional portrait for my mayoral campaign literature. Charlotte is holding Evan; behind us are Ricky, Rita, and Butch.

Senator Hubert Humphrey was very supportive of my mayoral campaign.

Governor Wendell Anderson also gave me strong, visible support.

DFL endorsed

Harry Davis for Mayor

My campaign literature reflected my desire to focus the campaign on issues other than school desegregation.

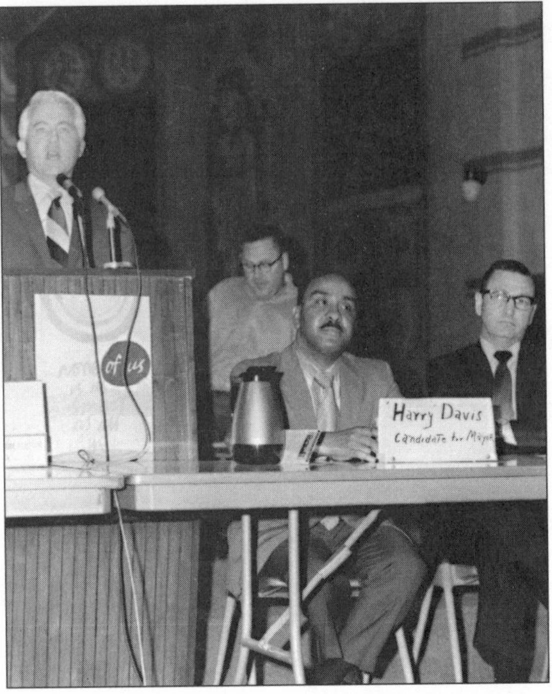

Mayor Charles Stenvig is at the microphone during our debate at Mayflower Church. To the right of me is City Council member Russ Green.

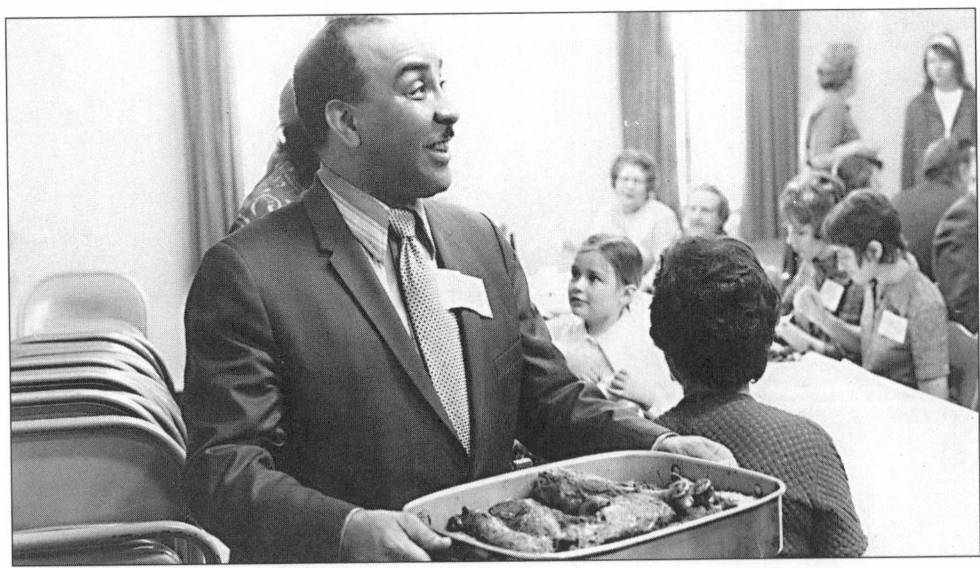

Campaigning takes many forms. I helped serve a meal at a community meeting in April 1971.

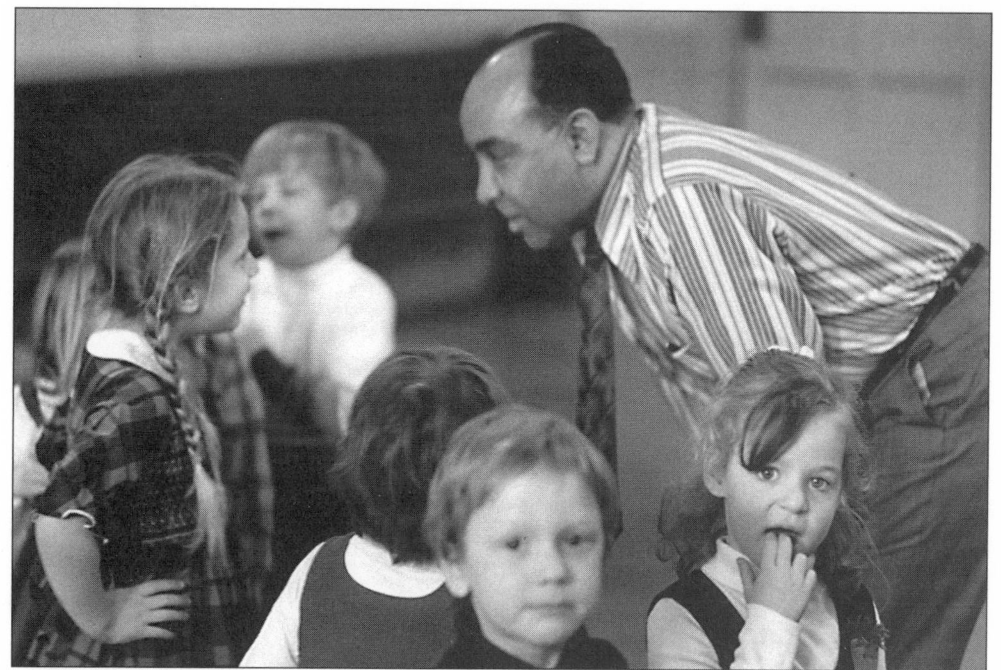

Seeking the youth vote, May 1971.

My concession speech at the Nicollet Hotel, June 8, 1971. From left: Ray and Mae Hatcher, Yvette and Butch Davis, me and Charlotte.

Bernie Kaye, far left, associate superintendent of Minneapolis schools, and I congratulate representatives of the Minneapolis Federation of Teachers, Dale Holstrom (second from left) and Norman Moen, on the signing of the first two-year contract with the city's teachers, September 12, 1972.

Corey and Evan visit Santa Claus in 1973.

John B. Davis and I became good friends while he served as superintendent of schools in Minneapolis. We celebrated his eightieth birthday in 2001.

IV
FULFILLING

17
Executive

EVEN BEFORE I LOST THE 1971 mayoral race, the possibility of yet another position change was placed before me. Governor Wendell Anderson called to say that if I lost the election, he would welcome me to his administration as the state human-rights commissioner. He went public with the offer after the election. He said, "Harry, you ran an outstanding campaign. We need people like you to make decisions in our government."

I thought it over for about a week, but could not work up any enthusiasm for the assignment. Those were dark days for me. I was weary in body and downcast in spirit. Moreover, I was well aware of how limited my scope of action would be as a state commissioner. Governor Harold LeVander had appointed me in 1969 to the Minnesota Board of Human Rights, an advisory panel that worked with the commissioner. I knew the job entailed overseeing the investigation of discrimination complaints to determine whether the state's narrowly constructed laws had been violated. I would have no authority to act more broadly to bring parity in housing, education, and employment opportunities between whites and minorities. I decided to reject the offer.

I went back to the Urban Coalition presidency, bruised but still firmly believing in the coalition's capacity to produce positive change. With Stenvig remaining in the mayor's office, the coalition would be needed more than ever. The coalition's focus was Minneapolis, and that was where I wanted my focus to remain. Disillusioned as I was after the election, I still loved my city. Charlotte and I gave no thought to leaving Minneapolis, though we did move within the city a few years later to a ranch-style house on East Sixty-first Street near Oakland Avenue South. I plunged back into my work.

It was a busy life. I would race from Golden Gloves meetings to Urban Coalition task-force sessions to United Way luncheons to school-board meetings to any one of a dozen or more other meetings of boards and organizations with which I was affiliated. I would be talking with Clyde Bellecourt about the American Indian Movement one minute and the governor or the CEO of a major corporation the next. I had a staff to supervise, community contacts to maintain, and a neighborhood bank to oversee. Art Naftalin once accused me of being unable to say no. He knows me pretty well.

Even though I had attended coalition board meetings during my campaign, there was a lot for me to catch up with after it was over. My campaign office was in the same building as the coalition headquarters in those years, so I had frequent contact with my staff. Moreover, several ideas I advanced during the campaign came right out of the coalition's task-force meetings. Still, it took me some months to get fully back up to speed and to begin to push again for the implementation of the next phase of our program. I was pleased to discover that when the coalition acted in the months after the campaign, people took notice. It seemed my campaign had brought some added prominence to our work. One task force that picked up steam in the months after the campaign was police/community relations. I had stressed the need for improvement in that area in my campaign. Soon there was a call throughout the city for block parties to be attended by cops on that beat so residents could meet their protectors in a friendly social setting, rather than a hostile one. The annual block parties we started then continue every summer to this day in much of the city.

We also concentrated on implementing and expanding the de novo program for underemployed men who had lived upright lives after brushes with the law when they were young. The MOER Board had TCOIC up and running, providing job training. The Urban Coalition's role was to seek out men who might benefit from that training, point them into the right program, and guide them into a job after they were finished. It was not uncommon for a man in that program to go from, say, a job as a janitor to one as a carpenter and to increase his hourly wage by $10 or $11 in the process. That enabled him to step up to home ownership and provide adequately for his children. We made sure the coalition board included top labor officials, in the hope that when our young carpenter was ready, he would qualify for union membership. I had seen in my campaign that labor was still a long way from being color-blind. Yet I knew organized labor's leaders well enough to believe they were people of goodwill who, if properly educated and motivated, could bring their organizations around.

My arrangement with Onan was for a three-year leave of absence that could be extended to five years, but no longer. I exercised my option to extend the leave in 1971, knowing that in 1973, I would have to either go back to Onan or sever my ties with my longtime employer. Though I appreciated my career at Onan, I was not eager to go back. Onan had been sold to the Studebaker-Worthington Corporation, and the Onan family was no longer at the helm. I could go back as director of personnel, which sounded less appealing than my old job as employee-services manager. I would have to report to a vice president for human relations in another city. Staying longer with the coalition was an option, but that position was seen as less than permanent. Our coalition was still going strong, but I was aware that elsewhere, as the threat of racial violence had subsided, Urban Coalition chapters disbanded.

What I should do with the rest of my career weighed on my mind, and Charlotte's too. She fretted about my health. I turned fifty years old in 1973 and was showing some wear. Ricky was finishing high school; Evan was starting kindergarten. I had grandchildren, with more on the way. "If something happens to you, we've got these children here," Charlotte said to me more than once. I was hospitalized in March with a kidney stone. My doctor urged me to take better care of myself. "Stress can have an effect on your health," he would remind me at every checkup. I began to wonder how much longer I could sustain the pace I was keeping.

I decided to explore my options and quietly passed that word to Donald McCarthy of NSP, the coalition president at that time, and other coalition board members. Their response was very generous. Several companies, General Mills and Pillsbury among them, contacted me for interviews. I was considered for positions in government relations, public relations, and corporate foundations. But my interest was piqued when the president of the Star and Tribune Company and scion of its owning family, John Cowles Jr., said to me after a meeting one day, "Harry, please send me your application." I replied, "John, what would I do for you? You have a publisher. You've got editors. You've got all the administrative people in place." He laughed a little and said, "There are other things you might not know about. We're doing a lot." That made me curious. My connection to the newspapers went back to 1943, when I became, in effect, a Star and Tribune employee as Phyllis Wheatley's Golden Gloves coach. I was indebted to the newspapers for their sponsorship of that program. If it had not been for the Golden Gloves, few people would have heard of Harry Davis. I sent my résumé to John.

A few conversations later, he offered me a new position: assistant to the publisher, concentrating on community relations and special projects. I accepted, and went to work for the Star and Tribune on August 13, 1973. I remained on the coalition board.

John's plans for me at the Star and Tribune Company, which was soon to change its name to Cowles Media, dovetailed with my Urban Coalition work. I would be much involved with a pet project of John's: landing a new professional-sports stadium in downtown Minneapolis, preferably on land in the Elliot Park neighborhood adjacent to the Star and Tribune building. That part of Elliot Park was a dilapidated slum; I would work on its redevelopment. I would still be engaged with the public, working to make things better for low-income people, just as I had done at the coalition. I was the company's liaison to the Chamber of Commerce and the Downtown Council, where I would continue to work with the same business leaders I had come to know. I was free to continue my work on the school board. I would work closely with another new Cowles hire, Tommy Thompson, who had been city coordinator in Naftalin's administration and was a good friend. I also had ties to the newspapers' whole circulation area, which then included North Dakota, South Dakota, and all of Minnesota. It was my Golden Gloves territory. I felt right at home.

I was aware that I had gone to work for a remarkable newspaper family. John Cowles Sr. came to Minneapolis from Des Moines (and the Des Moines *Register*) in 1935 to buy the *Star*. In 1939, he bought the competing *Minneapolis Journal* and merged the papers to create the *Star Journal*. The *Journal* name disappeared from the masthead in 1947, but it remained on people's lips for decades thereafter. John Sr. bought the venerable old *Tribune,* the city's oldest newspaper, in 1941. The *Tribune* was published mornings and Sundays; the *Star* was the larger afternoon sibling. For the next fifty-seven years, the Cowles name would be synonymous with newspapers in Minneapolis and John Sr. would be counted on any short list of business titans in the city. He had a forceful personality, great intelligence, and lofty ambitions for his newspapers and for his adopted city.

By the time I moved into my third-floor office at the Star and Tribune building at 425 Portland Avenue, John Sr. still appeared each day at his posh office across the hall. But he had relinquished control of the company to his erudite son John Jr. The younger Cowles was a civic booster but never brash or self-aggrandizing. He wanted the newspapers to take the lead in the city, but quietly, in a way that drew attention elsewhere. He never wanted to involve the newsroom in the things he was doing in the community. He went to extremes to avoid interference with the independence of his editors and reporters. John Jr. was not a commanding leader. He never raised his voice, but when he said something, you understood that he meant what he said. The adjacent offices of father and son in the Star and Tribune building provided a clue about their personality differences. John Sr.'s office had rich wood paneling, a fireplace, and a bar from which he would offer, "D'you want a little nip?" John Jr. favored stark white, straight lines, spartan furnishings, and a modest amount of modern art. When you walked in the door, you would think you were walking into a hospital. Here's another clue: John Sr. came to work in a chauffeur-driven limousine. John Jr. drove himself to work in a Volkswagen.

Those differences in personality and style did not diminish the Cowles influence in city affairs. Like his father before him, John Jr. was an unquestioned leader among his business peers. He was the guy they wanted on their side. He was the thinker behind much of what other spokespersons said publicly on behalf of the business community. And like his father, John Jr. was devoted to city betterment. To be sure, a healthy city and strong downtown are good for the newspaper business. But I think he pursued city projects as a matter of personal interest and pride. Both father and son sincerely loved Minneapolis and wanted to do their part to make it the finest city in the American Midwest. We had that passion in common. It helped cement my relationship with them.

John Jr.'s executive team included two men I knew well, Bower Hawthorne and Otto Silha. Bower had been an editor of the *Tribune* before moving into administration. He was the company's vice president for public affairs in the 1970s and was considered one of the city's consummate deal-makers and arts boosters. Otto rose from the *Star*'s copy desk to become publisher of the two papers, then president of the Star and Tribune Company as John Cowles Jr. moved up to chair. I considered Bower and Otto both allies on civil rights and school issues; they had contributed generously to my campaign. I also had friends in the newsroom, both on the city desk and in the sports department. The city-affairs and city-hall reporters, education reporters, and sports reporters knew me. Those connections gave me a family feeling toward the newspaper that lasts to this day.

As assistant to the publisher, I first reported to Robert W. Smith. He was a fine man and respected publisher with whom I got along very well. He left us too soon; he died suddenly in December 1975. In subsequent years, my title changed to assistant vice president for public affairs, then assistant vice president and employee-services manager, then vice president.

As if my mayoral campaign and school policy had not exposed me enough to the rigors of Minneapolis politics, my new job landed me in a political thicket. The siting and funding of professional-sports facilities have been perennially controversial in Minnesota. A new stadium was already an issue when I ran for mayor. The Minnesota Twins and Minnesota Vikings both played in open-air, no-frills Metropolitan Stadium in Bloomington, on the site where Mall of America now stands. The Vikings often played in snow and bitter cold in December—and in January too, since the team often advanced into the play-offs in those years. I went to some of those games and froze my tail off. The Vikings wanted to play with a roof over their heads, and most of their fans liked the idea. Twins fans were fonder of Met Stadium, but Twins officials knew that they lost money and goodwill when their fans shivered in April and May or were turned away because of rain-outs after long drives into the Twin Cities.

In my mayoral campaign, I supported building a domed stadium downtown, funded at least in part with tax money. Mayor Stenvig opposed the idea. My position sprang from my awareness of the good that comes from having professional-sports teams in a city. They provide a nucleus of role models for young people. Kids idolize professional athletes. The teams, in turn, cater to kids with sports training clinics and camps, equipment donations, admission discounts, and chances to meet players. Kids get inspired to get involved in sports rather than in some less wholesome pastime. The good players happily get involved in the community and do a lot for charity. That work is often overlooked as people try to tally the financial benefit of professional sports to a region. Stadium opponents often belittle the low-wage jobs a stadium provides; I did not. I knew many people who would grab at the chance for a low-wage, part-time job. I was excited about the possibility of bringing the Twins and the Vikings downtown. My view was not lost on John Cowles Jr. He was a great backer of the idea.

At first, downtown-stadium boosters had their eyes on a site adjacent to my old North Side neighborhood, where the Farmers' Market stands today. The thought was that a public subsidy would likely come from the city, not the state. But Interstate Highway 94 claimed that parcel, and other sites were considered. One was northwest of downtown, where the county garbage burner stands today. The other was in Elliot Park, on the east side of downtown, on land owned by the Star and Tribune. I had not been aware until I was hired how much land on the east side of downtown was Star and Tribune property. The company controlled upwards of a dozen blocks. The Cowles family had been buying land in anticipation of building a large new production plant close to their existing headquarters and newsprint warehouse. But the company's thinking about its production needs was changing as printing technology moved into the computer age. A new printing plant didn't need to be adjacent to the newsroom. The company could consider other possibilities.

Of course, there was one other option for a stadium: stay in Bloomington and either remodel the Met or rebuild. That idea had support among fans in the suburbs and in southern Minnesota who did not want to drive downtown for a ball game. That meant, in turn, that a Bloomington site had friends in the legislature. On most big issues in Minnesota, the legislature has the final word. It became clear in the mid-1970s that the stadium question would be no different.

It was Robert Smith who clued me in on the Cowles family's willingness to donate company land for a stadium. But they would look to others, either the business community or the taxpayers, to pick up the cost of clearing the land, installing utilities, rerouting roads, and building a stadium. Moreover, John Cowles Jr. was quietly lining up others to be large corporate underwriters of the project at that site. The pitch to the legislature would be that if the state were to authorize the sale of government-backed revenue bonds to finance construction of the stadium itself, the Minneapolis business community would cover the ancillary costs.

Housing stood on the Star and Tribune land in question—ancient, dilapidated single-family houses and apartment buildings that were long past their prime. The neighborhood had been among the city's finest in the 1880s and 1890s, but the intervening years had not been kind. Nearly all of the housing near the stadium site was rental property, in buildings not owned by the Star and Tribune but by several landlords who leased the land on which they stood. The area deserved its nickname, Cockroach Corner. But it was home to about three hundred people, and, thanks in part to the work of the MOER Board, those people had been organized into the Elliot Park Neighborhood Association. They were a force to be reckoned with. As soon as I knew the Star and Tribune's plans, I knew they would be controversial in the neighborhood. I told the Star and Tribune executive team that we had to make their stadium idea a win-win proposition: good for professional sports, but also good for the neighborhood.

The Star and Tribune was party to the establishment of a Downtown Neighborhoods Committee of the Downtown Council, an arm of the local Chamber of Commerce. I became its chair. We developed a proposal that reached beyond the immediate four-square-block site of a stadium. We said that it would be our responsibility to replace the housing lost on that immediate site with housing of a better quality nearby. We would clear out the trashy bars four or five blocks south of the stadium site, on and around Chicago Avenue, to make way for housing. We would also rehab old apartments there into something more livable but just as affordable as those that would be lost to the new stadium. To stabilize the neighborhood, we would place some middle-class housing and small businesses there too. The design of the new and rehabilitated area would be finalized in collaboration with the neighborhood association, which would then take the lead in administering the project. In addition, we would pay the relocation costs of displaced residents. I thought it was a fair proposal.

The Star and Tribune Company was not going to pay for all of this alone. The Downtown Council's Downtown Neighborhoods Committee solicited major businesses for contributions for a redevelopment financing pool. That pool could be tapped either for grants or interest-free loans. We raised about $5 million for that purpose very quickly. Money in the bank at the start turned out to be a major advantage as we went forward. How to dispense that money would be decided by the Elliot Park Neighborhood Improvement Corporation, a nonprofit entity created as a joint project of the Elliot Park Neighborhood Association and the Downtown Council. Seven businesses, including the Star and Tribune, put up $42,000 in seed money to start the corporation. The Downtown Council's committee specified that a significant portion of the work would be done only by small, locally owned construction companies, subcontracted through a general contractor. Our aim was to give minority-owned businesses a chance.

It fell to me to take the idea to the apartment-building owners and the neighborhood organization. As I predicted, there was considerable resistance. There were places on Chicago Avenue that were essentially rooming houses—flophouses—that we would not replace. Not everyone could continue to live in the area at the same cost as before. There was the issue of additional noise and traffic when a stadium became their neighbor. But one argument won over the law-abiding people in the area: this project was likely to reduce crime. Crime of all kinds, from petty thievery to murder, was a major problem in Elliot Park. Prostitution and drug-dealing on Chicago Avenue were running rampant. Clearing out undesirable businesses and buying out irresponsible landlords sounded good to people who wanted to stay in Elliot Park.

That recognition did not come overnight, however. Opponents of a downtown stadium planted seeds of skepticism in Elliot Park, including a group that thought neighborhood resistance was the way to keep the Twins and the Vikings in Bloomington. Some of our planning meetings with neighborhood people would get vocal. The meetings were chaired jointly by Brian Nowak, the executive director of the Neighborhood Improvement Corporation, and me. Even though we met frequently, sometimes three times a week, we drew a crowd. At first, we met at the Star and Tribune building, at 425 Portland, but we decided that a more neutral location, one less likely to draw protesters, was needed. The Valspar Corporation, a paint manufacturer a few blocks away, became our host. As people came to us with their questions, we soon got the sense that the residents' concerns centered mostly on timing and financing. The people who argued with us about the merit of a downtown stadium were typically not from Elliot Park. Sometimes the people who came to our meetings would start arguing among themselves. At one session, someone said, "You're coming in here and ruining our neighborhood." Before I could answer, someone else jumped up and said, "What's to ruin? What are these rat-infested buildings going to look like in ten years if nothing is done?"

The best way for us to establish credibility with the neighbors was to show results. "When can you start to produce?" the skeptics kept wanting to know. We decided to start the rehabilitation of several Chicago Avenue buildings in the summer of 1979, even before a state authorization for a new stadium had cleared its last legal hurdle. We would proceed with redevelopment and the relocation of residents in phases, rather than wait until we could make a big move. That way, we thought, neighborhood confidence and enthusiasm for the project would build. We could have a small amount of replacement housing available rather quickly in some of the vacant apartments in the rehab area that needed relatively little work. Vacancy rates were high in those years. In early 1980, the first section of housing in the prospective stadium site was demolished and the first wave of residents relocated. Two more waves would follow.

Some of the improvement in Chicago Avenue property was striking. The small contractors that the general contractor hired did good work. We had arranged with the Minneapolis Building Trades for our subcontractors to get any additional personnel they might need to do the job in a timely fashion. That in itself was breaking some new ground: some union craftsmen would be working for minority subcontractors for the first time. Just thinking of that today brings to mind the smiling face, twinkling eyes, and chewed-on cigar of union boss Dave Roe, whose leadership made that happen.

Between Fifteenth and Sixteenth Streets, two large old buildings contained two-story, balcony-style apartments. Spiral staircases connected the two floors, with the bedrooms on the balcony levels. They were just beautiful. The first showing we had of a renovated apartment was on a bitter midwinter night. It must have been minus twenty degrees. John Jr. and Otto Silha drove over for the showing and came in all ruddy with cold. They were pleased with how toasty warm the apartment was (we had upgraded the heating system) and with one of the heat sources: the contractors had found some previously concealed marble fireplaces in the building when they remodeled. They also found hardwood floors and beautiful original woodwork. These had once been posh quarters. John and Otto were so pleased to be party to making them beautiful again. Better still, the Elliot Park residents who saw the unit were agog. Word got back to the rest of the neighborhood, and my job suddenly got easier.

In starting the renovation before construction began for a new stadium, one might say we had "bet on the come." The business community proceeded, knowing that if a stadium did not go on the site they were clearing, something else would, and Elliot Park would still be better for it. That thinking was characteristic of the Minneapolis business leadership in those years. The city's CEOs had always been a close-knit, civic-minded group. But beginning with the Urban Coalition in the 1960s, and for the next decade and more, the city's top executives showed remarkable cohesion and capacity for joint community action. There was great confidence within the business community in their ability to do the right thing. People grumbled about money doing all the talking in Minneapolis, but for the most part, the business community encountered relatively little resistance to their projects. Their power was not in doubt, and their motives were seldom in question. The City Council was always supportive, it seemed. The idea that a new stadium would not be built where they wanted it, or that it would instead go to upstart Bloomington, seemed impossible to these business leaders.

Yet a Bloomington stadium was what a sizable share of the legislature wanted in 1979. A coalition of suburbanites and southern-Minnesota legislators jelled for that location. St. Paul legislators were ambivalent, and a few were hostile to Minneapolis. Most Minneapolis legislators were onboard, though a stadium held little interest for some of them. While I worked on site preparation, the attention of John Jr., Otto Silha, Bower Hawthorne, and the rest shifted to the legislature. Some serious lobbying was in order.

Governor Rudy Perpich, recognizing a political hot potato when one was headed his way, had appointed a citizens commission to study the matter and recommend a location to the 1979 legislature. At the head of the commission was Dan Brutger, a hotel owner and developer from St. Cloud. Dan was both a shrewd businessman and a good politician. He made the business calculation that the stadium belonged in the center of the metro area—that is, in downtown Minneapolis—and employed his considerable persuasive skill to make sure that was the commission's recommendation. On the last day of the session, the legislature finally concurred. But the bond sale was delayed by a last-ditch, ultimately futile lawsuit by two state-senate leaders that summer. Work finally started on the Hubert H. Humphrey Metrodome in October 1979, which became the home of the Twins and Vikings in 1982. I was pleased about that, but more proud of my role in finding better homes for the people the stadium displaced.

In the middle of the struggle to redevelop Elliot Park, I got a new intern in my office from Harvard University. His name was John Cowles III, but everybody called him Jay. His dad wanted him to examine up close the importance of community relations and civic improvements to the newspaper business—a business Jay would eventually make his own. Jay has many of the best traits of both his father and his grandfather and was a wonderful young man. I took him all around the Elliot Park neighborhood and exposed him to a few meetings. After one particular meeting, he shook his head and said to me, "How do you maintain your sanity?" I replied, "Jay, if you're around as long as I am, you'll be talking to yourself, just like I do."

18
Integrating

AFTER THE DRUBBING I TOOK in the mayoral election in 1971, I think some Minneapolis voters were surprised to find me still around. I still had four years to serve in my first six-year term on the Minneapolis Board of Education. Although my position on school desegregation was the club Charles Stenvig had used to beat me, mine was still the majority view of the seven-member board. We were still on track to desegregate Minneapolis schools in 1971 and 1972.

School-board meetings during the 1971–1972 school year felt like a continuation of the mayoral campaign. The issue at every meeting was desegregation, and the room was always full of emotional people. People supposedly came to the microphone to address the entire board, but often they wound up aiming their remarks just at me, the only black member. It was as if opponents of integration and busing held me personally responsible for the changes that were coming. I no longer had a bodyguard to protect me, but the harassing phone calls continued.

Other board members got their share of nasty comments too, of course. It was a time of considerable turnover on the board, and I always suspected that the strain that went with imposing unpopular change on the system was part of the reason. Stuart Rider quit unexpectedly in 1972; Frank Adams declined to run again in 1973; David Preus resigned in 1974, not long after he was elected president of the American Lutheran Church; Richard Allen retired from the board in 1975. I was proud of the Minneapolis School Board all the years I was part of it, but I thought the board that voted for desegregation was an especially strong one. The city was lucky to be served by people of such caliber just then.

Despite the criticism that hammered us, I had the sense that public opinion was changing. I like to think that my campaign's defense of desegregation got some voters in the city to begin thinking differently. In addition, as 1972 dawned, our desegregation pilot projects—the federally funded Southeast Alternative Program and the pairing of Field and Hale elementary schools in south-central Minneapolis—were well into their first year and operating smoothly. *Minneapolis Tribune* education reporter Gregor Pinney went to Hale and Field schools to investigate a host of complaints from desegregation opponents—from too much classroom noise to mice in the Field building—and found most of them groundless. One of his most encouraging findings was that students liked their new schools and that some former pairing opponents among the parents had changed their minds. At the time of the pairing of mostly white Hale with mixed-race Field, the schools also adopted a more modern teaching method involving more individualized instruction. Five additional teachers were assigned to the pair of schools to facilitate the change and bring down class sizes. We could claim with confidence that our plan of integration was not disrupting education. It was improving education for everybody.

Our schedule was to have in hand in mid-March a plan from Superintendent John B. Davis Jr. to implement desegregation citywide. We would take a last round of public testimony in early April, then vote on April 25. We were in regular contact with federal judge Earl Larson, who still had not ruled on the NAACP's 1970 desegregation suit. He served notice in February that he intended to bring the suit to trial on April 10. He was giving us time to act. We knew that he was watching, and that he would eventually either endorse our plan or order a different one.

As our work went forward, racial tensions erupted into fights at Washburn High School, not far from Field and Hale. The black student population was small but growing fast in that high school, which was in the heart of an affluent white neighborhood. Black students said the school ignored them, and they had a point. Though the incidents were minor, they called attention to the need to do more than put white and black bodies into the same classroom: they needed to come to know and respect each other. I began to speak out at board meetings about the need not just for desegregation, but integration, and to call for human-relations training for teachers and staff at all our schools. Davis was quick to pick up on the idea and run with it, and diversity training became a standard part of in-service education for Minneapolis teachers.

The superintendent's desegregation plan was a gem. It built on the strengths of our two pilot projects. Elementary schools in close proximity would be paired. No long-distance busing of students was required. Some new, larger schools would be built and populated by students from racially diverse areas of the city, while nineteenth-century buildings in areas with dwindling populations would be torn down. Attendance boundary lines would be shifted to raise the minority population at Washburn High School while reducing it at the city's most mixed high school, Central. (More boundary changes for secondary schools were to follow.) In all, forty-two of the city's one hundred schools would be affected by Davis's plan. I liked it in every respect but one: it would take three to five years to implement. Almost no change was foreseen for the 1972–1973 school year. I wanted faster action. I wanted ten elementary schools paired in the fall of 1972, and I also wanted to retain Lincoln School as a junior high to minimize busing of North Side junior-high students. But my motion died for lack of a second.

Davis's plan was approved by a five-to-two vote of the board on April 25. A crowd of four hundred people was on hand to watch the vote, and I worried that things could get ugly. But to my pleasant surprise, about half of the audience burst into long applause after our vote. David Preus, ever the eloquent preacher, was our voice of moral conscience that night: "Justice in the public schools means equal educational opportunity for all children. As long as we require children in money-poor families to cluster together in central-city schools isolated from the majority of privileged children, we cannot provide them equal educational opportunity."

We acted against the backdrop of a trial in progress at the federal courthouse downtown. The main issue at the trial was the very one I had raised, the pace of the desegregation plan. John B. Davis testified that delay was needed to prepare many school buildings for enrollment increases. The trial ended the day after the school board acted. We held our breath, waiting for Judge Larson's verdict on the plan we had adopted. It came on May 24: Minneapolis was found guilty of school segregation and ordered to implement, with only a few small modifications, the very desegregation plan we had adopted the month before. The judge's modifications had to do with teacher hiring and the distribution of minority teachers, not students. Big movement of students would wait until the 1973–1974 school year. Again by a five-to-two vote, the board quickly decided not to appeal. There was a burst of bluster from Phil Olson and Marilyn Borea, Mayor Stenvig's allies, about going to jail rather than complying with the court order, but the rest of the board ignored them. Judge Larson's order would govern school-desegregation efforts for much of the next two decades.

The court order gave the school board's policy the force of federal law. That made it much less likely that Stenvig's T Party or any other political force in town could reverse our decision. The community could no longer doubt that schools would be desegregated. I also think that Larson's order gave the city and the whole state reason to examine more critically the education their children were receiving. Determining school enrollment by student residence, once unquestioned, was now being reexamined. Did neighborhood schools really provide equal quality of education? If not, what remedy made the most sense? This city and this nation are not through wrestling with those questions. But I believe that in Minneapolis in 1972, for our era, we answered them honorably and well.

Not six weeks later, my role on the board changed. I was elected chair, succeeding Richard Allen. David Preus nominated me and engineered my election. I had no opponent, but the vote—predictably—was four to two. Phil Olson and Marilyn Borea were still opposed to desegregation, and hence to me.

But then David and John came up with an idea that began to change Phil and Marilyn's minds. We knew we had a big public-education job on our hands if our new policy was to be implemented smoothly. David and John suggested that each school-board member take responsibility for carrying the message to a portion of the city. We took care to send DFL board members to DFL neighborhoods and Republican board members to Republican neighborhoods. Each of us asked party people in our assigned areas to open their homes for informational meetings to discuss the changes that were coming. It was a low-key tactic that got information out in a friendly, nonthreatening way, and it worked very well. We knew it would be unfair to ask Phil and Marilyn to go out and defend a policy they opposed, but we were not about to excuse them from public-education duty. So we matched them up. David took Phil with him to visit people's homes, and I brought Marilyn. Our hosts were surprised. They would ask, "Harry, why are you bringing Marilyn? She was against you." I explained that she needed to be educated: "I want you to tell her about your children's education. I want you to tell her that you think our new policy is going to work, and why." Gradually, those meetings had a positive effect on the board as well as on the school system. Marilyn started voting with the board's majority on some desegregation matters in 1973; Phil followed not long thereafter.

I continued to be much involved in contract negotiations with the district's employees. The district had fifteen bargaining units in those year, far too many. Too much of our time was consumed in negotiations. The teachers contract always set the pace for the rest. Especially after the 1970 teachers strike, negotiations with the teachers took on added importance. As board chair I was automatically a member of the contract-negotiating team, but I was also still seen as the teachers' ally. I was determined to do all I could to avoid another strike. We simply could not stand the disruption a strike would bring while we implemented a controversial desegregation plan. I favored something the teachers wanted: a two-year contract to break the caustic cycle of perpetual negotiations. The board was originally divided on the question, but when David and I raised the issue with the board in 1972, my colleagues were ready to see the advantage of a multiyear contract for the district. We made the change with relative ease and signed the first two-year contract with the district's teachers on September 12, 1972. There has not been another teachers strike in Minneapolis since.

The school board's majority watched the 1973 city election approach with some trepidation. Two seats were at stake: the Rider seat, which had been filled by deputy state attorney general Jack Mason, and the Adams seat, which Frank was leaving. If antidesegregation candidates won those seats, our board's majority would tip. Our desegregation policies would still be in force because of Judge Larson's order, but a difficult situation would be created. News commentators kept telling the city that this would be an "all-important" school-board election. But in the end, it was pleasantly lacking in drama. Charlie Stenvig, standing for reelection, was in trouble this time. His weak leadership in city hall and his overuse of force in putting down a student demonstration at the University of Minnesota in 1972 had finally caught up with him. His T Party supporters were very slow to choose school-board candidates, and when they did, their choices were unknowns with skimpy credentials and whose platform was defiance of the Larson order. Meanwhile, people supportive of desegregation had gotten organized. A group calling itself CURE, Citizens United for Responsible Education, had been meeting for months to fend off a conservative onslaught. I met with them several times. They endorsed Jack Mason and Carol Lind, a Republican and a teacher. The DFL Party endorsed both in a rare show of bipartisanship for the sake of racial equality. Jack and Carol won, and everybody on the board took heart, save for Phil Olson, our only holdout. In the same election, Charlie Stenvig lost to City Council member Al Hofstede.

As the desegregation plan became reality, opponents whose focus had been on busing began to discover the plus that they had been overlooking: choice. It was always our intention to offer all families in the city the same curricular choices available in the southeast wedge of town, through the Southeast Alternative Program. We could not implement curricular choice concurrently with desegregation. Its logistics were simply too complex. The choice program had to wait until 1976 to get under way. At first, we offered contemporary curriculum, which was essentially traditional classroom learning; continuous progress, a team-teaching approach that allowed students of varying abilities to proceed at different paces; Montessori, which was very popular; and fundamentals, a stricter program that emphasized basic reading and math skills. There was also a Free School in the Southeast Alternative Program, which involved students in curricular choices and school operations. Eventually, we added an open-school curriculum that blurred grade lines. Those were the choices for families. We could not have given every family its first choice, or we would have needed ten thousand buses and a batch of new school buildings to make it work. But the vast majority of families in the city got either their first or second choice for their children. I have long maintained that if we had been able to offer families the whole package all at once, desegregation would have enjoyed broader support.

We also might have made things easier for ourselves if we had begun earlier to decentralize the district. John Davis wanted to move in that direction, but it was not until the mid-1970s that we split the district into three zones—north, west, and east—and put an area superintendent and staff in each zone. That moved the administration closer to the people and helped us explain and implement the curricular choices. We all were much involved in the selection process. We chose Marvin Trammel as the west-area superintendent, Ken Northwick for the east, and Melvin Hoaglund for the north. Each of them had been part of John Davis's cabinet and was well prepared for his new assignment.

A remarkable turnaround in public opinion occurred as we implemented what was being called the most sweeping change in the school district's history. The forecast in 1970 and 1971 was for a tidal wave of white flight, either out of the city or toward private schools. But when the numbers were in from our first year under desegregation, enrollments were up and no unusual increase had occurred in the number of students transferring out of the system. A survey of white parents in the Hale-Field area, the people who by then had lived with desegregation for three years, found 61 percent support for the change.

Another indication of the city's change of heart came in the 1975 city election. I was reelected to the school board by a comfortable margin, as was the member we had appointed to David Preus's seat, Jane Starr. This time I had won a four-year rather than a six-year term; that change in board structure came in 1973. I could not help thinking on that election night how different it was from the one four years earlier, and wondering if I had simply chosen the wrong time to run for mayor. On the other hand, mayoral politics was fraught with uncertainty in those years. Charlie Stenvig caught Al Hofstede's campaign napping in 1975, and my old nemesis sneaked back into the mayor's office for one final term.

I served three terms as board chair, becoming the first person in the district's history to serve three consecutive terms in that role. The board had become a close-knit, well-functioning group. We met often at the Minneapolis Club with John and his cabinet, so much so that we occasionally ran afoul of the state's new open-meeting law. Minneapolis was a model for desegregation around the country, receiving national publicity and visitors from school boards in other cities seeking to copy our success.

Then a blow fell. John B. Davis resigned in July 1975 to assume the presidency of Macalester College in St. Paul. It was a plum promotion for him but a terrible loss for us. I wanted us to hire a professional search firm to find a replacement, but my colleagues disagreed. They charged forward with some consulting help from the University of Minnesota and found Raymond Arveson in Hayward, California, to succeed John. Ray was a kindly, charming native of North Dakota who fit in with Minnesota's Scandinavian culture, but he was no superintendent. I wanted us to promote Marvin Trammel instead. Marvin had been at John's elbow all the while we designed and implemented the desegregation plan. He was ready to lead. But he was black, and the board apparently was not ready for him. The vote for Arveson was five to two, with Phil Olson joining me in supporting Trammel. What a turnaround that vote represented for Phil! Yet I was discouraged. It was the first time in more than six years on the board that I doubted the depth of my colleagues' convictions on racial equality.

During Arveson's tenure, minority enrollment in Minneapolis schools climbed steadily as overall district enrollment dropped. The baby boomers had become adults, and the "Gen Xers" who followed were fewer in number—and, in Minneapolis, more likely to be people of color. The district had an increasingly difficult time complying with Judge Larson's order that no more than 35 percent of the students in any school represent a single racial minority group. Meanwhile, citizens made very clear at several large public hearings that a more geographically expanded busing program was unpopular. The district pursued an alternative that was nearly as unpopular: school closings. Further, in 1978, Arveson asked Judge Larson to relax his order and let minority enrollments swell in inner-city schools. Instead, the judge gave the district only a little more wiggle room and criticized the board and the administration for not taking the desegregation imperative seriously enough. A new wave of busing was at hand. The board was divided over how to proceed. Four members, excluding me, voted to appeal Larson's most recent order to the circuit court, and then to the U.S. Supreme Court. I felt we were off course. It was clear to me that we needed a stronger superintendent, one whose commitment to desegregation was in no doubt.

By 1979, my colleagues agreed with me. Jack Mason, was outspokenly critical of Arveson's handling of many aspects of school management. We had given Ray's deputy, Vern Indehar, more responsibility, but the problems persisted. We were literally minutes away from voting not to renew Arveson's contract when he resigned in February 1980.

It was time for the school board to redeem itself. This time we promoted from within and hired a man steeped in knowledge of Minneapolis and groomed for leadership by John Davis. With a unanimous vote, the board turned to one of the smartest kids I ever coached in Golden Gloves boxing, west-area superintendent and former North High principal Richard Green.

Richard was born in Arkansas in 1936, one of three children in a sharecropper's family that fell apart soon thereafter. He and his mother moved to my old North Side neighborhood in 1938. By 1946, he was one of about fifteen boys on the cub football team I coached at Phyllis Wheatley. Already then, he stood out. He was both the best athlete and the most mischievous player on the team. He would carry the ball three-fourths of the time, and three-fourths of those times he would either get a first down or make a touchdown. But he would not listen to his coach. Richard did not have a father at home, and he didn't have real discipline—that is, he didn't until I started coaching him. In those years, Phyllis Wheatley required all boys age ten and older who participated in any of the house's sports to take Golden Gloves training. I told Richard I expected to see him there, and he came. He thought he knew all there was to know about boxing before receiving a single lesson. During one of his first evenings at boxing, he watched some boys sparring who were a little older than he was but about the same size. He said, "Let me get in there and box a couple of those guys." He had offered to take on Willie Jemison, Leroy Bogar, and Neil Frazier, all of whom became Golden Gloves champions. I told Richard he could take his pick of partners, and he chose Willie Jemison—the worst choice he could make. Willie just boxed his ears off. Richard couldn't touch him. His nose was bloody, and he started to cry, though he was careful not to let many people see his tears. I think that moment changed him. He wasn't the smart aleck with me after that. He started to understand that others were better than he was at some things, and the difference came from discipline and hard work. He was a natural leader, but at Phyllis Wheatley, he learned to be an intelligent leader.

Richard stood out in another way too: he had asthma. He was a terrific athlete but generally about once each game, he would start to wheeze. I would watch for that and send in a substitute so that he could take his medicine.

As a kid, he was able to recover just like that and get back into the game. It wasn't always that easy as he got older. I talked with his high-school coaches to help them understand Richard's illness. Managing asthma was a constant, lifelong challenge for him.

Richard was not out of the woods yet. He may have subdued his devilish streak around me, but it was still apparent in other settings. When he was about fourteen or fifteen, he spent a short stint in reform school. He returned chastened and serious about making a good life for himself. He enrolled in Vocational High School in downtown Minneapolis and learned how to be a shoemaker. But he also got straight A's in his classes and made All City in both basketball and football his senior year. It was plain to everyone who knew Richard that his talent would be wasted if he spent his life making shoes. A Phyllis Wheatley board member from Augsburg College connected Richard with the school, where he got a scholarship.

It was a wonderful choice for him. Augsburg is a serious school, strong academically, with a good athletic program. It allowed him to stay close to home and be active in the community. My kids and I could go over to the campus and watch him play football or basketball. While he was at Augsburg, Richard began to see his future in education. When he sat down and told me as much, I was not at all surprised. I had two thoughts about Richard: I thought he would go either into education or medicine. He was very bright, very interested in learning. He spent a great deal of his leisure time reading books in the library. But he also spent a lot of time helping kids. While in college, he coached a cub football team at Phyllis Wheatley. The kids and the Wheatley staff all liked him very much. It was like he was doing his practice teaching at Phyllis Wheatley.

I stayed close to Richard as he moved into adulthood. In fact, we were always in touch and always talking about every turn in his career. He went to teach at Glen Lake Boys Home, a reform school, right out of college in 1959. A few years later, he went to North High, where he was promoted to head basketball coach in 1968. He was the first black head coach in a city high school. People started saying to him, "Richard, you ought to go back to college and get a higher degree. You're not a regular classroom teacher. You're an administrator." We talked it over, and I encouraged him to do just that. I also put in a good word for Richard with the new superintendent in those years, John Davis. "There's a good prospect, that young man," I said one day to John. He assured me, "I've already got my eyes on him." John encouraged Richard, and together we raised some corporate money to help Richard go back to school. The funds we raised even covered housing. By then, Richard was a married man with four small children. He could not have returned to school without financial help. He earned his master's degree from St. Cloud State University and his doctorate from Harvard.

With each step up in his academic credentials came a promotion. He rose to being North High's principal, then west-area superintendent. In both positions, he tackled the tough issues head-on. When some black students beat up some younger white students at North in 1974, Richard called an assembly and expressed his disappointment in plain language. He said that, on that day, he was not sure that black was beautiful. He laid out standards of conduct in unmistakable terms for all to hear. Similarly, when a group of North High seniors refused to wear caps and gowns at commencement, he sat them down and spoke to them about the importance of taking pride in personal achievement. He had a confidence and a persuasive manner that could turn other people around. When he would walk out on a stage, he had the presence of a performer or a magician who was there to charm you. Parents, both at North and in the west area, just adored him—and he in turn was very smart about involving parents in the schools. He was an excellent politician. When John Davis left, he shared with us his assessment of the rising young administrators in the district. Of Richard he said, "In another couple of years, he will be the top."

The board was sold on Richard before Ray Arveson had cleaned out his desk. We went through the motion of interviewing a few others, but Richard stood head and shoulders above them. On June 10, 1980, the boardroom was packed as we made our final decision. We did the final interviews in public, then told the audience we would make our final decision in private, as state law permitted, and come back into the room with our candidate. As we walked by the room where the candidates waited, Richard caught my eye and I winked at him. He knew our decision then. I returned to get him a few minutes later. When we walked back into the boardroom with Richard, the place went crazy. I think it was thirty or forty-five minutes before the crowd quieted down. I doubt there has ever been such a moment of joy in that room. When Richard could finally address the crowd, he left the stage and stood among his friends. He said, "I'm here because of Phyllis Wheatley. I'm here because of this fellow sitting next to me," he said, putting his arm on my shoulder. I beamed like a proud papa.

I would rate John B. Davis as the best Minneapolis school superintendent in the modern era because he was the architect of our school-desegregation program. I place Richard Green right behind him. He completed the implementation of Davis's design and did it in a way that united the city around a goal of a high-quality education for every child. When Richard took over, things just moved. The momentum that John Davis created came back to the district.

Richard faced plenty of challenges. Eighteen schools were closed during his tenure as enrollment continued to decline. When I joined the school board, the district served seventy-two thousand students. At its low point during Richard's tenure, enrollment approached forty thousand. It was a precipitous change and brought financial pressure with it since the state tied school aid to enrollment. Each school closing was unpopular but the worst was that of Central High School. Richard proposed closing three high schools at about the same time, Marshall-University, West, and Central. Enrollment was down at both Marshall and West. Further, West's building had a serious problem. It had been built on a bog about a third of a mile from Lake Calhoun and was literally sinking deeper into the bog every year. Central still had strong enrollment, bolstered by a dedicated community of parents and alumni supporters. Its turn-of-the-century building had an elegant Gothic facade, but inside it was crumbling. Its wooden staircases and floors were buckling and warping. It was far from meeting modern codes for building safety. Richard and school-board members met with engineers for countless hours to discuss what could be done about problems with the Central building. Bringing it up to code was simply unaffordable. We could have built two new high schools for the cost. Reluctantly, we concluded that Central would have to go.

We had a terrible time with Central's parents and alumni. At a meeting to discuss the situation, Richard, in his magnificent way, got in front of them and said, "This school is not safe for our children. It may look nice on the outside, but that is just a shell. Inside, it has become a hazard. We are going to have to tear it down." People asked why a new school could not be built on the site, at Thirty-fourth Street and Fourth Avenue South. Richard explained that high-school enrollment in the district did not justify the expense. The area's children could be served at Washburn, Roosevelt, and South High Schools. The parents came around. But some of the alumni, including Rita Davis Lyell and Butch and Ricky Davis, have never quite forgiven us.

One reason we hesitated to close those schools was that, just a few years before, as board chair, I had spearheaded a gymnasium-building program at the high schools. I thought every high school deserved a decent spectator gym. Both Central and West had lovely new gyms that certainly were not ready for demolition. The YWCA came to our rescue and bought the West gym; the Central gym was taken over by the Minneapolis Park and Recreation Board. In the 1990s, a new elementary school, Richard Green School, incorporated the gym.

Another school our children attended, Warrington Elementary, was on the hit list too. That decision was better understood. Warrington was in an ancient building with wooden floors and stairs, and was widely considered a fire hazard. It went the way of the wrecking ball.

We were able to arrange a better outcome for the building that housed Bryant Junior High School, only a few blocks from Central High. The school was closing because of declining enrollment in the area, but the spacious, solid building was well worth saving. It had cement and steel staircases, two gymnasiums, a swimming pool, and lots of rooms that could be adapted for a variety of purposes. One possibility stood out: turning the building into a headquarters for social services so that those in need could find one-stop assistance.

A modest effort at such a collection was located right across the street: Sabathani Community Center. It was founded some years earlier in the hope of providing for the South Side something akin to what Phyllis Wheatley had long been doing on the North Side. It had not grown the way its founders had hoped, but it attracted the attention of some important patrons, among them Rhoda Lund of the grocery family, City Council member Gladys Brooks, and Virginia McKnight Binger, daughter of longtime 3M boss William McKnight. Alongside Sabathani in similarly inadequate quarters was the African-American Cultural Arts Center. I served on the boards of directors of both.

The school board liked the idea of selling the Bryant building to Sabathani and housing the cultural-arts center there too. Jack Mason joined me in spearheading a plan to sell the building at a reduced cost to promote the services that Sabathani would provide. We were criticized for doing that, but we felt that getting any money and keeping that building useful made better economic sense for the city in the long run than the alternative, which was tearing it down.

It's regrettable that the cultural-arts center is no longer in existence. At one point there was a plan for it to have its own home on a parcel of land owned by Central Lutheran Church. We envisioned a place where the history of African Americans—their hardships and their triumphs—would be interpreted through art, music, dance, and drama. It would incorporate arts-education programming provided by the school district. A black architectural firm from Chicago was hired to prepare a design modeled on an African village. Unfortunately, the plan got snagged by the recession of 1980–1982 and did not get off the ground. It was a worthy idea that should be reconsidered someday.

Richard sweetened the pill of school closings with new magnet programs that became some of the most popular in the district. Those programs helped the district stay on target toward desegregation and finally to be found in full compliance with Judge Earl Larson's 1972 order. The district was freed from federal-court supervision in 1986. Richard was a stickler for providing high-quality education in every school in the district. He set a citywide school-discipline code. He established uniform curriculum requirements on schools so that each offered advanced sciences and foreign languages. He imposed a regimen of benchmark tests and stopped the practice of social promotion of young children. He altered the district's contracts with principals so they could be assigned by the superintendent on an annual basis. Richard wanted full control of the deployment of his troops.

Some people faulted Richard for arrogance. Some called him demanding, even dictatorial. But he was also warm, funny, and considerate. When Phil Olson was ill with cancer, it was Richard who took time off work to drive him to radiation treatments. Richard was quick with bear hugs, considerate of his staff, and open and accessible to parents. But some of them disliked his outspoken nature. He did not mince words. He would not hesitate to fire back when other elected officials said something critical of him or the city schools. You couldn't tell him, "Richard, just forget it. It will come out that they're wrong." "No," he'd say, "I've got to tell them that they're wrong." More than once, I counseled him to control his temper. He did not recognize that when you acquire political enemies, sooner or later, they will try to do you in.

Richard's relationship with one principal, George Dahl, led to his stormiest episode as superintendent. George was a fine principal at South High School, popular with students and parents. Richard was well aware of his talent and wanted to apply it to a North Side school that was not faring as well, Patrick Henry High School. When Richard announced Dahl's new assignment, an outcry went up from South, orchestrated by Dahl himself. Dahl and a contingent of parents stormed into the next school-board meeting to protest. George got on the list to speak. Joy Davis, the board chair, was not inclined to let him speak, but Richard urged her to give him the microphone. George made his appeal to stay at South and invited some of the parents in the room to testify to his importance at that school. He concluded, "I am not going to leave."

That was the last straw for Richard. He was growing angrier by the minute as George engaged in what Richard considered rank insubordination. When Joy called on Richard to respond to George's comments, Richard asked George to come back to the microphone because he wanted to address his remarks directly to George. "I'm sure that you know that I have the right by law and by board policy to assign principals at the beginning of every year. I'm superintendent—that's my responsibility. When the schools do not achieve, the board and I are the ones that get the criticism. I have tried to make sure that I give each principal a chance to prove his ability, and I reward good work. I've done that to you. Because you've done an outstanding job at South High School, South High School now is where we want it to be. We have another school that's stumbling. We need good leadership. That's why I've assigned you to Henry. Now, you said you don't want to go. That's fine. I've fulfilled my responsibility to the board. All I have to say to you is—you can choose to go, you can choose not to go. If you don't go, you have only one option. You can retire."

That blew the lid off that meeting and caused lasting repercussions. George Dahl retired and ran for the school board in 1987, making Green himself the issue. It was the rockiest school-board election in years, as several DFL elected officials, City Council members, and legislators backed an anti-administration slate headed by Dahl. Four seats were up that year; the Dahl slate won three of them. That meant support for Richard on the board was now four to three. He saw the precariousness of his situation and confided to me that he was looking for another job. I noticed something else then too: More frequently, he would start wheezing during board meetings and have to excuse himself to take his asthma medicine.

I counseled him against leaving. "Richard, nothing is going to happen to you here," I told him. "Those new board members can't do anything to you. You're the best superintendent we have had since John Davis, and people recognize that. Your roots are here, your family is here, you have a nice home, your kids are still in school." But Richard wanted an adventure. Offers started coming in, from Miami, Houston, New York. The New York Teachers Federation sent a delegation here to meet with him. He asked me to sit in. I could see how drawn he was to the challenge there, to turn around a district that had been called ungovernable. I played my last card. I told him I thought moving to New York would be bad for his health. "If you think it's a strain here in Minneapolis, the one in New York is a hundred times bigger," I said. "They've got a million students. The unions control everything. Richard, your health won't permit you to take that job."

Richard wouldn't listen. "Ahhh," he said, "I'll make it. I'm in good shape yet. I'm still young." He was fifty-one. New York offered him more than it had ever offered any chancellor. The job came with a furnished Manhattan condominium, a limousine with a chauffeur, bodyguards, everything. He had calls from Governor Mario Cuomo begging him to come. He had the prospect of being one of the nation's most recognized educators. For a kid from north Minneapolis, it was heady stuff.

Richard became New York City chancellor of public education in March 1988 in an elaborate, formal inaugural ceremony. Charlotte and I were there; I spoke at the ceremony, describing Richard's early years. Richard invited a busload of people from Minneapolis, including his family and other board members. He put us up in a luxury hotel in Midtown and provided limousines to take us around. He gave us a bus tour of the city and one evening reserved a famous Harlem restaurant entirely for us. We were there for four days and it didn't cost us a quarter. Yet it was hard for me to enjoy myself. I was proud of Richard but sad and worried at the same time.

Richard was soon working ten times harder than he had before, bringing Minneapolis ideas about alternatives and options to the New York system. He was very popular. We talked often, and I knew he was pleased with the way things were going. In early May 1989, he just bubbled over the phone about how he was working with corporations like New York Life to sponsor new schools in downtown locations. He sounded good—no wheezing.

At about 3:00 a.m. on May 10, we got a phone call from Richard's aunt. Richard had died about two hours before, she told us. He had a severe asthma attack and did not recover. Gwen, his wife, was with him when he died and was in a state of shock. It was a terrible, terrible loss. His funeral in New York was at St. Patrick's Cathedral, then we brought him home for a Minneapolis funeral at Hennepin Avenue United Methodist Church and burial at Crystal Lake Cemetery. In the years to come, I would help bury many of my former boxers. Richard's burial remains the hardest.

I did not have the heart to run for reelection in 1989. With that election, I ended twenty years on the school board. But I continue to follow school affairs closely. I was one of those cheering in 1997 when one of Richard's protégés, Carol Johnson, became the district's first female superintendent.

One of my favorite memories from those twenty years was a Washburn High School graduation ceremony in about 1984. Richard was there as superintendent and one of the speakers, and I was there to represent the school board and help pass out diplomas. Some of the graduating seniors were kids from the Field and Hale schools who had been in kindergarten when we paired those schools for desegregation purposes. A couple of big boys came to me, and one said, "Mr. Davis, I remember when I was in kindergarten and you came over to Hale School and spoke." The other said, "When I was a little boy, I watched you when you had a meeting at my house. My mother told us to go to bed, but we didn't go to bed. We stood and peeked out of our bedroom doors and watched the meeting downstairs." Then they thanked me for the good education they had received in those pioneering schools. I wanted to hug them. In fact, I think I did. And then I looked over at Richard, who was surrounded by happy students, black and white, exchanging hugs. I said to myself, we have come a long way—Richard and me, and Minneapolis.

19
Olympian

BOXING IS WHAT BROUGHT ME to the party—that is, to opportunity and recognition in Minneapolis. I never forgot that. I stayed involved in boxing, one way or another, for more than fifty years.

I moved from coaching into administration of the Golden Gloves program in 1960. At first, that meant I was still what I had always been: an employee of the Star and Tribune. Star Tribune Charities ran the Golden Gloves program from its inception in the Upper Midwest. But all of that changed in the early 1960s. Beginning with the newspapers that founded the Golden Gloves, the *New York Daily News* and the *Chicago Tribune,* newspapers around the country decided to sever themselves from athletic programs like ours. The growing professional and ethical consciousness in journalism was behind the change. New generations of sportswriters did not think it right for the newspaper to sponsor sporting events they covered.

The Star and Tribune Company informed me in 1963 that it intended to discontinue Golden Gloves sponsorship. I was quickly in touch with my fellow board members of the national Golden Gloves, based in Chicago. We concluded that the end of newspaper sponsorship need not be fatal. The Golden Gloves tournaments were moneymakers. We could raise funds from other sponsors and keep the program going as an independent association: the Golden Gloves Association of America. We promoted one of the regional directors, making him national director, and paid him a salary. I agreed to continue to manage the Upper Midwest region, which included Minnesota, North Dakota, and South Dakota. I kept control of all of the fights and reported to the national association. My counterparts around the country also signed on with the new organization. No one was of a mind to discontinue a program that we believed did so much good for so many young men.

Back home, Charlie Johnson, George Barton, Dick Cullum, and others from the Star and Tribune Company helped me ease the transition. They called all the coaches from the Upper Midwest region to a meeting and joined me in explaining the change. It went very smoothly. I was well known to all of them, and all were willing to keep the organization going. The external agreements we needed, such as contracts for the Minneapolis Auditorium and arrangements for gym space, all were in place. We just extended them. I enlisted a sports-minded attorney, Irving Nemerov, to help me raise a base of funds. He summoned well-to-do boxing fans, including Minnesota Vikings investors Max Winter and Arne Fliegel, to a fund-raising meeting at their 620 Club restaurant on Sixth and Hennepin. We also contacted Golden Gloves alumni from Phyllis Wheatley and all the other gyms in town and asked them to contribute. We got thirty-three people to give $300 apiece. That $9,900 was the financial foundation of Upper Midwest Golden Gloves, Incorporated. That base, combined with tournament revenues and corporate sponsorship, kept us in the black for many years.

Later, when we needed more money, we combined forces with the American Legion All-Star Corporation. It was headed by Dick Grant, an Upper Midwest Golden Gloves heavyweight champion and, with his brother Norm, a successful investment banker. His American Legion All-Star Corporation sponsored the annual High School All-Star football game, which was a big moneymaker. When Dick agreed to sponsor the Golden Gloves, we changed our name to the Upper Midwest Golden Gloves All-Star Corporation. Dick and Norm also agreed to serve on the board of the Golden Gloves Alumni Association that was organized to provide additional support. The alumni were very helpful with publicity and pro bono professional services of various kinds.

The organization I inherited from the Star and Tribune Company was a well-oiled machine that did not make huge demands on my time. Our volunteers were old hands who did not need to be told what to do. We had people to put on and remove the gloves at matches. We had people to transport the rings. We had judges and referees. We had a state committee to supply rules and regulations and adjudicate disputes. We had people to sponsor shows and entertainment to keep the boxers busy before their matches. The *Star* and *Tribune* sportswriters were happy to keep supplying publicity. It was a joy to head such an organization.

There were eleven settlement houses in Minneapolis in the 1960s, each with a gymnasium and a Golden Gloves program that ran from fall to spring. It was typical for upwards of one hundred kids to box at each settlement house in a given year. We were able to run special shows and tournaments to showcase Minneapolis youth boxing. In the summertime, we would take the rings to city parks—Logan, North Commons, Nicollet Field, the Parade Grounds—and put on training camps. Coaches were paid a small sum to work with the kids at those camps. We were reaching a lot of young people, so many that we added more age divisions to our program.

Phyllis Wheatley teams had been dominant in Upper Midwest tournaments for fifteen of the seventeen years I coached there, and they continued to be strong for a few years afterward. The experienced kids continued to work with the younger ones in the style in which I had taught them, emphasizing physical fitness, mental alertness, and spiritual awareness. But eventually, my successors abandoned my scheme of older boxers helping the younger ones, and the Wheatley program began to fade. Much as I enjoyed my work with the entire region, watching my old program decline was hard.

I became president of the Golden Gloves Association of America in 1969. That put me in a good position to bid to bring the national Golden Gloves tournament to Minneapolis. For many years the tournament was a fixture in Chicago. But under our new administration, its venue rotated in an effort to build interest around the country and maximize our proceeds. I knew how other cities won hosting rights. They came to the national board with cash in hand to underwrite the tournament and with a persuasive pitch about the area's facilities and fan interest in boxing. I enlisted fund-raising help from Golden Gloves heavyweight champion Ching Johnson, a member of our alumni association board. I enticed my counterparts in Detroit and Cleveland to come and see what it was that gave the Upper Midwest teams a disproportionate share of victories through the years. Together, we got the job done. Winning the 1972 national tournament for Minneapolis was a highlight of 1970 for me—that, and being chosen the national Golden Gloves Man of the Year.

The 1972 national Golden Gloves tournament was at the Minneapolis Auditorium, bringing boxers from thirty-one cities to town for six days of competition, Monday through Saturday. Our local alumni network was in full force, helping me develop and run the national event. To us, it was just a larger, longer version of the regional tournament we were accustomed to operating. It was three rings instead of two, five days instead of three or four. I had plenty of help arranging hotel accommodations and publicity. We were at home in the old Minneapolis Auditorium. It seated eleven thousand spectators—and we needed every seat because we had a major draw in young Duane Bobick. Duane, an up-and-coming boxer from Bowlus, Minnesota, who would go on to an outstanding professional boxing career, was in the navy at the time. He could have qualified for the Olympics through the navy's own boxing program, but he wanted to come home and box in the tournament here. He did, and he won. Before the year was over, he had also won the Olympic trials; he went to Germany to represent the United States. He lost there to Teofilo Stevenson from Cuba, who was unbeaten. Still, we were very proud that one of our Upper Midwest boxers was competing at that level.

That should have been boxing thrill enough for me that year. But there was more. In 1971 I had been selected to represent the Golden Gloves on the United States Olympic Boxing Committee. The Golden Gloves had an automatic seat on that committee as the largest amateur-boxing program in the country and a longtime feeder program for the Olympics. Winners of our national tournament qualified to go into Olympic trials. In fact, the most famous American professional boxers, including Muhammad Ali, Willie Pep, Sugar Ray Robinson, and Joe Louis, rose through Golden Gloves ranks.

It was a momentous but also disheartening time to become affiliated with the Olympics. The quadrennial summer games were in Munich in 1972 and were marred by the assassination of eleven athletes and six others from Israel. The militant Palestinian group Black September held the athletes hostage during a twenty-one-hour standoff, during which the gunmen demanded the release of 236 Palestinians from Israeli jails and five others imprisoned in Germany for terrorist acts. The German officials failed to react effectively and refused to let Israeli antiterrorist units step in. The world was horrified when the standoff ended in mass murder. It was hard to think of the Olympics as mere games after that.

The 1976 Summer Olympics were in Montreal. That year, I was selected along with another of our Golden Gloves coaches, Biff Holstein, to go to England as team manager of our second-place trial team. We would box with the British champions. I was pleased to have the opportunity to work with such talent—and in London! I had always dreamed about going to London and seeing all the sights I had learned about in school—Parliament and Buckingham Palace and Westminster Abbey. It was my first trip overseas.

As team manager, I was in charge of logistics and living arrangements for eleven boxers, four coaches, and the doctor and nurse who traveled with us. I worked closely with our British counterpart, who, to my surprise, was a member of the royal family, a duke. The duke was in charge of all of his country's official amateur athletic programs. I don't think he had ever so much as held a tennis racket, but he arranged for us to fight at Wimbledon, site of the world-famous tennis tournament. We stayed in an old hotel with an elevator, or "lift," like a closet. With its beautiful old woodwork and marble floors, the hotel looked like something out of a movie. We all were charmed by the place.

Our British hosts went out of their way to make our visit memorable. The duke ordered a bus to take us as a group to Buckingham Palace to watch the changing of the guard. It then took us to the palace guards' quarters, and we were shown where the guards' horses were trained. We were invited to stay for dinner in the officers' quarters. Another time, we were given a tour of a beer brewery, and though the team was not allowed to drink, the coaches were not under such restrictions.

I became well acquainted with a member of the British Olympic committee named Harry Haden. We had breakfast together on several occasions. We teased about the pronunciation of our shared name. He insisted it should be pronounced "Air-ee." He arranged for us to have a shopping trip to Harrods, where I bought Charlotte a lovely tea set—cups, saucers, teapot, sugar, and creamer. I regretted that spouses were not invited on that trip. Charlotte would have loved it.

We had a joint news conference with the British team at the London Press Club soon after our arrival. It fell to me to introduce our team. The first question the reporters asked was, "Where is Sugar Ray Leonard?" He was the undisputed star of the U.S. Olympic boxing team that year and, as such, was not part of the second-place squad in London. I explained that Sugar Ray Leonard was representing the United States in the Olympic games and that our rules did not permit him to box for a specified number of days before the Olympics. I offered in his place his runner-up, Tommy Hearns of Detroit. Tommy had lost to Leonard in the qualifying finals, and later would challenge him for the world championship. Tommy was an impressive fighter, but Sugar Ray held all the fascination that year. The British press taunted, "You didn't bring Sugar Ray Leonard, because you knew that our boxer would beat him."

When the matches started, we were down to ten boxers. Our flyweight contender was sidelined with a fever. We had won four matches, they had won five. It was down to the last fight of the evening, Tommy Hearns's match. Wimbledon was packed. We discovered that the Brits liked a little beer (or a lot of beer) with their sporting events. By the last bout, the audience was pretty well schnockered up. The bell rang, and Tommy's opponent (whose name escapes me) came out swinging. He backed Tommy into the ropes. Tommy hit him as he came in with an uppercut, then with a right, and he knocked him colder than a mackerel. Down he went. He appeared to be having a convulsion. Our doctor rushed for the ring, only to be stopped by the referee. Some sharp words were exchanged before the referee did the responsible thing—stopped the fight and got the British boxer the medical attention he needed. That knockout punch took the best British fighter out of the Olympics for that year. So much for Tommy Hearns being a second-place fighter.

An Olympic team and its managers live and work so closely together that they get to know each other well. I got to know fine, upstanding young men like Tommy Hearns and Michael Spinks. Then there was Michael's light-heavyweight brother, Leon. He was a devil! He would sneak out of training camp, get drunk, and wind up fighting in the street. Still, Leon Spinks was the one who came away from the 1976 Summer Olympics with a gold medal. We had a terrific team that year and picked up a majority of the eleven gold medals in boxing.

In about 1978, Congress required all amateur-sports organizations that produce Olympic qualifiers to come under the jurisdiction of the U.S. Olympic Committee. The sports could continue to have their own organizations, but they were required to adhere to rules and regulations set by the Olympic Committee. That changed boxing. Golden Gloves Association of America would no longer be the feeder program to the Olympics. Instead, a smaller group called the Amateur Boxing Federation, which had been centered in East Coast cities, was enlarged as the Amateur Boxing Federation of America. That body provided the structure that would lead to the Olympics. Golden Gloves would be its affiliate; so would some of the smaller boxing programs that had popped up around the country. It was a complete reorganization of amateur boxing. The federation administered the federal tax money allocated for the establishment of Olympic training camps. The boxing camp was located in Colorado Springs, Colorado, in the old air-force base there. The federation also took charge of Olympic-level traveling teams, of the sort I took to London. The federation was well funded because it was able to attract private sponsorships and charge admission to events, and it even got television contracts for Olympic trial matches. From the beginning, it had a contract with Caesars Palace in Las Vegas for hosting the trials and international shows. Exhibition matches between the U.S. Olympic boxing team and squads from Russia, Germany, and Britain were conducted with some frequency and drew big crowds.

After the 1976 Summer Olympics, I was one of four Americans chosen to serve a four-year term on the World Olympic Boxing Committee, which brought together representatives of eighty-seven different countries. I also continued to serve on the U.S. Olympic Boxing Committee and continued as a director of the Golden Gloves. Those multiple roles required me to attend a number of the tournaments at Caesars Palace. It was tough duty! Charlotte would often accompany me, and sometimes we were joined by Ray and Mae Hatcher. Caesars Palace treated us royally, putting us up in luxurious suites. We were a long way from the cramped gym at the Wheatley.

Boxing brought me more excitement in 1978, when the World Olympic Boxing Committee met in Madrid, Spain. It was the meeting that would select committee leadership for the 1980 Summer Olympics, so it was highly charged with politics. All eighty-seven participating countries would have a vote. The committee's leadership had been in Russian hands for some time. Our meeting took place more than a decade before the Soviet bloc's breakup. The Russians were adept at pressuring their satellite nations to vote for them. We four Americans on the committee were determined to make a change. Before we went to Madrid, we huddled at our training center in Colorado Springs to decide on a strategy. The other three Americans on the committee were Don Hall, a retired army colonel; Bob Sircon of the University of Illinois athletic department; and Thomas Johnson, an army boxing coach. Our plan was for Don to run for International Boxing Federation chair. We were well aware that most of the countries that were not controlled by Russia were countries of color: the Arab countries, the African countries, the South American and Central American countries, the Pacific and Caribbean islands. Every one of them had a vote. We decided to expose them to some American-style politicking. We reserved rooms for use as a hospitality suite and arranged for a bar and the best hors d'oeuvres from the countries we were courting. We had an amazing buffet of Arab, Latin American, and African cuisine. We enlisted the head of the Olympic Committee in the Virgin Islands, a person of color who was fluent in both Spanish and English, to serve as our interpreter. Thomas Johnson and I would serve as hosts of the hospitality suite and would extend invitations to come and meet our candidate, Don Hall. Our wives were with us, and they pitched in. We must have done a good job because Don was elected.

One might say that the Madrid trip was my first exposure to international relations, of both the political and the social kind. Somehow we learned to overcome the language barriers with a mixture of body language and a few phrases we picked up by listening to the interpreters at the general sessions. Those sessions were like mini–United Nations assemblies. The delegates from North Korea and South Korea, both of them military officials, gave us a taste of their mutual hostility by screaming insults at each other. We got a sense of

Arab attitudes toward the West just from observing the bearing and tone of the delegate from Iraq. The bravado of a delegate from Mexico gave us one of the meeting's most humorous moments. He wore a pure white suit and a big white, silver-tasseled sombrero on a trip to a bullfight and a bull ranch. By the time the group got there, they had been served a number of alcoholic beverages at previous stops, and at the ranch the food and wine just kept coming. After the meal, we were invited to watch the training of young bulls for the ring. The Mexican delegate in the white suit boasted that he was an experienced bullfighter. "Come down. Let's see what you can do with this little bull," our host said. Sure enough, the bull brushed by him and he landed with a splat in a place where animals had been doing what animals usually do. Oh, he looked terrible! He suffered all the way back to the hotel.

Hotel assignments were made in national clusters so that we could get to know a few other countries' delegations especially well. Poland, England, Brazil, and Italy were in our cluster. Already at that time, Poland was pulling away from the Soviet bloc. One of the Polish delegates and his wife were especially friendly to Charlotte and me. We occasionally ate meals together, and when we had an interpreter at hand, we would talk. He said, through the interpreter, "Harry, I'd like to have you bring a team over to Poland. Why don't we do that next year, or just before the Olympics?" The idea sounded good to me. I thought I could arrange a team visit modeled after our 1976 trip to England with our runner-up boxers. I gave him an encouraging response, and it paid off. The voting for committee president was the next day, and Poland's vote went to the American candidate.

All of our planning for American participation in the 1980 Summer Olympics was for naught. President Jimmy Carter ordered a boycott of the Olympics by Americans that year in protest of the Soviet invasion of Afghanistan. The games were to be played in Moscow, and the Carter administration did not want American athletes to be party to strutting by the Soviets of the sort Olympic hosts sometimes do. It was very disappointing. I understood the politics of Carter's decision, but political calculations overlooked the purpose of the program. We were athletes, not soldiers. Our goal was to give deserving kids a chance to compete at the world's highest levels. Most of our boxers were inner-city kids for whom the Olympics meant a chance to climb out of the ghetto. For them, the boycott was a terrible disservice.

The boycott gave us an excuse to expand our trip to Poland in March 1980 by including our first-team boxers as well as some of the runners-up. We wound up with a squad of eighteen boxers, plus coaches, referees, and medical personnel. Altogether, it was a troupe of about thirty people. I was the team manager once again, the guy in charge of logistics for the group. Our plan was for the team to assemble at JFK Airport in New York and leave together for Poland aboard a Russian-made aircraft flown by Lot, the Polish national airline. Charlotte and I were to fly from Minneapolis with two boxers, Steve Adams and Monroe Gage, both Upper Midwest champions. Our plane leaving Minneapolis taxied to the runway, then stopped. The flight crew announced that they had indications of a mechanical problem and that we needed to deplane. We were told to expect a delay of a couple of hours. That delay stretched to upwards of six hours. When we finally got to New York, we had missed the flight to Poland.

I always felt afterward that it was God who delayed our flight from Minneapolis. The plane carrying the rest of the squad crashed on the runway in Warsaw on March 14, killing all eighty-seven people aboard. Engine failure was cited as the official cause of the crash. Charlotte, Steve, Monroe, and I got the news while we were at the airport in New York, waiting for our flight to Poland. It was an enormous blow to me personally, and to amateur boxing in America. I have always considered that huge loss the real tragedy of the 1980 Olympic boycott. If those fine young athletes had been going to Russia instead of Poland, they wouldn't have been on that plane.

Soon after that terrible loss, at a somber meeting in Colorado Springs, I was elected vice president of the Amateur Boxing Federation of America. Loren Baker, a young boxing referee and official from Georgia, was elected president. We tried to work together as a leadership team, and though we were different in style and outlook, we got along well. He was the schmoozer, I was the guy with the detailed reports.

We were determined to take steps to reinvigorate our program and offset our tragic loss. We brought in teams from Europe for exhibitions. We boxed Cuban fighters in Reno. We boxed the Russians at a special tournament of heavyweights at Caesars Palace. We promoted the Pan American Games and the World Championships, an international program conducted between Olympic games, to give our up-and-coming youngsters a chance to test themselves against strong foreign competition.

Then came the 1984 Summer Olympics, the one that would finally lift the cloud over U.S. Olympic boxing. The games were held on home turf, in Los Angeles, and the United States had the best boxing team yet. It included Evander Holyfield and Pernell Whitaker. Of our twelve first-team fighters, nine won gold medals, one won a silver, and one a bronze. It was an amazing sweep.

I was team manager again, which put me in charge of the team's housing, meals, transportation, credentials, and other logistics. We were assigned to a large complex at the University of Southern California that included track and field, polo, swimming and diving, and boxing. We competed on the campus where we were housed. Each meal was served outdoors in big tents and offered an amazing array of fresh fruits and vegetables, meats and fish, and an abundance of milk to accommodate the various dietary needs of the athletes. Each of our boxers had a daily diet to follow, depending on whether he needed to gain or lose weight or build up certain reserves. We made out diet slips for our boxers each day, and coaches ate with the boxers to make sure they followed the regimen. It was always a little bit of a thrill to walk into a tent at mealtime and see athletes from various countries, wearing the warm-up clothes of their teams, congregating and conversing in a babble of languages. A swimmer from Germany might be next to a track star from South Africa and a boxer from Minnesota. Whether they spoke the same language or not, they understood each other and got along well.

I was housed in the Olympic Village with our boxers. We were in apartments that had four bedrooms clustered around a living room, a kitchen, and a little dining room. I assigned two fighters to each bedroom. Our first and second teams, twelve boxers each, were housed in the same building but in separate clusters. Also with the team were four coaches, two doctors, two nurses, and some judges and referees, about three dozen people in all. I assigned three first-team and three second-team boxers to each of the four coaches responsible for seeing the athletes through their schedules, monitoring their diet and training regimens, and keeping track of their uniform and equipment requirements. The crucial thing for Olympic boxers is to get through the weigh-in. A boxer who does not make his requisite weight is disqualified. The coaches and doctors worked together to get the boxers past that critical hurdle. Boxers who come in overweight have an hour in which to shrink down. It's possible to lose four or five pounds in an hour if one has to, but the exertion required leaves one weak for a day or so afterward. Competitors watch for that and try to take advantage of boxers who had to bring their weights down quickly to qualify at weigh-in.

I was no longer coaching directly, but I was often involved in conversations with other coaches and with coaches and boxers, discussing strategy and training options. I also helped scout other countries' teams as my time permitted. We had the tournament schedule posted on a big board, listing all twelve weight divisions and our likely competitors at each step. I made sure that someone would scout the competition in advance and got the right people together afterward for strategy sessions. The scout would report on a competitor's strengths and weaknesses, and we would discuss options for working those traits to our advantage.

Charlotte did not come with me to Los Angeles. She was active in the Links, a national organization for black women, and was attending their convention in Philadelphia while I was in Los Angeles. That meant that sixteen-year-old Evan was home alone—or would have been, had I not arranged for him to join me in L.A. It just so happened that we had an extra bed in the second-team suite because one boxer went home early. I got Evan all the credentials necessary to put him in that bed. His roommate? Mike Tyson, the future heavyweight champion and boxing's bad boy of the 1990s. It did not occur to me that I was making a dubious choice. Mike was only seventeen then, the youngest member of our team and still under the sway of Constantine "Cus" D'Amato, his trainer/manager. Mike was a much tamer person in those years than he became after Cus died in 1985. Evan had the time of his life. He ate with the team; he traveled in official Olympic Village minivans with the team; he wore an official warm-up along with the rest of the team. He told me afterward that he even signed autographs when asked, just like the other boxers did.

The U.S. boxing team that year stands out in my mind not only because of the success they had, but also because of the fine young men they were. I got to know quite a few of them well because we had been together at the Olympic training camp in Colorado Springs or at previous international tournaments. Our relationship was such that if the boxers needed anything, either equipment or something of a personal nature, they called me. They were bright kids; in fact, I would call some of them brilliant. They were not overly boastful, but they had plenty of self-confidence. Of course, they were kids, and kids need guidance. The adults who lived with the team often discussed how best to give each athlete the guidance he needed. Still, after living with the team for nearly a full month, I came away believing anew in the power of boxing to shape boys into admirable young men.

Holyfield, the future heavyweight champion, was very easy to work with. He was dedicated, confident, always in good shape, and pleasant to everybody. He was cheated out of a gold medal in Los Angeles. In his semifinal bout, the crowd was so noisy that no one could hear the bell ring. Holyfield hit his opponent and knocked him unconscious after the bell had rung. The judges debated what to do for some time before disqualifying Evander from that match. Their decision provoked a howl of protest. Evander ended up with the bronze medal in the light-heavyweight division. His reaction to what happened made us proud. He did not fuss and fume that he had been cheated; he thanked his opponent, shook hands with the referees, and bowed to the judges. He handled himself with a lot of grace.

Holyfield was not the only member of that team who went on to distinction as a professional boxer. Paul Gonzalez became the 105-pound flyweight champion of the world. Steve McCrory later became flyweight champion of the world. Meldrick Taylor won the featherweight, lightweight, and welterweight championships as a pro. Another three-time world champion was Pernell Whitaker. He won the world's lightweight championship, the welterweight championship, and the super-welterweight championship. Our 147-pound gold medalist was Mark Breland. He had the biggest following before the games; he had won the New York Golden Gloves several times and had been in movies and on television. He won the 147-pound championship of the world. Our 156-pound medalist, Frank Tate, won the world championship in both that division and the 160-pound division. Virgil Hill, from Williston, North Dakota, was the team's silver medalist. He went on to win the light-heavyweight championship of the world. Henry Tillman had the distinction of beating Mike Tyson in the Olympic trials. He stands out in memory as a disciplined athlete, always in at curfew time. That meant he was the opposite of our heavyweight medalist, Tyrell Biggs. He was our problem case. He weighed about 240 pounds, stood about six-foot-five, and boxed beautifully. He wanted to be watched, especially by the ladies. The girls would be around him in droves. He was never in his room for the 9:00 p.m. curfew. Most nights, we were still wondering where he was at 10:00 or 11:00. We discussed replacing him with his alternate from the second team, but he had a big following in the media, which made him hard to replace. He won his gold medal by the skin of his teeth.

For every athlete, the Olympics offers a powerful lesson. Young athletes work and sacrifice for years to get there, only to find that their competitors in other countries have done the same thing and that they are just as deserving. Athletes develop a great deal of respect for each other. They live in close proximity to athletes from other countries and develop friendships that cross barriers of language and culture. Seldom does bad sportsmanship mar an Olympic event. Competition is keen at the Olympics, but so is the recognition that other athletes just might be better. Athletes come away thankful for the experience, even if they do not win. I consider the 1984 Summer Olympics the greatest experience I ever had working with young athletes.

I did not realize it at the time, but the Los Angeles games would be something of a last hurrah for me in the Olympics. Only a few months after the Los Angeles games, the Amateur Boxing Federation of America met to elect officers in Rapid City, South Dakota. The federation's bylaws called for the vice president to move up to the presidency at the next election. I had been preparing to take charge. But as the Rapid City meeting approached, I got wind of opposition. The nominating committee was either all-white or very nearly so. I had spoken out at some of our meetings about ensuring equal opportunity for all races. I was allied with another black federation member from the University of Ohio, a well-educated man who was controversial within the organization for his advocacy of racial inclusion. Our remarks were not universally well received. Further, I was told, some members of the federation resented the large influence the Golden Gloves program had, and, by extension, resented me. I learned upon arriving in Rapid City that an organized effort was afoot not to have "a Golden Gloves man" head the federation. A challenger had stepped forward. To my surprise and chagrin, it was Don Hall, the man I had helped elect to the International Boxing Federation chair in Madrid six years earlier.

It was plain to me that the Golden Gloves excuse was a red herring. My color was the issue. I was so disillusioned; I thought we had risen above racism in this country. After all, this was the 1980s. It hurt that Don Hall was willing to alter the federation's bylaws to keep me out of the presidency. But that is just what he did. Don had the stature to carry the day.

After that blow, I decided it was time to pull back my involvement in the administration of amateur boxing. I declined reappointment to the Olympic Committee but agreed to continue as administrator of boxing's Olympic feeder program in the Upper Midwest. It was much the same responsibility I had known since the 1960s with the Golden Gloves. I chose not to attend national meetings or manage future Olympic teams. In 1991, I was pleased to be given the U.S. Olympic Committee's outstanding-service award. I finally retired as a boxing administrator in 1993, fifty years after I started work as Phyllis Wheatley's Golden Gloves coach. My successor was a terrific choice—Chuck Hales, one of my former Golden Gloves boxers from Phyllis Wheatley. Chuck was a boxer from Staples, Minnesota, but when he graduated from high school, he enrolled in college in Minneapolis just so he could join my team at the Wheatley. The way he tells it, every young boxer in rural Minnesota wanted to have a chance to learn from Harry Davis. Chuck became the owner of a successful computerized machine-tool business. He is a strong manager of people and skillful at organizing events. We talk often, commiserating about all the politics in sports organizations, but we enjoy the satisfaction of making a difference for young people.

I often told my boxers, and anyone else who would listen, that the squared circle we enter as boxers is an imitation of life itself. "There's the squared circle," I would say. "That's where you are headed. That's life. You are in training to go into that circle and be something in life. If you want to succeed there, you must prepare your body, your mind, and your spirit. If you prepare today as boxers to enter this squared circle, then when you are an adult and must perform in life's larger circle, you will know what to do." That is what boxing did for me. It's what I hope I've taught every young boxer I've known.

20
Harvesting

FEW, IF ANY, EMPLOYEES of major American newspapers can say they rose in corporate ranks from boxing coach to corporate vice president. The latter years of that unconventional career journey were rich and varied. I had assignments in the areas of property acquisition, public and community affairs, and human resources. I was involved in corporate planning and philanthropy too. Every day was interesting.

But I also associate my last years at the Star Tribune Company with something else: cancer.

With the exception of bouts of pneumonia and kidney stones in the early 1970s, I had enjoyed good health through most of my adult years. I had pushed myself hard, and my body had, for the most part, kept up with me. But in 1983, during a routine annual physical, a bump was discovered in my groin. My doctors, Paul Nelson and Robert Schultz, recommended a biopsy. Dr. Schultz arranged to have it done at Metropolitan Medical Center, which was the old Swedish Hospital, only a few blocks from the Star Tribune building. The biopsy tissue was analyzed by an oncologist I was to come to know well, Dr. I. E. Fortuny. He determined that I had cancer, and that it was already present in my lymph glands as well as in the tumor in my groin. He and my surgeon, Dr. Harrison Farley, wasted no time. They removed the tumor and some glandular tissue from my groin and also opened my belly to examine my liver. Knowing whether my liver was diseased would help my doctors determine the course of any additional treatment.

Charlotte and all four of my children were at the hospital as I had surgery, waiting for news. The report was serious but not catastrophic: I had Hodgkin's disease, or lymphatic cancer. It appeared concentrated in the lymph glands of the groin. My liver did not appear to be affected. The doctors explained treatment options briefly to my family and later, in more detail, to me. We talked about radiation, but radiation would treat only one area of the body. The presence of cancer in the lymph glands suggested that a more systemic treatment was the wiser course. That meant chemotherapy, the first and second Mondays of every month, for a whole year.

It was a dreary prospect but one I had to face. At the start, I would receive treatments at Metropolitan Medical Center following a checkup. The doctors would adjust the chemotherapy regimen depending on what their examinations showed. Later in the program, I went directly to Dr. Fortuny's office for the treatments, on the corner of Chicago Avenue and Twenty-sixth Street, near Abbott Northwestern Hospital. I was told not to drive home, so I would pick up Charlotte beforehand and she would sit with me during the long treatment sessions and drive me home afterward.

I would be ushered to a reclining chair, like the ones used at blood banks, and a long needle would be injected in the blood vessels of my hands. That is, we started with my hands. After a few treatments, those vessels began to collapse and the chemotherapist had to search for vessels in my arms. During the last few sessions, she had to use hot towels to heat my arms in order to find blood vessels to use. Dr. Fortuny worked with a chemotherapist named Diana, a gentle, caring woman with a sunny personality that was well suited to her job. It seemed that her touches had healing power.

The routine was that I would arrive at noon. The first step was the injection of saline solution, both to avoid burning the skin with the strong poisons used in chemotherapy and to make sure the needle had been properly placed. By 12:30, the real stuff would begin flowing. It would not end until nearly 4:00 p.m., four long hours after my arrival. I would go home, knowing what would come next: extreme nausea. It was like a terrible case of stomach flu. I did not stay sick very long, however; often I could go to work the next day, though I was not at full strength.

That went on for a full year, twenty-four treatments in all. In between I had two bone-marrow biopsies. My doctors were also concerned about the cancer spreading to my colon. As the treatments drew to a close, Dr. Fortuny suggested exploratory surgery to check the condition of my colon. When I mentioned this to the family, they didn't like the idea. They felt I had endured enough surgery. My son Ricky had played football in school with a son of Dr. John Najarian, then chief of surgery at the University of Minnesota. We had also come to know the Najarians at Hennepin Church. Unbeknownst to me, Ricky contacted Dr. Najarian about my case. He in turn called Dr. Fortuny to recommend involving another oncologist at the university, Dr. B. J. Kennedy. It was the kind of suggestion many a doctor would resist, but not Dr. Fortuny. He was a great guy, affable and cooperative. He had followed my career in politics. In fact, he would come and chat about political matters with me while I was receiving treatments in his office. He was eager to do anything he could to help me. He arranged for me to check into the University of Minnesota Hospitals (now Fairview-University Medical Center) for two days and be thoroughly examined by Dr. Kennedy.

By coincidence, the year of my chemotherapy was also the first year of our involvement with a program called Christian Ashram. It is something Charlotte and I came to know about through Gail and Don Dahlstrom. Gail had been Butch's social-studies teacher at Bryant Junior High School and, later, my strong campaign supporter; Don is a radiologist and a fine person. We became good friends through the years. Gail and Don were members of Augustana Lutheran Church, whose pastor, the Reverend William Berg, was much involved in Christian Ashram.

The Ashram concept originated in India as a Hindu spiritual discipline. Originally, it involved withdrawing from the world, from everything, and abiding in silent prayer for several days. When the Reverend E. Stanley Jones adapted the concept for Christians, the requirement of intensive silence was dropped. But it was still a program of regular retreats, three or four days long, taking participants away from work and home to concentrate on God. The Christian Ashram involves Bible study, discussion, and individual and group prayer. One or more clergy leaders or evangelists guide the sessions.

I had arranged for the new senior pastor at Hennepin Church, the Reverend David Tyler Scoates, to serve as our evangelist at the Ashram at Villa Maria, a former Catholic girls school on Lake Pepin near Red Wing. The Ashram ran Thursday through Sunday, but Charlotte and I decided we needed to leave after the Saturday-evening session. I was to check into University of Minnesota Hospitals on Sunday night for my battery of tests. On Saturday evening, before we left, Pastors Berg and Scoates led a healing service. Charlotte and I sat in the center of a circle as Pastors Scoates and Berg and Gail Dahlstrom joined us and put their hands on us. Other participants then put their hands on them and so on until the whole group was connected by touch. I had a strange sensation as they prayed for me. It was as if I were a light bulb and somebody had turned me on. I had the sensation of being very bright, like I was glowing. I was warm, but not feverish, and everything I looked at seemed unusually clear and bright. When the prayer ended and hands were removed, the glow faded. When I described the sensation to Charlotte, she said she had felt the same thing while we were holding hands in the circle. We knew we had experienced something profound.

The next night, I was admitted to University Hospitals and went through all the examinations in the book (and a few that weren't) over the next two days. My team of doctors—Kennedy, Fortuny, and Schultz—met with me after all the results were in. "We cannot find a trace of cancer," they reported. Further surgery was not needed. I told Dr. Fortuny about my experience at the Ashram. He said he too believed God played a role in healing. "Harry, we are the doctors, but Christ is the teacher," he said. "He teaches us how to treat illness. When we perform surgery or administer chemotherapy, we are doing the work of the Lord, through us to you." It made so much sense.

My year of chemotherapy ended with the cancer in complete remission. I continued a regimen of tests for a time, but I have never had a recurrence of the disease. When I describe my Ashram experience to people, they ask whether I believe I was healed at that prayer service. I know it played a role, but I believe that the knowledge and skill of the doctors and therapists and nurses also healed me, and that knowledge is God-given. God is the greatest surgeon. God works through medicine as well as prayer. God also works through the love of family and friends. I was healed by the way Charlotte cared for me. She was my closest nurse and friend. I never saw her crying or giving up. She would go with me to the treatments and the checkups, and always be there for me when I came out. Her devotion said to me, "You can't give up. You've got to fight it." When I say today about my cancer, "The Lord was there and brought me through it," I think of all of those things. And I am grateful.

The Ashram program became an important element in our spiritual lives in the 1980s, and it remains so today. It is a relatively new program in the United States, but it traces its origins to India in 1930 and the work of the Christian evangelist E. Stanley Jones. He organized the Ashram as a non-denominational movement, centered on the discipline of annual retreats. The North American Ashram owns no property and is headquartered wherever the current general secretary of the organization lives. The chair of the Ashram board of directors is a retired United Methodist bishop, James K. Mathews, E. Stanley Jones's son-in-law. Our spiritual leader through the years has continued to be Pastor William Berg, who is said to be "in the four" in the Ashram organization. That means he was one of four leaders chosen by Jones years ago to direct the Ashram movement in the United States after his passing. I am a founding member of the Minnesota board of directors and am serving my third term on the board of the national organization. My friend Don Dahlstrom remains the chair of the Minnesota organization.

Ashram retreats are conducted in a variety of settings. In recent years, the Minnesota group has met for four days the third weekend in August at St. John's University in Collegeville. That is our annual Ashram. We generally draw about 250 people, many of them families with young children, from all over the state and region. People are encouraged to bring their whole families. We have three floors of a dormitory to ourselves. People attend classes and listen to speakers, then break into smaller groups of about a dozen people for discussion and prayer. I have been a leader of those groups. The focus is on our relationship with God and how that relationship affects our daily lives and our relationships with other people. That includes the people in attendance, people who have become close friends. We make a commitment to pray for each other, often about very personal problems and needs. There is something about coming together around a focus on Jesus as Lord that quickly creates a close connection among people. It doesn't seem like anyone is a stranger at an Ashram. Everyone who goes there gets refueled with love for other human beings. Charlotte and I look forward to seeing the people who come year after year. We also see the local participants at "mini-Ashrams" that are conducted three or four times a year in the Twin Cities. We often meet for a day at Augustana Lutheran Home, near Bill Berg's Augustana Church. It is common for a hundred people to attend those sessions.

My faith in God has grown and become dearer to me as I have matured. It has grown because I've seen things happen. I have seen the way that God has touched people's lives and been with them through both tribulation and celebration. I see God more clearly in my own life as I reflect on my childhood and youth. It almost seems like a special power kept me from winding up in prison or addicted to drugs and on the streets. I have watched children and grandchildren grow and have seen them change as they have made a spiritual connection to God. I have come to a deeper understanding that God reveals himself through relationships with other people. More than ever, I see that it matters how we treat each other. It is a statement of faith to say of someone else, "That's my brother. That's my sister. Whatever happens to him or her happens to me. I will laugh when they laugh and mourn when they mourn. If they have nothing and I have something, I will share my something with them." To live a life of faith is to always strive to serve others.

So many people think that life slips away from you as you age. I believe just the opposite: you gain life as you get older. You first gain knowledge, the stuff of school and church and family. Then comes experience. As you put the two together, wisdom results. You learn that life is more than what you know or what you do. Its richness lies in the meaning you grasp from the viewpoint that you develop. For me, a key to grasping life's meaning has been faith in God.

After my recovery from cancer, I wanted to dedicate myself more fully to serving God and the people around me. But I was aware that I had to establish a new, slower pace. During my year of chemotherapy, I had several frank conversations with my doctors about my workload. Hard work may not cause disease, but hard work and stress make it more difficult for one's body to fight disease. I came to understand that it was important to my survival to reduce the stress in my life. I began to approach life differently. I tried not to let myself get so wrapped up in the routine conflicts that arose on the school board, the boxing federation, or at the office. When someone approached me in anger or opposition, I could almost hear the Lord say, "Just let it go. Let it go. Don't let it affect you. They'll turn around."

I decided to retire from the Star Tribune Company in January 1987. The top executives at the newspaper could not have been more supportive during my illness. They adjusted my duties to free me to concentrate on recovery. When we began to talk about my retirement, they took a personal interest in the adequacy of my retirement income and benefits. School-board members received only a modest per diem, and the boxing work I did in those years was not salaried. But I maintained one paid position: since 1980, I had been a member of the board of directors at TCF Bank.

My TCF board membership resulted from my acquaintance with TCF's chair, Harvey Kuhnley, on the Urban Coalition board. He was a fan of the Broadcasters' Skills Bank that we founded at the coalition to train and hire minority people for broadcasting jobs. He surprised me when he announced that he wanted me to replicate that program at TCF. "If you are interested, I'd like to have you come on my board," he said. I was pleased to do so, given his bank's strong reputation and my admiration for him. Harvey was a smart businessman and a very decent, friendly man. TCF stands for Twin Cities Federal. When I joined the board, TCF was a savings and loan institution, the largest in this part of the country. Kuhnley's goal was for TCF to become a full-service bank. It would be a move that would require great caution. Full-service banks are expected to make commercial loans. A large new bank was bound to be deluged with applications for such loans from businesspeople in other cities who had been turned down by the banks in their own locales.

I had some experience with commercial loans at First Plymouth Bank, but none of them were the large loans TCF would be asked to provide. Only a few other board members had any background in that area, though as the board grew, we added people with that experience in their portfolios. As the transition toward a full-service bank began, Kuhnley was also becoming less active. He built a home in Arizona and spent fewer days in Minnesota. He hired Roy Craven, a full-service banker from the East, with the title of president and groomed Craven to succeed him. Craven pushed Harvey to go faster into granting commercial loans than many board members wanted. When Harvey announced he would retire, the board's jitters over the direction and speed of change at TCF became more apparent. We were split on a very visible decision, a $34 million loan to the brand-new Canterbury Downs horse-racing track. I was among those who considered it a risky act for a bank that had little history with commercial loans. The temporary board chair, Norm Lorentszen of Burlington Northern Railroad, agreed with me. But we were on the losing side.

Not long afterward, I was invited to a meeting with Norm and a few other board members at the Perkins restaurant near Augsburg College—away from the downtown crowd, I noted. "What kind of meeting is this?" I asked. The first thing they said was, "Are you satisfied with the way the bank is going?" I hesitated, then put the question back to them: "Let me get you to respond first. Are you satisfied?" They looked at each other and said, "No, we're not." They began to tell of their discomfort with promoting Roy Craven to succeed Harvey Kuhnley. My thinking was much the same as theirs. Craven had led the bank to invest in a $650 million real-estate venture that was going badly. He not only advocated larger commercial loans than these board members thought prudent, but he also tried to goad and even intimidate board members who disagreed with him.

As a result of that luncheon, I wound up on a five-member search committee assigned to recruit a different successor to Harvey Kuhnley. In the interim, we installed as chief operating officer Jim Fox, a former executive vice president at TCF who had left the bank but still served on the board. We interviewed several candidates with an eye toward hiring someone with solid commercial-bank experience. Some of the people we interviewed were actually more experienced than the man we chose but weaker in the commercial-loan area that we felt was crucial to the transition TCF was trying to make. Our choice: Bill Cooper. He had a wealth of the experience we were seeking. He had not been a CEO before, but had been the in-the-trenches lending officer and executive vice president who had to make day-to-day decisions about large commercial loans and defend them to a CEO and a board. Listening to him talk about his modest family background in inner-city Detroit, and how he started in banking as a teller to put himself through college, gave me confidence in him. I thought, he must be exceptional to have risen from teller to executive in a large Michigan bank the way he did. We gave Cooper the TCF reins in 1985.

Cooper has now been with TCF for seventeen years, making him one of the longest-serving bank CEOs in the region. The team of senior officers he brought with him has also stayed in place, giving TCF the important advantage of stable leadership. I consider my work on the search committee my most important contribution to TCF in the thirteen years I served on its board.

In my retirement, I drew satisfaction from watching the flourishing of a program that bore my name, the W. Harry Davis Leadership Institute. It was a summer-camp leadership-training program for African American high-school juniors and seniors, sixty each year, funded by a foundation established in my name as a parting gift when I left the Urban Coalition in 1973. Each summer for twenty years, students and counselors assembled at a camp in the St. Croix River Valley and studied through reenactment about slavery, the Underground Railroad, the Civil War, and Reconstruction. At the end of the two weeks, Charlotte and I were always on hand with the parents for a meal and a program that the young people themselves would prepare to reflect what they had learned. It was a moving experience. Unfortunately, the program was overly dependent on a few key staff members. When one of them died and another mismanaged foundation funds, the camping program folded. What remains of the foundation today funds a scholarship for graduates of Summit Academy OIC to go to college. I hope the camping curriculum we established will be used again someday.

I have not abandoned community activities. I served a stretch on the Hamline University board of regents and on the board of the Minneapolis Area Red Cross. I faithfully attend Rotary Club meetings and keep my hand in at Phyllis Wheatley and Sabathani Community Centers. Every fall, I also go on the lecture circuit, giving speeches on behalf of the United Way as a member of its speakers bureau. I served two five-year stints on the United Way board of directors, 1968–1973 and 1977–1982, and became a firm believer in its collective approach to community philanthropy. When attorney Marvin Borman was United Way fund-raising chair, I was in his cabinet as a committee chair. A loaned-executive program to beef up United Way staffing was initiated, modeled after the loaned-executive program developed at the Urban Coalition. We sold the loaned-executive program with the argument that charity involves gifts of time and talent as well as money. That is the philosophy I am putting into practice, and promoting, when I contribute to the United Way speakers bureau now.

The greatest blessing of my retirement years, of course, has been extra time for Charlotte and our growing family. Our four children have thus far given us thirteen grandchildren, enough to fill our hearts—and our house at our monthly family meetings—to overflowing. They represent a variety of racial colors and backgrounds, continuing the rich mixing of humanity that has always been characteristic of the Davis family.

Rita and her husband, Joseph Lyell, have two children who are now adults, Corey James and Charlotte Jean. Rita has had a long career with Wells Fargo Banks that started when she was a student in the first computer-science program at the Minnesota School of Business and was given an internship at Northwestern National Bank—which through merger has become today's Wells Fargo. The bank was so taken with her that it paid for the rest of her education. Rita has risen to a vice presidency and oversees part of the bank's technical center. She is also a dedicated volunteer in the community and has remained active at Hennepin Avenue United Methodist Church. Rita's husband, Joey, is a management troubleshooter for Burger King. He has taken some of that chain's most troubled franchises and turned them around. He helped Corey and Charlotte Jean go into restaurant management too, and both have shown a lot of ability in that field. Today, Charlotte is a manager for Pizza Hut in north Minneapolis; Corey is a customer-services agent for Express Scripts.

Butch's career has also involved computer science. Always self-disciplined, he was an outstanding high-school athlete as well as a strong student. With some mixed feelings, I steered him away from boxing and toward football and basketball because boxing offered no hope of a college scholarship. Charlotte and I wanted all of our children to go to college, and that goal was a financial stretch for us in the early 1960s, when I was still working for the Onan Company. We needed whatever scholarship help was available. Butch landed a football scholarship at the University of Minnesota and played for legendary coach Murray Warmath. He ultimately graduated from the University of Minnesota–Duluth.

Butch went to work for Control Data and married Yvette Johnson, a young lady with similar career interests who worked for IBM. They have one son, Ramar, who graduated recently from Minnesota State University–Mankato. Yvette and Butch were divorced, and Butch then married a wonderful woman, Bobbi Denison. Butch adopted Bobbi's two daughters, Nasstasha and Rekia, and then they had a third daughter, Chloe Elizabeth. Butch's career focused on mainframe computers, of the sort used by government. He went from Control Data to Ceridian to General Dynamics and rose well into management ranks before taking a buyout when General Dynamics downsized in 1999. He and his family live in Eden Prairie. Bobbi and Butch's first grandchild, Keyon Spencer, was born April 13, 2002.

Like Joey Lyell, our second son, Ricky, has made a career of owning and managing restaurants. He lives today near Mankato, where he is working for Slumberland. Like his brother Butch, he was an outstanding high-school athlete, winning all-state status four years running for Central High School in track and several times in football. But Ricky was not as interested in academic study as his older siblings. He attended Black Hills State University, Willmar Junior College, and Lincoln University in Jefferson City, Missouri. The football coach at Lincoln had been his coach at Central High School; he gave Ricky both a scholarship and the motivation he needed to stay focused on his studies. It was there that he enrolled in the hotel/restaurant management program and became acquainted with another young athlete whose family owned a Creole restaurant in New Orleans.

It was only a few years after Ricky graduated that a break came his way. A barbecue restaurant on the North Side was failing due to bad financial management, and the city's economic-development authority wanted to keep it alive. The City Council member for that ward was my old friend from Phyllis Wheatley, Van White. He knew about Ricky's college training and invited him to propose a rescue plan for the restaurant. Before long, it was Rick's Café Americana, styled much like the place Humphrey Bogart ran in the movie *Casablanca* and serving a mixture of American, barbecue, and Creole food. Ricky's college friend from New Orleans was the original chef. It was a successful business for Ricky for more than ten years. He married Barbara Pendleton, a woman he had known in high school. Barbara became involved in the restaurant as well as in her own career as a mortician. It was the breakup of that marriage that led to the end of Rick's Café. Ricky sold the place to his chef, who eventually closed it. Ricky is single now and the father of four beautiful children, sons Myles William and Melik Evan and daughters Angelina Marie and Mikayla Geraldine.

Evan, the baby of our family, is now a big man with a beautiful wife, Blythe Richie, and three children, Jaylyn Maleesa, Juwan Malik, and Jaliya Marie. Evan was a basketball player at Roosevelt and Washburn High Schools and at Minneapolis Community College. He went on to St. Cloud State University and got a computer-related job in downtown St. Cloud through the good offices of one of his professors. He also got more than a taste of racial profiling, as St. Cloud police made it their habit to follow him home from work at night. That experience contributed to his decision to leave St. Cloud before graduating and take a job at TCF Bank. Blythe, whom Evan first met while at Roosevelt High School, worked there too. When their daughter Jaylyn was tiny, Charlotte and I were her day-care providers. I used to rock her and sing her to sleep at nap time every day. I cherish the chance I have had to take care of our grandbabies since I was so seldom at home while our own children were small. Blythe now sells Mary Kay cosmetics and is a licensed day-care provider. Evan left TCF and is working for ADP Hollander, a procurement-management firm in Plymouth.

One reason I appreciate my children and grandchildren so much is that the family of my childhood is nearly gone. Of the six children of Lee and Libby Davis, only my sister Geraldine and I remain.

My eldest sister, Charlotte, and her husband, Clemens Rooney, had four children, all girls. (The family always called Charlotte "Dooney," so after her marriage she was stuck with the name Dooney Rooney, the poor dear!) Three of their children, Arlene, Muriel, and Frances, lived to adulthood, and each of them had families of their own, making me a great-uncle many times over. After her children were grown, Dooney worked as an aide in the public schools. She died in 1990 at age seventy-seven, after a rewarding life.

Menzy was the first of us to move to Minneapolis's South Side and buy his own home. He ended his career as a mechanic for the Volkswagen Company. He and his wife, Ginger, had no children of their own, but she had a son from a previous marriage that Menzy regarded as a stepson. Neither he nor his wife enjoyed a long retirement. Not long after she died of a heart attack, he was found to have an inoperable tumor between his stomach and liver. He died at age sixty-seven.

The family always considered Retie Marie's childhood death a case of murder. My sister Eva might be considered a homicide victim of sorts too, for her death was hastened by a deadly crime. Eva's first husband was a boozer and a bit of a goofball. He led her into what we called "the life," meaning vice. She finally had the strength to divorce him, get training as a nurse, and land a legitimate job at the Sister Kenny Institute. She married again, this time to Richard Anderson, a mechanic who worked at Grossman Chevrolet. He loved to fish, and the two of them bought a boat and spent many summer weekends happily fishing on Minnesota lakes. I was so pleased by the turnaround in her life. Then tragedy struck. One day as they were preparing to leave town to go fishing, they stopped at Grossman's to pick up Richard's paycheck. Just at that moment, an irate customer was at the garage, arguing with Grossman employees. Richard got caught up in the argument. The customer threw a punch, which Richard returned with such force that the man wound up on the ground. While he was down, he reached into his pocket, pulled out a pistol, and shot Richard dead on the spot. Eva witnessed the entire incident. She went into a state of shock and never fully recovered. We had to put her into a nursing home eventually, as she retreated ever further from reality. She was sixty-seven when she died.

Geraldine lives now in pleasant circumstances in Edina, but her life has not been easy. She married a jazz guitar player named Stanley Morgan. He was very talented and played for a time with Duke Ellington and with the original Ink Spots. They had one son, Franklin, whom they raised in California. He became a terrific jazz saxophonist, but he has had a troubled life. His dad introduced him at a young age to Charlie Parker, a sax player who was legendary for both his musical ability and his appetite for drugs.

Franklin's attraction to drugs got him arrested repeatedly and landed him in San Quentin prison. Even there, Franklin's musical ability shone through, so much so that the warden would give him special privileges if he would play the saxophone during lockups to help keep prisoners calm. He was featured on an NBC television special hosted by Jane Pauley as the prison sax player. His talent was such that between brushes with the law, Franklin was able to continue his career, playing in the Broadway orchestra for *Jesus Christ Superstar* and performing on the soundtracks of a number of major motion pictures. He joined a band that traveled to jazz clubs all over the country and performed on luxury cruise ships. All that hard living took a toll on his health. He had a stroke some years ago while on an airplane en route to a gig in New York. They had to land the airplane in St. Louis to rush him to a hospital. He survived, and was even able to perform at a benefit for the hospital where he was treated. He is married today and lives in Albuquerque, New Mexico.

Geraldine couldn't forgive Stanley for getting their son mixed up in drugs. She divorced him and moved to Stockton, California. She remarried, but again, things did not go well. Her second husband, Ted Smith, was addicted to alcohol and gambling, and while he was kind when sober, he could be a wild man when he was drunk. When he died of cancer, I convinced Geraldine that it was time for her to come home to Minnesota.

I started life as the baby of the family and wound up as the patriarch. I understand that role in a way that I believe is consistent with my Sioux Indian heritage. When Indians pray, they call God "Grandfather." I am the grandfather, which means I am to be the spiritual leader of my family. I am to be the guardian, watching out for the best interests of each one and for the continuity of the clan. When the Davis family gathers—which we do, very intentionally, one Sunday a month—I always convene the group and offer the prayer. I ask the family members to join hands in a circle. I stand in the middle and say the prayer. My grandchildren always seem eager for that moment—and I don't think that is so only because they get to eat afterward. I always begin by thanking God for the family. I then thank God for any experience that any of us has had in recent weeks that will better our lives or lead to a closer relationship with God. Finally, I ask God's blessing on the food and give thanks for it. I like to think that those monthly prayers give even the youngest children a powerful sense of belonging and of connection to something holy.

Rich as my years of retirement have been, they have not been free of concern about my health. Just as I was leaving the school board in 1989, I suffered a heart attack. Dr. Schultz discovered that one of my major arteries was closing. He treated me with angioplasty, an artery-clearing procedure that has become rather commonplace in subsequent years but was rather novel in 1990. The procedure succeeded in keeping me free of heart problems—for a few years.

I had another heart attack in 1996. That was the cue for more drastic treatment of my clogging arteries: double-bypass surgery. It was a serious procedure, but I approached it without a trace of fear or nervousness. I was pleased that two pastors from Hennepin, the Reverends Verda Aegerter and Jan Pettit, came to Abbott Northwestern Hospital to be with me and my family as I went into surgery. Pastor Berg from the Ashram was on hand as well. They prayed with me before the procedure began.

During surgery, I had a vivid vision. I was lying in bed, but not in a hospital. My bed was surrounded by women, all dressed in beautiful colors and surrounded by an iridescent light. Something on their backs that could have been wings reflected the light. It was an extraordinarily beautiful scene. I did not recognize any of the women, who were sitting at tables scattered around my bed. On the tables were arrayed beautiful fruits and vegetables, but I did not see the women eating. I could hear them talking, but I could not make out what they were saying. I asked them, "What am I doing here? Why am I here?" They acknowledged me with smiles and nods but did not speak to me.

When the surgical procedure was over and I was in intensive care, I woke up with this scene still clear in my mind. Two nurses were there, adjusting the tubes that were inserted in various parts of my body. After they left, I had the sensation of once again being surrounded by the group of women, arrayed in the same arrangement around me. It was the very scene I had witnessed before. I thought, My goodness! Can this be a dream? What is happening here? Then the smiling women faded away, and I was again in my hospital room.

I mentioned my vision to Charlotte but no one else. It seemed too personal and a little too unusual to tell anyone else. I was afraid that if I mentioned it, word would get around that Harry Davis is crazy! I am telling it now because I saw the same scene once again, in February 2000, when I again had major heart surgery. This time, a heart valve needed replacement, and two of my arteries were closing again and needed stents. During the valve surgery, I had the same sensation of awakening in a room surrounded by women bathed in beautiful light and radiating colors. I was in the middle of them again, in bed, and once again they were talking, but I could not engage them in conversation. Watching them gave me a radiant feeling. I said, "What am I doing here? Can I get out of bed? Can I join you?" They would only smile. I could move, but I felt unable to get out of bed. Then I saw something at the other side of the room that I had not seen before: a tunnel. It seemed as if my bed was moving toward that tunnel. I asked the women, "Am I going down that tunnel?" They looked and smiled, and then kind of shook their heads no.

This time, when I regained consciousness after surgery, I learned that at one point during the procedure the surgeons had difficulty controlling my bleeding. If the blood flow had not been stopped when it was, I would have died.

I concluded that my recurring vision was a prelude of death. I had heard reports from other people who have had near-death experiences who say they had the sense or vision of moving through a tunnel. I decided to relate here what I saw, with the thought that I could add my confirmation to those stories and help others who might themselves have a similar experience. I believe I saw the tunnel I will one day enter. I am convinced that the women I have seen so clearly these three times are guardian angels. They are there to help and encourage me on my journey. I expect to see them again.

21
Reflecting

I HAVE LIVED ALL MY DAYS in Minneapolis. Yet the place I knew as home is gone. The city's near North Side, the old Hellhole, is like a blackboard that was written on first by Jews, then blacks, then erased, rewritten, and erased once more. As I write these words, a large portion of it is being swept away and rebuilt again. A massive new housing program is in the works, recently given the name Heritage Park. My prayer is that it will bring new life and new hope to a neighborhood that I believe has a lot more to contribute to a great city.

As I drive through the old neighborhood, I see very few landmarks from my childhood. There's an empty field at the corner of Eleventh and Emerson Avenues North. To see it today, one might think it always had been a park or some other undeveloped parcel. But there stood one of the homes of our early marriage, 1107 Emerson. There was a store on that once-busy corner and houses all around. Across the street was Goodman's, another fine store. All are gone now.

In fact, just about all that is left is little Sumner Library, across Olson Memorial Highway from where Sumner School once educated children of so many backgrounds and races. The old library is scheduled for a face-lift soon, and I am glad. It has fallen on such hard times that it is now closed on both Saturdays and Sundays. That's not the kind of library service any Minneapolis neighborhood deserves.

Otherwise, I see modern, widely spaced buildings where the old stores and houses once stood so close together. The streets look clean and well kept. The houses are few but tidy. The apartment complex named after my old mentor Cecil Newman offers decent, low-cost housing. Telling from appearances, the neighborhood would not meet anyone's definition of blight.

Yet there is a lifelessness about my old neighborhood that saddens me. The population is down substantially from its heyday. Even on a warm summer afternoon, there are few children playing and few adults walking on the streets. Places that I remember as teeming with activity are now empty fields, waiting for development. The retail hubbub that I remember so well is nearly all gone. Only a few shops remain, and there is just one well-known restaurant: Lucille's Kitchen. It has become a community gathering spot almost by default. There are few other places for neighborhood people to come together.

One might say that the change in that part of the city is the unavoidable consequence of something very positive. The overt discrimination that once confined Jews and blacks to that part of the city is gone, I hope for good. The black community has scattered throughout the Twin Cities. The upbringing that people of my generation got in this neighborhood, at Phyllis Wheatley and Sumner School, enabled us to move into the larger community when the barriers fell and to make a middle-class life for our families. I like to think that we can be an example for the low-income people who live on the North Side today. Just as it was finally possible for us to get an education and make something of ourselves, so can they, especially if we help them.

The forces of change on the North Side have not all been positive—or, at least, not respectful of the good that was present in my old neighborhood and that should not have been tossed out with the bad. Too often, change came to the North Side in the form of a bulldozer, pushing aside everything in its path. It came to install someone else's vision of what the North Side should be, not the vision of the people who lived there.

The result has been a loss of community. Too many churches and synagogues went the way of Border Methodist and are gone now. Too many institutions—Grant School, Sumner School, all the old stores and restaurants—were lost. Too many families—whole families, not just the young—turned their backs and left. Closeness within the black community has been a casualty. Gone, for example, is the annual Union Picnic, when all the black churches in the area would come together for a big celebration, with food, music, kids' programs, and great speakers. Gone are the three barbecue restaurants, all within a block of each other, where friends could count on meeting friends. Gone are the little grocery stores and clothing shops that fed and clothed the neighborhood through good times and bad.

The public school that now serves the neighborhood, Mary McLeod Bethune School, is a fine facility, built just before I joined the school board in 1968. Soon after it was built, federal funds were available to combine schools with parks and social-service agencies. By then, I was on the school board and was chair of the Wheatley board. I made sure we tapped those federal funds to keep Phyllis Wheatley alive at a time when the United Way was closing settlement houses around the city. With a valiant fight and the help of my allies on the school board, in May 1970 the Wheatley moved into shared quarters with Bethune School, where it was able to sustain a scaled-down roster of programs.

Settlement houses were out of vogue with the social-service experts in the 1960s, a time when immigration was at a low ebb. The expense of those programs, all housed in buildings that were in need of repair, became too great for the United Way to handle. Maintaining the Wheatley building was becoming especially costly, since it was built over the buried Bassett Creek. Its footing was unstable. We had no choice but to acquiesce to its demolition. The dear old building came down in 1971. Moreover, the old Women's Christian Association that had been the Wheatley's founder and financial guardian angel was weakening as members who had been its mainstays died. It would eventually become today's WCA Foundation, dispensing some $200,000 a year in grants to community organizations, drawn from an endowment built with the sale of the last of its boardinghouses in the late 1980s.

When Phyllis Wheatley moved into quarters shared with the Bethune School and Park, it had only about one-fourth of its former space. Its mission changed. It became a community center, not a settlement house. The number of people it served fell dramatically. It has access to the Bethune gymnasium but only when it is not needed for park and school programs. There is no room for boxing. In fact, nearly all of the Wheatley athletic programs are gone, though some have been supplanted by park-board activities. Gone too are most of the classes that taught young people self-respect and self-reliance. The music and drama activities for kids are no more. The comprehensive, cradle-to-grave programming that was once there has been scaled back. There is still a Wheatley-related nursery school, at the Mary T. Wellcome Child Development Center near the Bethune building. But older kids don't turn to the Wheatley as their second home the way my siblings and I once did.

I maintain that the change in Phyllis Wheatley is the most grievous blow that the Minneapolis black community has suffered in the past thirty years. The molding of young people that happened there for fifty years is not happening nearly as effectively now. Phyllis Wheatley no longer sees its mission as lifting a whole community out of poverty. It is no longer a rallying point for people to come together as a community, to teach adults to be good parents and kids to be good citizens, to keep merchants in business, to get a bank going, to pressure city hall to keep the streets patrolled and safe.

There are many fine community-service programs operating today, but they each look at one slice of a community's needs. They don't come together very often or speak with a collective voice. On the North Side, they aren't housed together in a way that allows people in need to conveniently get help. There is no one leading institution that brings community leaders together to develop strategy for achieving mutual goals. That is what the Wheatley once did, and what I believe is sorely missing today.

I am an honorary emeritus member of the Phyllis Wheatley board and still involved in the organization. I want to help the current executive director, Carl Jones, redevelop the Wheatley camp, the place that Charlotte and I and our children hold dear in memory. I am trying to convince the Wheatley alumni of my generation to help, either financially or materially. I point out that today's Wheatley board and staff members are the products of our generation's effort to send our children to college. They ought to be the role models for the next generation, but for that to happen, places like the Wheatley camp have to be available so that the generations can interact. We know how valuable that camp was for us, and we have a moral obligation to make sure it is there for kids today.

Housing remains a major problem for the North Side, which is why the Heritage Park project is badly needed. When it is completed in 2008, it will bring nine hundred new, mixed-income housing units to what should be a prime location, close to downtown, with impressive views of the skyline. The project includes a nice mix of housing for rental and ownership, some available with federal housing subsidies, some intended for conventional financing. That mix is important; the North Side needs all types of housing—affordable single-family houses, townhouses, duplexes, and apartments. But it should not have large apartment buildings, in the style of a 1950s or 1960s housing project. That kind of housing concentrates poverty too strongly in one place and tends to put families side by side with people who prey on children in a variety of ways. We should not make that mistake again.

I take pride when I see the older houses near Olson Highway and Penn Avenue that were among the first in the city to offer scattered-site, publicly subsidized housing to low-income tenants. The Urban Coalition bought those houses during my years there and hired minority contractors to rebuild and remodel them. The coalition also helped make some of those houses available for purchase by low-income people by arranging financing through its member banks. As the city addresses a shortage of affordable housing that is moving from chronic to acute, it needs to remember to stay focused on affordable home ownership, not just low rent. That is the real key to neighborhood stability and health.

Racial discrimination has not been eradicated in Minneapolis or anywhere else in America. But even in the old days, when racial hatred was often right out in the open, I felt lucky to live in Minneapolis. I always went to integrated schools. Both races always used city buses and streetcars freely. Our parks, pools, and lakes welcomed all comers, as did most downtown businesses. Our political leaders by and large were men and women of goodwill who were willing to take on overt racism and try to end it.

That legacy ought to be both a point of pride and a summons to greater progress for today's generation. Minneapolis ought to be able to approach the whole question of diversity, of making the most of all of its human resources, with a leg up on other major cities. We have a lot less to overcome than most places.

We have time-tested tools in place for giving people of color the boost they need to overcome disadvantages. Our Urban League is growing and taking on more responsibility for employment services. Summit Academy OIC is doing an excellent job of training people for employment. Seed Academy has a terrific alternative educational program for children of color. Public schools are better than ever too, offering diverse teaching styles, foreign languages, and higher skills in mathematics and computers. Education is the hope for tomorrow. My sense is that many black kids in Minneapolis are catching on to that fact and are taking better advantage of their opportunity to learn than their counterparts did a decade or two ago.

It is vital that we secure a high-quality education for children of color and make jobs available to them when they are grown. But if all of this city's citizens are to reach their full potential, there is still more to be done. Minneapolis must root out the covert discrimination that still holds back people of color. Too many people find that, in business, they are allowed to advance only so far. Too many are bothered by a persistent coolness in business relationships. Too many face a stern judgmentalism that allows no forgiveness for mistakes. Minneapolis has seen some important breakthroughs by people of color—school superintendent Richard Green, Mayor Sharon Sayles Belton, school superintendent Carol Johnson, and parks superintendent Mary Merrill Anderson among them. But they would tell you that they are conscious of being harshly judged by the larger community and of being blamed for the mistakes of others over which they had no control. The racial prejudice that persists in Minneapolis today is sometimes hard to get your teeth into. But its subtlety does not make it any less real or damaging.

It was the unity of the black community, which developed in places like north Minneapolis in the 1930s and 1940s, that helped produced the civil-rights movement of the 1950s and 1960s. If there is to be a second wave, a new push for truly equal opportunity for all races, there needs to be another coming together of people of color. In the middle of the twentieth century, the black community carried the load of combating discrimination. What's needed now is a coalition among many races.

Minneapolis became more like every other American city in the 1990s. The 2000 census found that the overwhelmingly white city of my youth is now less than two-thirds white. The city has become a gathering place for people from around the globe. The city's Hispanic and Southeast Asian populations are growing fast. Newcomers from Somalia, Ethiopia, and the Middle East have joined us, as have Jews from Russia, students from India, and business-people from Europe and Japan. I am sorry to report that these newest Minnesotans have not always been made welcome, nor have they always ingratiated themselves with the existing population. Negro Hispanics don't always get along with African Americans, who don't always get along with Somali immigrants. If those divisions escalate into hostility, the cause of racial equality is going to suffer.

We need a mechanism to bring the Asian-American, Hispanic, Middle Eastern, and black communities together with white people of goodwill around an agenda of mutual advancement and support. What is happening now is that each racial subgroup is forming its own organization. They are vying with each other for funding and community recognition when they need to be working together. We need a different kind of grass-roots organizing, not along racial lines but across them. We need to build the understanding that no one racial group is strong enough alone to make a great difference, but together we can change society. We need a renewed awareness that the fate of one minority group affects all—that, for example, the defeat of a black mayor is a setback for all minority groups in the city.

Trustworthy leadership is crucial to the continued advancement of people of color. I have learned from experience that the ability to earn and keep people's trust is an essential component of leadership. Trust is earned over time. It comes from consideration of others, dedicated effort, and integrity. It comes from constancy and persistence. It comes from doing one's homework—preparing the body, the mind, and the spirit to step alone into the squared circle of life and apply oneself fully to the task at hand. It comes from standing up for what's right in the face of opposition.

I learned to value those things from John Wesley Harper and Armintha Jackson, Gertrude Brown and Ray Hatcher, Hubert Humphrey and Cecil Newman, Art Naftalin and David Preus, and Charlotte NaPue Davis. I hope I taught them in turn to Rita, Butch, Ricky, and Evan Davis, Richard Green, Sharon Sayles Belton, and the many other young lives I touched through the years. They are my legacy.

I took the gavel as school-board chair in 1974. Front row (from left): Phil Olson, Marilyn Borea, me, Superintendent John B. Davis, and staff secretary Virginia Tinsley. Back row (from left): Carol Lind, Dick Allen, Jane Starr, and Jack Mason.

These were the trophies the U.S. boxing team I headed won at the 1976 Britain-USA team match in London.

Receiving the Distinguished Merit Citation from the National Conference of Christians and Jews in 1969 from Roland Minda, the longtime rabbi at Temple Israel, whom I first met thirty years earlier on a picket line protesting discrimination.

Governor Wendell Anderson (second from left) and Mayor Charles Stenvig (fifth from left) were on hand in 1971 as we cut the ribbon opening First Plymouth Bank, the first bank on the near North Side.

I met the founder of the National Urban Coalition, John W. Gardner, at a meeting in Washington while I headed the Urban Coalition in Minneapolis.

I received Metropolitan State University's Community Service Award from president Reatha Clark King in 1986.

Minneapolis school superintendent Richard Green.

I spoke at Richard Green's installation as chancellor of the New York City school system. At right is New York governor Mario Cuomo.

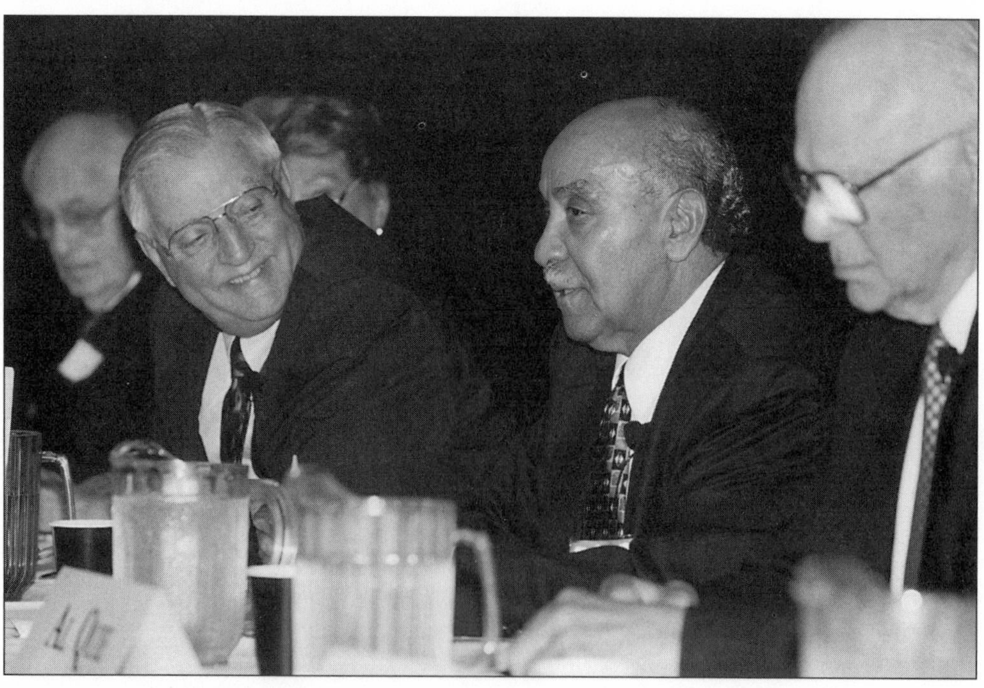

I spoke in June 2001 at a University of Minnesota program remembering Hubert Humphrey, convened by former vice president Walter Mondale. From left: Art Naftalin, former ambassador Geri Joseph (barely visible), Mondale, me, and former governor Al Quie.

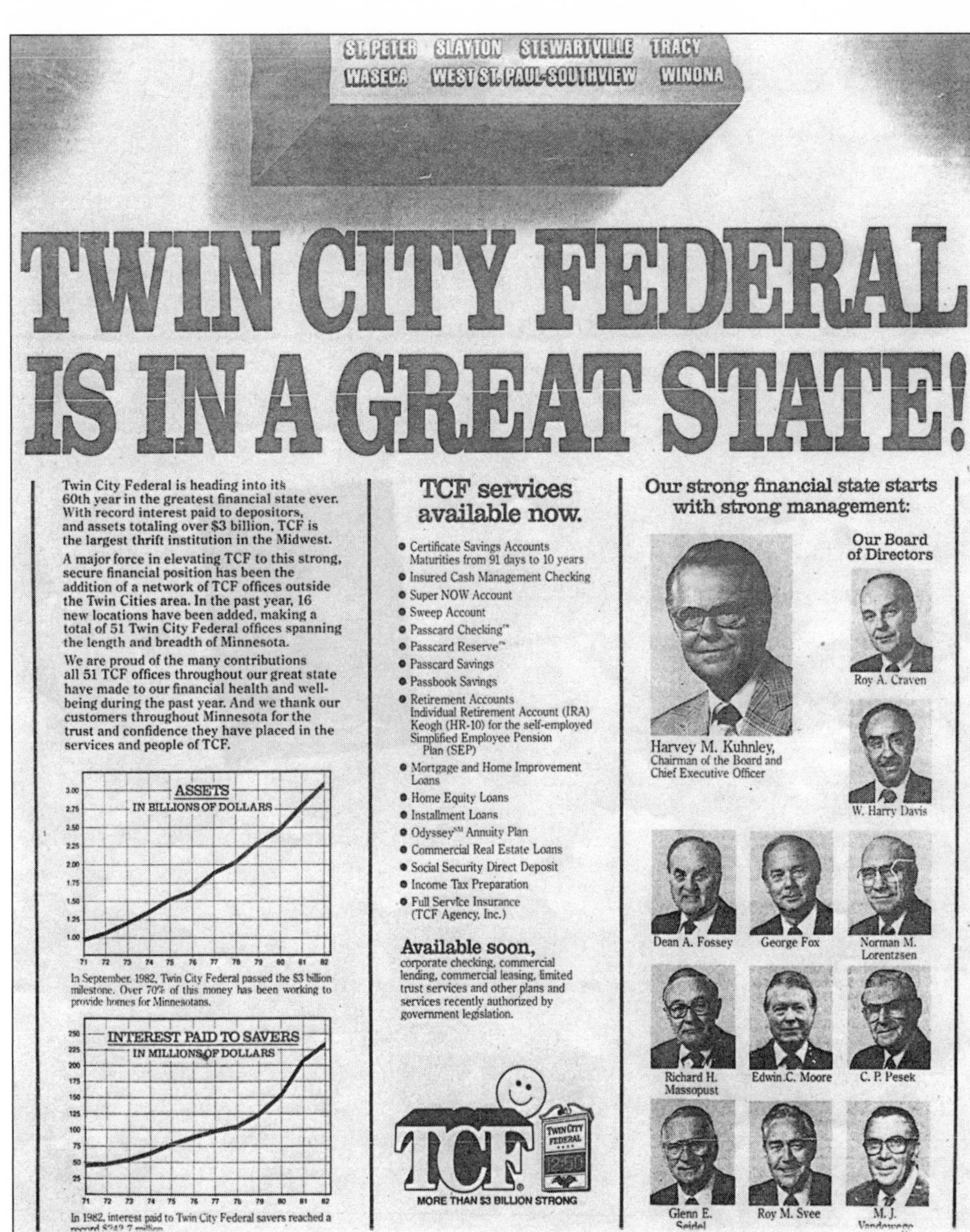

The TCF board of directors in the early 1980s. This was the board that changed the bank's leadership in 1985 and, some say, saved the institution in the process.

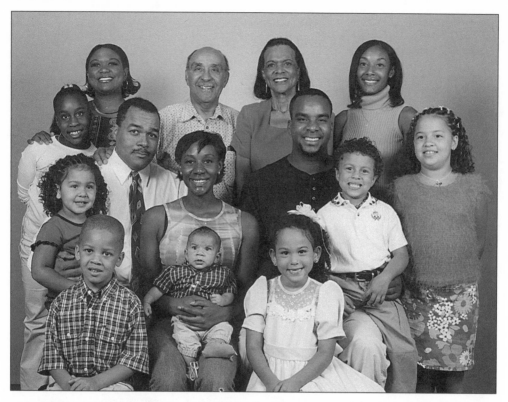

Our grandchildren all were present for Charlotte's seventy-fifth birthday in August 2001— all but little Jaliya, who would be born three months later. Front row (from left): Myles, Melik, and Angelina. Second row (from left): Mikayla, Rekia, and Juwan. Third row (from left): Chloe, Corey, Ramar, and Jaylyn. Fourth row (from left): Charlotte, Grandpa, Grandma, and Nasstasha.

Charlotte and I with our longtime friends and Christian Ashram associates Don and Gail Dahlstrom.

Our granddaughter Jaliya was born on November 15, 2001.

Charlotte and I at the Rotary Club Christmas party at the Minikahda Club, December 2001.

Appendix

W. Harry Davis may have received more awards for civic service than any other living Minnesotan. Here is a roster of some of them.

1963—George Barton Award, Old Guards of the Ring
1967—Urban Service Award, Hennepin County Mobilization of Economic Resources Board
1969—Distinguished Merit Citation, National Conference of Christians and Jews

1970—Governor's Prayer Breakfast Award, Governor Harold LeVander
1970—Achievement Award, Twin Cities Opportunity Industrialization Center
1972—National Industrial Club of America Award
1972—Governor's Award, Governor Rudy Perpich
1973—Honorary Doctor of Laws Degree, Board of Trustees, Macalester College
1973—Board of County Commissioners, Hennepin County
1975—Outstanding School Board Director, Minnesota School Board Association
1975—Service to Minnesota Youth – Viking Ring Award, Minnesota Vikings
1975—Partnership Award, National Alliance of Businessmen
1975, 1980, 1982, 1983, 1989, 1991—WCCO Good Neighbor Award, WCCO Radio
1976—Hall of Fame, Golden Gloves Association of America
1976—Distinguished Service Award, United Way of Minneapolis Area
1979—Service Award, Hennepin County Bar Association
1979—Governor's Award, Governor Albert Quie

1980—Elliot Park Service Award, Elliot Park Neighborhood Association
1980—Outstanding Community Support Award, United Way of Minneapolis
1981—OIC Torchbearer Award, Opportunity Industrialization Center
1981—Outstanding Service Award, USA/American Boxing Federation
1981—Outstanding Leadership Award, Control Data United Way
1982—Service Award, National Medical Fellowship
1982—Governor's Service to Youth Award, Governor Albert Quie
1983—Presidents Award, National Golden Gloves
1983—Minneapolis Board of Education Award
1983—Lifetime of Outstanding Service Award, United Way of Minneapolis
1983—City of Minneapolis Proclamation
1983—State of Minnesota Proclamation
1983—Minneapolis City Council Resolution
1983—National OIC Service and Leadership Award, Opportunity Industrialization Center
1983—Leadership Award, Downtown Council of Minneapolis
1983—Dedication Award, Kansas City Golden Gloves
1983—City of St. Paul Proclamation
1983—Minnesota AFL-CIO Award

1984—Cecil Newman Award, Urban League of Minneapolis
1984—Service Above Self Award, Minneapolis Rotary
1984—Distinguished Service Award, Minnesota Elementary School Principals Association
1986—Community Service Award, Metropolitan State University
1986—Lifetime Board Member Award, Sabathani Community Center
1986—Rotary Foundation Paul Harris Fellowship Award, Rotary International
1986—Minnesota Human Rights Award, League of Human Rights Commissaries
1987—Service to Competitive Sports Award, National Football League Alumni of Minnesota
1987—Distinguished Service Award, City of Minneapolis
1988—Bishop Stanley Neil Frazier Leadership Award, Minnesota Church of God in Christ
1988—Outstanding Leadership Award, Minnesota Opportunity Industrialization Center State Council
1989—Appreciation Award, W. Harry Davis Charity Basketball Tournament
1989—Community Service Award, Central Community Gymnasium
1989—Outstanding Leadership Award, Minnesota Alliance of Black School Educators
1989—Outstanding Leadership Contribution to the Education of All Young People and Advocacy for Students with Exceptional Needs, Special Education Department, Minneapolis Public Schools
1989—Lifetime Commitment Award, Minneapolis/St. Paul Urban Coalition
1989—Loaned Executive Award, United Way of Minneapolis

1990—B. J. Reed Wise Volunteer Service Award, Community Schools Organization
1990—Pennell Award, Minnesota Federation of Teachers
1990—Fathers of Waters Award – City of Minneapolis Highest Service Award
1990—Minneapolis Commissioner of Civil Rights Award
1990—Governor's Award, Governor Arne Carlson
1991—Outstanding Service Award, USA Olympic Committee
1992—Loaned Executive Award, United Way of Minneapolis
1992—Minneapolis Black Achievers Award
1993—Loaned Executive Award, United Way of Minneapolis
1993—Distinguished Service Award, TCF Bank Board of Directors
1993—Distinguished Service Award, Minneapolis Rotary
1993—50 Years of Service, Upper Midwest Golden Gloves
1996—Leon H. Sullivan Volunteer Award, OICs of America
1996—Special Recognition Award, City of Minneapolis
1997—St. Paul Humanitarian Award, City of St. Paul
1997—Citizenship Award – Building Community
1997—Housing and Urban Development Award, Summit Academy
1998—Outstanding Director Award, Directors Association of Businesses and Banks

2000—Individual Humanitarian Award, Minneapolis Community and Technical College
2001—Whitney Young Award, Boy Scouts of America
2001—Many Years of Service Award, Phyllis Wheatley Gladiator
2002—Honorary Doctor of Education, Board of Trustees, Hamline University

Index